RECORDS OF CIVILIZATION

SOURCES AND STUDIES

EDITED UNDER THE AUSPICES OF THE

DEPARTMENT OF HISTORY, COLUMBIA UNIVERSITY

NUMBER XV

THE LITERATURE OF THE NEW TESTAMENT

THE LITERATURE
OF THE
NEW TESTAMENT

BY

ERNEST FINDLAY SCOTT

EDWARD ROBINSON PROFESSOR OF
BIBLICAL THEOLOGY
UNION THEOLOGICAL SEMINARY

COLUMBIA UNIVERSITY PRESS

NEW YORK: MORNINGSIDE HEIGHTS

PREFACE

The aim of the present book is to do for the New Testament what Professor Bewer has done so admirably for the Old Testament in a previous volume of this series. Some change in the method of treatment has been inevitable in view of the radical differences between the two parts of our Bible. The Old Testament covers a period of centuries, while the New Testament writings all belong to the same age. The Old Testament is concerned with the life of a nation, and cannot be rightly understood without some knowledge of general history during the millennium before Christ; the New Testament was written for the Christian community, and has little relation to the wider interests of the time. The Old Testament is not only a book of religion but a national literature, which needs to be studied, like any other literature, from an esthetic and historical point of view. In the New Testament the religious purpose is everything. It may indeed be claimed for Paul and the evangelists that in their religious fervor they unconsciously became great writers. The sheer literary excellence of the New Testament has too often been overlooked, and emphasis has been laid on it in the present volume. Yet it is not merely as literature that we read the New Testament. What we seek from it, almost to the exclusion of all else, is a first-hand knowledge of the origin and nature of the Christian religion.

In the following chapters I have tried to explain the New Testament in the light of the modern investigation. I have kept three objects more especially before my mind: (1) to put each of the writings into its historical setting; (2) to examine the critical problems involved in it; (3) to indicate its value for its own time and its permanent religious interest. New Testament criticism is now a highly complicated study, in which no one can be thoroughly at home without years of special training. Yet it works by methods which have come to be recognized as valid in every field of knowledge, and all intelligent students can appreciate its main conclusions. My effort has been to avoid the technical terms and academical issues and to offer a plain account of the essential difficulties. I have also done my best to keep my own conjectures and prejudices in the background. A book of this kind ought to represent the general findings of modern scholarship, not the private and perhaps fanciful views of any one scholar.

Broadly speaking, I have taken the New Testament books in the order in which they were written, but this scheme has been subject to necessary modifications. In some instances the date of a book is doubtful; in others, the book belongs in substance to an earlier period though in its present form it may be late. The Synoptic Gospels have a clear right to be considered first. Although they were later in composition than the Epistles of Paul, they not only contain the message on which all Christian teaching was based, but are compiled from sources which reach back to the earlier time. The book of Acts, too, cannot be separated from Luke's Gospel, to which it was meant to be the sequel.

Here and there I have quoted New Testament passages of special significance, but have confined myself for the most part to exposition. The New Testament is a short book, and some acquaintance with its contents may fairly be assumed. It is a book, moreover, which cannot be reduced to a brief collection of extracts. There is hardly a verse in it which is not, in some way, important, and even its greater utterances lose half their value when they are isolated from the rest. No book has been so much misunderstood, and the reason chiefly is that it has seldom been read as a whole. It is familiar to everybody, but only as a bundle of texts and chapters which have no relation to one another. The present volume will have served its purpose if it leads to some genuine reading of the New Testament.

NEW YORK   E. F. SCOTT
May, 1932

CONTENTS

CHAPTER I

CHAPTER II

CHAPTER III

CHAPTER IV

CONTENTS

CHAPTER X

CHAPTER XI

CHAPTER XII

CHAPTER XIII

CHAPTER XIV

CONTENTS

CHAPTER XXI

CHAPTER XXII

CHAPTER XXIII

CHAPTER XXIV

CONTENTS

CONTENTS

CHAPTER XXVIII

CHAPTER XXIX

CHAPTER XXX

CHAPTER I

THE ORIGIN AND NATURE OF THE NEW TESTAMENT

1. *Form of the Book*

The name "New Testament" was at first applied to the Christian religion itself. Jeremiah had declared in a sublime passage that the present relation of God to his people would give place in the future to a more inward and personal one.

Behold the days come, saith the Lord, that I will make a new covenant with the house of Israel and the house of Jacob, not according to the covenant that I made with their fathers, in the days when I took them by the hand to bring them out of the land of Egypt. But this shall be the covenant that I will make with them: I will put my law in their inward parts and write it in their hearts, and will be their God and they shall be my people. [Jer. 31:31-33.]

On the ground of this prophecy, Paul describes the Christian message as the New Covenant, and contrasts it with the Old Covenant which was given in the books of Moses (I Cor. 3:4 ff.). The same idea is conveyed in the words attributed to Jesus at the Last Supper, "This is my blood of the Covenant which is shed for many," and is fully developed in the Epistle to the Hebrews. When the primary Christian writings were brought together, they came to be known as "the books of the New Covenant," and this title was shortened into the "New Covenant" or "New Testament." This latter term, by which the book is now universally known, is due to a mistranslation. The Greek word for "covenant" was also the word for a "will" or "testament," and this was the sense in which it was commonly understood when the writings were translated from Greek into Latin. It was assumed that as a man disposes of his possessions by his will, so God had drawn up two "testaments," of which the later had superseded the first.

As we now have it, the New Testament consists of twenty-seven documents, some of considerable length, others confined to a few chapters or only one. Something will be said later as to how these writings came to be set apart as sacred, but at present it will be enough to think of them as the literature of the primitive church, or at least that part of it which was considered most valuable and authoritative. In the age when these documents were composed, the general writing material was papyrus, made by slitting into thin strips the pith of the papyrus stem, and glueing a number of horizontal strips over the same number laid perpendicularly. The result was a sheet about a foot square, and twenty or thirty of these sheets joined together made up a roll, which the reader held on his knees or rested on a table, unwinding it as he read. These mechanical conditions have to be borne in mind when we consider the nature of the New Testament books. The writers worked under severe restrictions of space. A roll that could be conveniently handled had not to exceed a certain bulk, and the authors of the longer books (e. g., Matthew, Luke, Acts) were evidently anxious to compress their material so as to bring it within the necessary limits. It is noticeable that these books, different as they are in character, all run to about the same length — the extreme length of a manageable roll. On the other hand, we have several short writings, each of which contains approximately the same number of words (II and III John, Philemon, Jude). The presumption is that the writers of these letters wished to make the utmost use of a single sheet of papyrus.

Our New Testament is now bound up in one small volume and the illusion is thus created that although it had a number of authors it is a unity, and that the various writings are meant to illuminate and supplement each other. A great deal of misunderstanding on matters of vital importance is due to the mere fact that since the invention of printing and the vogue of thin-paper editions, the New Testament has been before us in a single book. We speak of "New Testament religion," "New Testament teaching," "the authority of the New Testament."

It is forgotten that the writings at first existed separately and that each of them circulated by itself. An important church would no doubt possess a number of the rolls, but perhaps a century elapsed before any church had access to all of them. The process of gathering them together seems to have been slow and uncertain. Apparently the first step was taken when churches associated with Paul tried to form collections of his surviving letters. Rome, Corinth, and Philippi would make copies of the letters addressed to them and send them to each other, so that all might have a complete set of his writings. In course of time the Gospels were similarly brought together, then the letters ascribed to other Apostles than Paul. Thus the main portion of the New Testament is made up of three separate collections, and to these were added three books, which have nothing in common with each other, Acts, Hebrews, and Revelation. As the sequel to Luke's Gospel, the book of Acts had a natural claim. The Epistle to the Hebrews, though it was certainly not written by Paul, found its way, with some difficulty, into the Pauline collection. For a long time Revelation, which could not be brought within any group, was regarded doubtfully, but was added at last as a sort of appendix to the whole volume.

When we turn from the collections to the individual books, we find that they all have certain characteristics in common. (1) They bear some relation, more or less direct, to the practical work of the church. Their authors were not mere scholars or thinkers, bent on the furtherance of knowledge, but active missionaries. The Gospels, for instance, were drawn up for the fuller instruction of new converts. Paul's Epistles were written for the guidance of his churches when he was unable to visit them personally. The book of Revelation and the First Epistle of Peter were meant for the encouragement of Christians under persecution. There is not one of the writings which cannot be linked in this manner with some practical aim. (2) They are *occasional* writings, intended to meet some given situation. It may almost be said that they belong to the class of pamphlets, rather than literary works, and they cannot be properly understood without some knowledge of the special emergency which called them forth. From this it does not follow that they were mere ephemeral tracts, hurriedly thrown off and meant to be forgotten when they had once served their purpose. Almost all of them bear the marks of careful composition. Although the authors never dreamed that they would have readers after two thousand years, they yet aimed at producing something of real value. Paul was aware that his letters would be read at a full meeting of the church, preserved in its archives, and copied out for circulation in neighboring churches. Luke intended that his Gospel should be a standard work, replacing the defective narratives which had hitherto been in use. The author of Hebrews had obviously studied every phrase in his Epistle; whatever may have been his original purpose, he meant that it should be reread and treasured. (3) These writings, occasional as they were, claimed from the first to carry authority. At a later date the New Testament was accepted as an inspired book, every word of which had an eternal value. This was certainly far from the mind of the authors, who were intent on some particular difficulty which they had met with in their missionary work. Yet at the time when they wrote, the idea of the Spirit was intensely real. It was believed that Christian teachers were not dependent wholly on their own wisdom, but spoke out of a divine illumination. Paul is everywhere conscious that his mind is that of the Spirit, and this is true in some measure of all the writers. The later view of the New Testament as an inspired book was not based wholly on arbitrary dogma. The writers themselves never doubted that they were inspired. They meant their words to carry a divine authority.

2. Language and Style

The New Testament is written in Greek, which in the first century was the language generally employed in the Eastern half of the Roman Empire. There were many local dialects, but every race could be counted on to understand the Greek language in addition to its own. Since Christianity began as a Jewish religion, some of the writings may go back to originals drawn up in Aramaic, the language of Palestine. It is practically certain that the first three Gospels have Aramaic documents behind them, and this may also be true of the earlier part of the book of Acts. There are peculiarities in the style and grammar of the book of Revelation which would seem to indicate translation from Aramaic or perhaps from Hebrew. With such exceptions, the New Testament was composed, from the first, in Greek.

When it is compared with that of classical literature, the Greek of the New Testament is rough and irregular, and used to be regarded as a sort of jargon, employed by half-educated Jews who were trying to express themselves in a language other than their own. But it cannot be doubted that a man like Paul, born and brought up in one of the chief centers of Greek culture, knew Greek as his native language, and this is probably true of all the other writers. The whole subject has been placed in a new light by the discovery in recent times of numerous papyri and inscriptions which reflect the Greek of common life, as distinguished from that of literary convention. The New Testament language is found to correspond almost exactly with this spoken Greek. It was, in fact, the so-called classical writers of the time who used a jargon — a language copied from ancient models and understood only by bookish men. In the New Testament we have the living Greek of the first century. Applied to Christian purposes it is colored, inevitably, by idioms and phrases borrowed from the Old Testament, in much the same way as the English of many of our writers reflects their familiarity with the Bible. Sometimes, as in the two opening chapters of Luke's Gospel, the author deliberately adopts a biblical style of language in order to produce a special effect. But the general rule holds good that the New Testament is written simply and naturally in the current language, so that its teaching might be at once intelligible to all classes of readers.

The authors differ widely from each other in the skill with

which they manipulate this Greek of their day. Mark's Gospel, while vivid and expressive, is frequently uncouth in its language, and this is true in yet greater measure of the book of Revelation. Luke and the author of I Peter, while they make no pretence to a polished diction, write easily and correctly. The author of Hebrews is a man of literary culture, and there are passages in his Epistle which might serve as models of Greek style. Paul is not only a great religious thinker, but a master of language. It is true that he is often loose in construction, to the point of obscurity. His ideas crowd on each other, as they do sometimes in Shakspeare's later plays, and he makes room for them as they come with little regard to elegance or even to grammar. Yet he expresses himself always with wonderful force and directness. It was his task, not merely to frame a Christian theology, but to devise the words and phrases in which it should be formulated; and this he did so skillfully that most of his terms have become a living part of our religion. His language is always adequate to his theme. In passages of argument he is terse and logical; in personal appeals he never fails to discover the most moving words: now and then, when he deals with the loftiest Christian truths, he breaks without effort into splendid poetry. The Apostle to whom we owe some of the most exalted passages in all literature may justly be ranked among the world's great writers.

3. *Time and Place of Origin*

The New Testament books extend over a period of almost exactly a hundred years. Paul's First Epistle to the Thessalonians, which is generally agreed to be the earliest book, was probably written in 51 A.D. The so-called Second Epistle of Peter dates from about the middle of the second century. By far the larger number of books, and all the more important ones, belong to the sixty years between 50 and 110 A.D. This cannot be regarded as a pure matter of accident. In the history of every literature there are flowering periods, when work of the highest order seems to come of its own accord, and there was such a period for Christian literature in the latter part of the first century. In the generation before, the church was still groping its way towards an understanding of the new message. In the century that followed, the message had become familiar, and was set forth in a number of conventional doctrines which were accepted as a matter of course. For some fifty years men were alive to the wonder of the new revelation. They had thought it out, and yet were able to respond to it with a fresh emotion and to express their faith and enthusiasm in living words. This was the age that gave us the New Testament. The church during the centuries since has produced writers who were no less gifted than those early ones, and far superior to them in literary genius. It has sometimes been suggested that a new Christian scripture might be formed, made up of all that is best in devotional literature throughout the whole history of the church. But the instinct which assigns a unique place to the New Testament writings is sound. They come to us from the time when men's minds were most impressionable to the essential meanings of the gospel. The saints and thinkers of later days may have understood much of its teaching more profoundly, but those men of the New Testament could interpret it with a freshness of vision which could not, in the nature of things, be repeated.

All the books were written during a narrow period, while the church was still engaged in its early struggle; but it had already established itself at a number of centers, widely apart. We can determine with certainty where the books originated only in the case of some of Paul's Epistles. Palestine was the cradle of the new religion, and the very earliest records must have been Palestinian, but that primitive literature is preserved to us only in so far as it was incorporated in the Gospels. Of the Gospels as we now have them, Mark was most probably composed in Rome. Matthew and Luke offer no indication of where they were written, but Matthew has been assigned on several plausible grounds to Antioch. As to the birthplace of Luke's Gospel, we are quite in the dark. A generation after Paul's death, the church at Ephesus, which he had founded, became the chief center of Christian thought, and in this neighborhood, according to trustworthy tradition, grew up the literature which is associated with the name of John. I Peter appears to have been sent from Rome, and Hebrews was pretty certainly the work of a Roman teacher, although he indicates that he wrote the Epistle during a temporary absence. The local origin of the remaining books can only be conjectured. In the New Testament, therefore, we have a collection of writings which come to us from many different places, and to this we must attribute not a little of its value. The early churches were not united in a single system as they were in a later age. Each of them stood by itself and developed its own character and its peculiar type of teaching. The New Testament is thus a fully representative book. We have the common gospel put before us in all its various aspects by writers who worked, for the most part, independently of each other.

Although they were resident in Gentile cities, these writers seem all to have been of the Jewish race. Already in the time of Paul, Christianity had broken with Judaism, and towards the end of the first century the majority of its converts were recruited from the Gentile world. But for its teachers, it still relied on men of Jewish origin. They had the necessary background of religious knowledge and training. They had an instinctive sympathy, which even the most devout of Gentile converts found it hard to acquire, with the ideas and aims of Jesus. At the same time these men of the Jewish race belonged to the Gentile world. Not only was Greek their native language, but their outlook was more Gentile than Jewish. It is perhaps unfortunate that we have no interpretation of Jesus' message by men who understood it from the purely Jewish point of view. We should have been glad, for instance, to have their own version of the gospel by those Jewish opponents of Paul who tried to thwart him in his mission. They were narrow-minded, but just as sincere as Paul himself, and perhaps had laid hold of elements in Jesus' teaching which Paul, with his Gentile sympathies, had overlooked or obscured. Jesus, it must never be forgotten, was himself a Jew, and we now know him only through a Gentile medium. Even the Gospels in which his words are preserved to us were written in a Gentile environment and are colored by Gentile ideas. For historical purposes, this Gentile bias in our New Testament is a perpetual cause of confusion, though it is easy to see that without it the book could never have achieved its task of making Christianity a world-wide religion. Those writers of Jewish origin were able to grasp the message which Jesus had given under Jewish forms of thought, while with their Gentile upbringing they could divest it of all that was local and accidental, and transform a Jewish gospel into a religion for the whole world.

4. *Problems*

From this brief survey of the conditions under which the New Testament was written, it will be apparent that there are certain questions which we must ask ourselves in the study of all the books. Each book has its own special problems, but there are these more general ones which have always to be considered:

(1) We must try to ascertain, as nearly as we can, the *date* at which the book originated. These writings are not, as was once assumed, mere timeless statements of what all Christians must do and believe. They are indeed of permanent value, but were intended, in the first instance, to meet difficulties which the church encountered at some particular point of its history. Before they can be properly understood, they must be fixed into their right place in the historical framework. It sometimes happens that an interval of only a year or two in the dating makes all the difference in our interpretation of the whole purport of a book.

(2) The question of *authorship* is also of primary importance. This was recognized by the early church when it made

the name of the supposed author an integral part of every book. The name was a guarantee that the teaching of the book could be accepted as fully authoritative. It has become evident, however, in the course of modern inquiry, that the traditional notices of authorship are often misleading. That Paul was the writer of most of the Epistles attributed to him cannot well be doubted, but the titles of almost all the other documents are open to question. It has to be noted that the books themselves, for the most part, contain no hint of their authorship. In several of them an introductory verse has apparently been thrown in by a later editor, to connect them with a well-known name; but these initial titles must always be regarded as conjectural. We require in every case to examine the book itself and to judge its authorship on the ground of the intrinsic evidence. Even when a book seems openly to profess that it is by a given man, there is always need for caution. It must be remembered that ancient sentiment with regard to literary property was different from ours. The man who puts the name of another to his own work is now deemed guilty of a serious offence, but in the first century this was considered permissible and even praiseworthy. A disciple could show no greater honor to his master than by issuing in his name a book which aimed at presenting his ideas. There is reason to believe that in several New Testament writings a practice like this has been followed (e. g., I and II Timothy, Titus, I and II Peter); and in such cases no question of dishonesty arises, as it would undoubtedly do if we were dealing with modern works. New Testament authors were much less anxious about their literary rights than critics have been on their behalf. They were quite content to keep themselves in the background. They seem indeed to have preferred that their work should go forth without any name attached to it, so that it might be received as the testimony, not of a man, but of the Spirit which spoke through him. To us the name of the author would often supply the key to his message, but at the time this need was not anticipated.

(3) It is necessary to inquire not only who wrote a given

book, but *where* he wrote it and *to whom*. If we only could be certain of the places where the writings were composed, we should be able to estimate the influences which entered into the author's thinking. We should also be able to determine, in a manner which is now impossible, the course of Christian development in the Greco-Roman world. Perhaps it is still more important to ascertain the particular audience which the author had in view. The documents, as we have seen, were all intended to meet special situations, and the nature of the situation is obscure unless we know something of the persons addressed. What was the public, for instance, which the author of Matthew's Gospel had in view? Did the writer of Hebrews send his Epistle, as the present title would imply, to some group of Jewish Christians? Who were the earliest readers of the Gospel of John? These questions have a vital bearing on the interpretation of the several books.

(4) The chief thing necessary for the study of any work of literature is a right conception of the author's *purpose*. A mathematician once began to read *Paradise Lost*, but soon threw it down because it did not seem to be proving anything. He was approaching the great poem with a false idea of its intention, and naturally it had no value for him. Most of the foolish judgments which are constantly passed on the works of artists and thinkers are due to a similar cause; and when we read a New Testament work we must always consider with peculiar care the purpose with which it was written. It is necessary, in the first place, to keep in mind that the author is primarily concerned, not with science or history or economics, but with religious truth. The Gospels, for instance, are historical works, but when they are examined solely from this point of view it is not difficult to show that they are often confused and inadequate. Account must be taken of the larger purpose which the evangelists had before them. They were possessed with the sense that God had spoken to men through Jesus Christ, and they tried so to picture his earthly life as to bring out something of its divine significance. So in all the writings, the

religious motive is primary. They have much to give us in the way of information, of social and ethical counsel, even of literary pleasure; but unless we approach them in the religious spirit they will never reveal their true meaning. In a more specific sense, however, the purpose of the books must always be considered. They are occasional writings, dealing in every case with the special needs and difficulties of the early church. Whatever permanent meaning they may convey is always bound up with the immediate object for which they were written. The First Epistle of John, to take one example, is perhaps the most purely religious book in the New Testament. It takes us beyond all changing forms to what Christianity must always be in its very essence. Yet the Epistle is directed against a particular type of error which had arisen in the beginning of the second century, and everything in the writer's thought has a fuller significance when we understand it in this context. In like manner, each of Paul's Epistles was called forth by a special occasion. Some question has been put to the Apostle which he tries to answer; some report has come to him which has caused him anxiety. His letters are all, in their different ways, like dispatches sent out by a commanding officer during a difficult campaign and, without some knowledge of the precise difficulties, they convey little meaning. Thus we have always to ask ourselves the purpose of a given New Testament book. Sometimes it lies on the surface; sometimes it is only to be inferred from vague allusions, which would be plain enough to the first readers but at this distance of time are hardly intelligible. What, for example, was the trouble in which Paul was involved at Corinth, and which led him to write his Second Epistle to the Corinthians? The whole Epistle turns on it, but Paul is so anxious not to revive a bygone quarrel that he refers to it only in elusive terms. Sometimes the purpose of a document is complex, and allowance has to be made for all its elements. The author of Acts sets himself to recount the early history of the church, but he also wishes to create good feeling between various parties in the church and at the same time to convince the outside world that Christianity has never been politically dangerous. The Fourth Evangelist also writes with a number of purposes all blended together, and in a minor degree this is probably true of every New Testament writing. There is always a danger of laying the whole stress on some one purpose and neglecting the others.

(5) In the study of any New Testament book, we must allow for a possible *controversial interest*. It used to be assumed that the early church developed peacefully, and contrasts were often drawn between the dissensions of our modern Christianity and the perfect harmony of those first days. We have now grown aware that, almost from the beginning, the church was divided into parties. Jewish and Gentile Christianity were opposed to each other; within the Gentile churches, every prominent teacher had his own following; towards the end of the first century, heresies arose which threatened to break up the church altogether. It was through this clash of opinions that Christian beliefs gradually defined themselves, and a creed was at last formulated on which the whole church could unite. The New Testament writers are all, in one way or another, controversialists. Each of them maintains his own view of the gospel in the face of some other which he deems inadequate, and his teaching must be explained in terms of this opposition. It is unfortunate that the contrary opinions have left no record of their own. We know how Paul answered the Judaists, but there is no writing in which they speak for themselves. We hear much in the later books about "false teachings," but all that we learn of these is from the evidence of their adversaries. At the best, this evidence is vague and unsatisfactory. The New Testament writers take for granted that the opposing views are generally familiar, and do not think it necessary to specify their nature. Probably there is not one of those heretical opinions of which we can now form anything like a just estimate. Yet however dim may be our perception of that controversial background in the New Testament, we can never afford to forget that it is there. Without

some notion of what the writers are opposing we cannot rightly appreciate what they say.

(6) There is one further question which can never be entirely left out of sight — that of possible changes and additions in the writings, as we now have them. It has to be remembered that for a considerable time the books of the New Testament were not treated as scripture. The church valued them highly, but thought of them as its own property, which it was free to deal with as it chose. Their position was somewhat similar to that of hymns in our modern worship. Familiar hymns are given differently in every collection, and all the versions differ in some points from the originals. While using the hymns, the church has modified them from time to time, omitting and adding and rewriting so as to adapt them to new ideas and new moods of devotional feeling. In much the same manner, it dealt in the early days with the New Testament books. Whenever they were recopied some changes were introduced to make them more effective for their purpose of instructing and exhorting a Christian community. Not only so, but the accidents of transmission under the imperfect conditions of ancient bookmaking must be taken into account. Leaves in a manuscript may now and then have got displaced. Two letters of Paul may have been bound together for the sake of convenience, and so have come down to us as a single letter. A stray fragment of uncertain authorship may have seemed too valuable to lose, and have therefore been inserted in one of the recognized documents. Probably there is no book in the New Testament of which we can say with absolute certainty that we now possess it just as it left the writer's hands.

5. *Religious Value*

The study of the New Testament is thus beset with problems which become more numerous and involved, the more we examine them. The whole book is no greater in extent than many a daily newspaper of our time, but the investigation of it is now a science by itself, so wide in compass that no one can pretend to know more than a portion of it. The language or text or exegesis or literary criticism or theology of the New Testament will each afford ample scope for the industry of a lifetime.

This exhaustive study which has been devoted to one small book is due to its supreme importance as the fundamental document of the Christian faith. It is from this book that we derive almost the whole of our knowledge of the life and teaching of Jesus. It is through the New Testament that we can trace the beginnings of the church and the meaning of its worship and institutions. It was the New Testament writers who laid down the primary beliefs on which the church has ever since based its teaching. Their account of Christianity would in any case have been of cardinal value, since they came first and were in immediate touch with the authentic message of Jesus. But their understanding of the message was not merely of this accidental kind. The more their writings are studied, the more they reveal a depth of insight and a fullness of comprehension which are not to be found in any subsequent literature of the church. However we explain it, the pulse of Christian devotion beat at its strongest in that first age. All revivals of our religion since have been due to some recovery of the principles set forth in the New Testament. Nothing, indeed, is more wonderful than the continued vitality of the book. Sacred writings, more readily perhaps than any others, become antiquated and are kept alive only by the reverence paid to their venerable claims. The New Testament has never ceased to appeal to men as a fresh and living book. Since it was written, the world's thought has passed through many phases, but each of them, instead of outdating it, has only unfolded some aspect of its teaching which had previously been overlooked. It is not too much to say that in the intellectual upheaval of the present day, the New Testament is the only book from the past which has not been found wanting.

This perennial freshness of the book is due, in no small measure, to the very fact that it is made up of occasional writings, each of them called forth by some passing crisis. The writers do not address some fanciful, impersonal audience. They do not deal with abstractions, but with concrete and pressing questions which have sprung immediately out of life. Thus there is a reality about their thinking which is not to be found in the works of professional sages. To be sure, they wrote in an age which was different from ours, and their teaching was meant for the special conditions of that age. But human life under all surface differences is in all times much the same, and the New Testament has always a close grip on the facts of life. The questions it seeks to answer are those which repeat themselves in all generations, changed in form but in substance unvarying.

6. *Literary Value*

Considered purely as literature, the New Testament has many shortcomings, which were inevitable from the manner in which it came into being. A pamphlet, thrown off in the heat of some crisis, does not aim at literary excellence. It loses its effectiveness when it is polished too carefully and has qualities which can be appreciated only by the discerning few. The New Testament writers did not aim at producing literature. Their object was to reach their immediate public and to get practical results in the shortest possible time. We cannot expect to find in the New Testament the noble poetry of the Psalmists and Prophets, or the perfection of art which marks some of the narratives in Genesis and the books of Samuel and Kings. Yet, in its own way, the New Testament is wonderful, even as a literary achievement. Intent as they are on the truths which they seek to utter, the authors express themselves unconsciously in great language. They often attain to a force and pathos which are quite beyond the reach of art. This is most of all true of the Gospels, which tell the story of Jesus simply, just as it had come down in the popular tradition. Many have since attempted to tell the same story, adorning and elaborating it with all the resources of literary skill. Yet we always fall back on the Gospel narrative, not only because it is the earliest, but because it is incomparably the best. The other writings all share, in their different manner and degree, in the qualities which impress us in the Gospels. Paul, as has been said already, has given the world's literature some of its grandest passages. The eloquence of the eleventh chapter of Hebrews has never been surpassed. Imagination has never risen to sublimer heights than in some of the visions in the book of Revelation. The First Epistle of John is the most exquisite of all religious meditations. Every New Testament writing contains sayings which have stamped themselves on the world's memory, as much by the aptness and beauty of their expression as by the truths they express. The Christian religion has no more precious asset than the New Testament. A book will permanently endure only by its sheer worth as literature. It may be acclaimed as sacred but, unless it lays real hold on the mind and the emotions, it will not be read. The New Testament, even apart from its message, is one of the finest and most interesting of all books. So long as men value great thoughts uttered in splendid language, they will continue to treasure it, and through the book they will know the Christian religion.

CHAPTER II

THE SYNOPTIC GOSPELS

1. *The Four Gospels*

The New Testament begins with the four Gospels, which record the life of Jesus and his message, as he himself proclaimed it. Although they stand first, they are later in date than many of the other books; the Epistles of Paul, for instance, were all written considerably earlier than any of our present Gospels. But when the New Testament was gathered into a volume, the place of priority was naturally given to those four accounts of Jesus' ministry. His Apostles after his death had expounded his message, but it was necessary first to know the message itself, and the life which had given it meaning.

Even on chronological grounds, it was only right that the Gospels should be placed first. They were not written down in their present form until the latter part of the first century, but they consist, for the most part, of material which had long been accumulating and needed only to be put together. Luke tells us at the beginning of his Gospel that, at the time he wrote, there were many narratives of Jesus' life in circulation, and that his object was merely to present their contents in a fuller and more orderly form. These earlier documents, of which Luke made use, appear to have been written in Greek, which had become the language of the church after it had identified itself with the Gentile world. There are many indications, however, that these Greek records had been translated from earlier ones, drawn up in Aramaic, the language of Palestine. Even with these lost primitive writings, we do not reach the beginnings of the process which had its final issue in our Gospels for, before anything was written, there was a

period when all Christian teaching was by word of mouth.
The written Gospels were, in the last resort, the precipitate of
this oral tradition. It used to be assumed that at a late period,
when the immediate disciples of Jesus were all vanishing from
the scene and every one could see that any clear memory of his
life and words would soon be lost, the idea occurred to several
men to put the tradition into writing. On this assumption one
of the favorite arguments against the historical truth of the
narrative was built. Our Gospels are confessedly late, and can
embody only the hazy reminiscences that still lingered after
the lapse of fifty or sixty years. Admitting that our evangelists may have written in perfect good faith, do we have any
guarantee that their record is trustworthy? In the course of
two generations the memory of any event becomes hopelessly
blurred, and we have also to reckon, in the present instance,
with the Christian imagination weaving legends, as time went
on, around the sacred figure of Jesus. Since nothing is known
of his history except from these belated Gospel testimonies, is
it not permissible to doubt everything, even whether he ever
lived at all? This reasoning, however, is based on premises
which cannot now be granted. The Gospels, as actual compo-
sitions, may be late, but they are made out of materials which
had existed long before. Almost from the time of his death,
the work of recording the life of Jesus must have been in process, and our Gospels represent the work in its final literary
stage. It may indeed be that some things in the story had become dulled or exaggerated, that it had been colored, more or
less consciously, by subsequent beliefs; but the record as a whole
had come straight from men who were themselves eyewitnesses
of the events. There is little more reason for challenging the
Gospels than for distrusting a history of the American Civil
War because it was composed only the other year. The author, it is true, can have taken no personal part in the battles,
but he has had access to previous histories, and these in turn
were based on letters, newspapers, and stories told by the
combatants. His work may be defective, owing to biased

judgment and inaccurate writing, but no one doubts that the main record is true history.

Our Gospels, therefore, are the result of compilation, and in each case the work has been done with remarkable skill. It has often been a matter for wonder that the church, at the very beginning, was able to produce these little biographies, which are as perfect in their own way as anything that has ever been written. But here, as always, perfection had come through long experiment. If one of the earliest narratives could be recovered, it would doubtless be found to consist of rude jottings, clumsily put together, with little attempt to draw a portrait or to sustain the reader's attention. We must remember, too, that the art of biography was by no means a new one. Our evangelists had before them the historical books of the Old Testament, where the stories of Joseph, David, Elijah, are so marvelously told. Luke in particular appears to have steeped himself in the Old Testament narratives, and uses them constantly as his models. Moreover our Gospels were written in Greek, and may have owed something to Greek example. The age in which they appeared was also that which produced Plutarch's *Lives*, their nearest parallel in classical literature; and Plutarch himself took up a prevailing fashion. Towards the end of the first century, there seems to have been a widespread taste for the short biography, illustrating the character of a famous man by a selection of sayings and anecdotes. It has happened constantly in Christian history that some popular type of literature has been turned to religious purposes, and of this practice our Gospels may furnish the earliest example. Yet when we allow for every influence which may have helped to shape them, they stand by themselves. The need for recounting the life of Jesus created a new literary form, which was brought to perfection in the Gospels.

Thus far we have looked at the four Gospels as if they constituted a single group, all of them composed in the same manner and with the same purpose. In a broad sense they may fairly be thus classed together, and ever since the New Testament books were collected, they have stood side by side. So much were they regarded as similar that towards the close of the second century an attempt was made to combine them in a single work, the *Diatessaron*, or *Four Gospels in One*. Down to our own times, there have been efforts of the same kind to harmonize the fourfold narrative. Yet every one who reads the documents, one after another, must perceive that the fourth is different from the other three. The difference is apparent even in the cast of language, which in John is abstract and uniform, instead of varied and picturesque. It is still more striking when we turn from the manner to the substance. The fourth evangelist includes material of which we hear nothing in the other Gospels; when he repeats the incidents they have described, he places them differently and sets them in a new light; he rearranges the whole history of Jesus and, above all, brings Jesus himself before us in another character, not as a Teacher sharing the life of his disciples, but as a divine being, manifest for a time on earth. For all these reasons the Fourth Gospel stands apart from the others. It is beset with a number of difficulties peculiar to itself, and needs to be considered separately at a later stage. For the present we must confine our attention to the Gospels of Matthew, Mark and Luke, which have been known since the middle of the eighteenth century as the Synoptic Gospels. This name denotes that they can be "viewed together." Their contents may be arranged in three parallel columns, showing at a glance where they agree and where they differ. For the purposes of critical study, it is necessary to have them so arranged. A number of "Synopses" of the Gospels, both in Greek and English, are now available in convenient form, and one of them should be in the hands of every serious student.

2. *The Synoptic Problem*

The three Gospels of Matthew, Mark and Luke are independent works, and yet bear a very close relation to each other. They cover much the same ground; they give nearly the same selection of incidents; when one of them records a saying of Jesus, it is usually repeated in one or both of the others. This similarity might be set down to the fact that all three writers are telling the same story and inevitably overlap. When you read the reports in several newspapers of an event that interests you, they show a close agreement. This is not because the reporters collaborated with each other, but simply because they saw and heard the same things, and could not but write about them in much the same way. This parallel, however, does not apply to our Gospels. They not only agree in facts, but frequently in their very language, so that it is not uncommon to find whole sentences verbally the same. Not only so, but incidents and sayings which have no intrinsic connection are often placed in the same sequence by all three evangelists, proving that they must have drawn from a common source. But while the agreements are striking, the differences are no less so. Again and again what is obviously the same incident is given in conflicting versions, or a saying of Jesus is reported in terms that are widely at variance. Why is it that the three writers who seem to be constantly using the same source are yet so independent? In almost every paragraph these two phenomena of agreement and difference are found together; on what theory of origin can we account for both of them? Here we have the synoptic problem, which has occupied many of the acutest minds for the best part of a century, and does not yet appear to be near a solution. Perhaps it will never be solved, for in some of its crucial aspects we have to deal with unknown quantities — documents that have now been lost and cannot be reconstructed except by doubtful inference. Of all literary problems this one which concerns the three Gospels is the most intricate and baffling, as it is incomparably the most important. Our knowledge of the life and work of Jesus is derived mainly from these Gospels, and the value of their testimony must depend on the conclusions we can form as to their origin.

It is only in modern times that the nature of the synoptic problem has been fully recognized. The Bible, during the greater part of Christian history, was placed in a different category from any other literature, and all critical inquiry into the Gospels, which were manifestly the central portion of the Bible, was forbidden. Anything that seemed peculiar about them was easily explained by the doctrine of inspiration. Four men had been led under divine guidance to tell the story of Jesus, and their agreements and differences were alike to be accounted for by the operation of the Spirit under which they worked. They were in close agreement because they wrote as the one Spirit instructed them. They were led at times to differ in order that they might supplement one another and thus impart a full knowledge of the truth. It had been ordered by divine providence that the four varying accounts should be like views in a stereoscope which give the complete picture only when they are all blended together. So far as the human authorship was considered, room was allowed for some interdependence. Augustine, at the beginning of the fifth century, had laid it down that Matthew wrote his Gospel first and the other evangelists had followed him in the order in which their books now stand, confirming his narrative and adding to it, according as a new light was vouchsafed to them. This was the theory on which all exposition proceeded until the eighteenth century. The main object was not to explain how the Gospels came to differ, but to prove that in spite of apparent conflict they always agree. Endless ingenuity was displayed in that work of *harmonizing* to which reference has been made already. It was taken for granted that whenever the same event is recorded in ways that seem mutually exclusive, it must have happened on several occasions. Jesus, for instance, must have cleansed the Temple twice — at the beginning of his ministry, as John tells us, and at the very end, as we learn from the other evangelists. He was anointed perhaps four times. He had a number of favorite sayings, which he repeated again and again in somewhat different words. No effort was ever made to explain the repetitions by some intelligent theory of the relation of the Gospels to one another.

With the rise of the critical spirit in the eighteenth century the insufficiency of the accepted methods came gradually to light. The doctrine of inspiration was not yet called in question, but it was perceived that a literary problem was involved in those curious agreements and differences in the Gospels. It was in Germany that interest in the problem was first awakened, and the work of investigation was carried on, not only by biblical scholars, but by distinguished men of letters like Lessing and Herder. Valuable assistance was also given by experts in classical literature. Towards the close of that eighteenth century, the world of learning had been stirred by the new theory that the Homeric poems had grown up by degrees out of a number of separate ballads or "rhapsodies." Some of the great scholars who had taken part in the classical discussion turned their attention to the Gospels and tried to explain their origin by methods which had proved fruitful in the other field. It was fortunate that in the earliest period of the inquiry such a variety of knowledge and talent was enlisted. Poets, philosophers, theologians, philologists all examined the Gospels from their various points of view, with the result that many theories were brought forward, all of them valuable, although none was fully adequate. The later advance has been made possible by the effort to combine and correct and supplement these different theories.

They fall into four main classes. (1) The primitive Gospel theory, which held that one original Gospel was the basis of our present three. (2) The oral theory, which found in the Gospels three different transcripts of a tradition which had come down by word of mouth. (3) The fragmentary theory, according to which the Gospels were made up of a large number of separate fragments pieced together. (4) The documentary theory, which derived them from earlier written documents. It was this last hypothesis which came to be finally accepted as the starting point of all sound investigation; but the others cannot be dismissed as the mistaken guesses which always precede the discovery of a genuine trail. They all laid hold of real elements in the problem, and the suggestions of-

fered by them have still to be taken into account. It is necessary, therefore, to look a little more closely at those older
theories, which held the field about the beginning of the nineteenth century.

(1) The favorite one was that of a primitive Gospel, underlying those which we now possess. It was assumed that in
the generation following the death of Christ, an account of his
life and teaching was drawn up in Aramaic and was employed
by the church in Palestine. In the course of the Gentile mission, this Gospel was translated into Greek by the various
evangelists. While translating, they took the opportunity of
modifying it and introducing new information which had come
to them from other sources. Thus it came about that, although
the broad outline of the original Gospel was preserved, it took
on a different character in each of the translations and, instead
of the one record, we now have the three independent records
of Matthew, Mark and Luke. This theory seemed to explain
the difficulty that these Gospels, while agreeing so closely, are
yet so often at variance. It seemed also to be supported by
one of the few accounts of the Gospels which have come to us
from early Christian times. "Matthew," according to Papias,
who wrote about 140 A. D., "composed the Discourses in the
Hebrew language, and each one interpreted them as he was
able." Here there seemed to be distinct evidence of a work
which had been written by an immediate disciple in his native
tongue, and translated by various hands into Greek.

It is doubtful, however, whether Papias was rightly informed, and in any case the meaning of his statement is far
from clear. Whatever he meant by the "discourses" (Logia),
he cannot have referred to a narrative of the life of Jesus,
such as the theory postulates. That there were narratives earlier than our present ones is indeed possible; all modern inquiry has tended to prove that they existed and have been
incorporated in our present Gospels. Almost certainly, too,
the theory is right in maintaining that at least some of them
were in Aramaic. But the idea of a single original Gospel,

which changed by a process of editing into our present three, is demonstrably wrong. For one thing, no whims of translation can possibly account for all the differences in the Gospels. Where they agree in their material, they constantly change the *order* in which they give it. Their material itself is often so different that they cannot have taken it from one original. The Gospel of Mark, moreover, is so much shorter than Matthew and Luke that it cannot be a version of the same document. But the decisive argument against the theory is to be found in the very agreements on which it is based. In all three Gospels there are passages which are almost word for word the same, and it is inconceivable that different translators should thus have hit on identical terms when they turned one language into another. They must be working, not on an Aramaic document, but on sources which already existed in Greek.

(2) The theory of an original written record was obviously open to criticism, and it gave place to that of an oral Gospel. That the teaching of the primitive church was by word of mouth cannot be doubted. The disciples, probably all of them, were unaccustomed to writing, and the public they addressed was not a bookish one. In those early days, too, when the story of Jesus could be heard from those who had actually known him, there was no inclination merely to read about it. The message went home with tenfold force when it came directly from the lips of eyewitnesses. From this fact, that the early teaching was by word of mouth, the oral theory sought to explain the origin of the Gospels. It was assumed that the disciples, like guides who are continually showing visitors over historic ground, fell into a set manner of telling their story. The incidents they selected, the words in which they described the incidents, became stereotyped. There was at last a narrative, more or less fixed, which was taken over by one missionary from another. Wherever the message went, the life of Jesus was presented in much the same terms. A time came when it was deemed advisable to have the story in writing, and

our three evangelists put it down as they remembered it. Since
it had been transmitted orally, it had always been in some degree fluid, and had reached the several writers in varying
forms. Since it had run into a conventional mold, much of it
remained the same in all the versions. The oral hypothesis
thus appeared to explain both the agreements and the differences. One has only to think of popular legends or fairy tales
which have been taken down from the lips of different narra-
tors. It is found when they are compared that the story in all
essentials is the same, yet each of the versions has peculiarities
of its own, since they have come down by different channels.
Does not this parallel hold good for the three Gospels?

It cannot be denied that the theory on the face of it is
plausible, and some scholars have clung to it almost to our
own day. In one respect it has permanent value, for it brings
into relief the undoubted fact that the earliest Christian teaching was by word of mouth. The records as we now have them
do indeed run back to an oral tradition; and this fact has been
put into the forefront by the very latest school of Gospel
criticism. Yet the oral theory as it was maintained by its first
champions cannot now be accepted. It is hardly credible, for
one thing, that some passages should have been orally transmitted without any change, even in language. This might happen in poetry, where the words are fixed by rhythm and meter,
but a prose narrative could not be verbally preserved without
the aid of writing. Again, there is a large amount of special
material in each of the longer Gospels which cannot be accounted for on the ground of a single tradition, written or
oral. But the fatal objection to the theory is to be found in
the *order* of the different narratives. Every one who has tried
to commit a speech to memory is well aware that when the
sentences get out of place the thread is hopelessly lost. Yet
the Gospel writers are able to vary the order of their narrative at will. The Sermon on the Mount, to take one conspicuous instance, appears in one single piece in Chapters 5-7 of
Matthew. Most of it is reproduced in Luke, but in a number

of separate passages, widely removed from each other. How was it possible for any one, relying wholly on his memory, to preserve the discourse and yet break it up in this fashion? It is still more remarkable that the evangelists continually interrupt their main narrative and resume it again when they please. Matthew, for example, will sometimes run parallel with Luke for a considerable stretch, and will then digress and devote a chapter or more to the teaching of Jesus. Yet he never fails to return to his narrative at just the point where he broke off. Luke at one place interrupts his story for nine chapters together, bringing in a varied mass of incidents and parables of which, for the most part, we hear nothing in the other Gospels. Yet when he has finished, he falls into line again with his companions, exactly where he had left them. The oral theory cannot possibly account for this freedom with which the evangelists vary the order of their record. They must have worked with written documents to which they could refer at leisure, taking a piece from one and a piece from another, and transposing where they thought fit. Writing from their memories, they could never have exercised this freedom.

(3) The third theory is connected with the name of Schleiermacher, the famous philosopher and theologian. He observed that the Gospels, when analyzed, are found to make up a mosaic of a great number of separate pieces, connected for the most part by quite artificial links. He threw out the suggestion that here we may discover the real clue to their origin. What the evangelists had before them was miscellaneous fragments — a mass of flyleaves on each of which was recorded a single anecdote about Jesus, or two or three of his sayings. Their task was that of combining the fragments, and so weaving the Gospels into their present form. This hypothesis also has proved of the highest value, and is coming to play a very important part in modern investigation. There can be little doubt that the Gospels do, in the last resort, consist of fragments, and criticism is now bent on discovering how these originated and how they were gradually brought together. Yet the theory

cannot offer a solution of the synoptic problem, for the material used in the Gospels, whatever it may have been at first, cannot have come to the evangelists in fragmentary form. This is evident as soon as we compare the three narratives in their general structure. With all their variations, they conform to the same plan, showing that the material had already been collected and arranged. They all begin, for instance, with an account of John the Baptist, and then proceed to describe the Baptism and Temptation of Jesus and the course of his ministry in Galilee. They close with a history of the Passion and Resurrection, in which the various episodes are placed very much in the same order. When we come to examine the evidence in detail, it is still more convincing. We meet continually with two or more sections which are joined together in all three Gospels, although it does not appear that the incidents described in them took place at the same time. This agreement in the grouping of separate passages cannot be accidental. It proves that the evangelists had taken over the tradition when it was well past the fragmentary stage. They must have worked with sources in which the material, whatever its original form, had been shaped into a more or less coherent whole. Not only so, but these sources must have been written documents. Thus only can we explain how the sequence of unrelated passages had become fixed, so that it is adopted as a matter of course in all the narratives.

(4) So we come to the documentary theory, which is now accepted by practically all scholars. It has been subjected during the last fifty or sixty years to every possible test, and has never failed to maintain itself. The other theories all have value, but only when they are used to complete and elucidate this primary one. It assumes that underlying our present Gospels there were written sources which can in some measure be determined. Occasionally the evangelists may have drawn on traditions which had come to them by word of mouth, but in the main their work consisted in the revising and combining of documents. It is apparent from our brief survey of the other

theories that the phenomena presented by our Gospels cannot be accounted for on any other ground. Here are three works in which the material is often verbally the same and is yet arranged differently. The authors must be extracting passages, just as it suits them, from a written record. At the same time they cannot be confining themselves to any single document for, while they are sometimes in striking agreement, they often differ. It constantly happens that a passage found in two of them is unknown to the third; and there are verses, and at times whole sections, which occur in one Gospel alone. We must therefore conceive of each evangelist as making use of various documents. Among these there are clearly one or two which they had in common, but there would be others which each of them had to himself.

That our Gospels had their origin in some such way may be gathered from that opening passage of Luke, to which reference has already been made. This passage must always form the starting point of synoptic inquiry, for it is here alone that an evangelist speaks in his own person about the aims and methods of his work. It was customary, in ancient times as now, for an author to dedicate his book to a friend or patron, and Luke follows this practice. He makes it plain by doing so that his Gospel has literary pretensions. It is not a rough manual put together to serve a practical need, but a regular book, which is meant to appeal to cultivated readers. The author selects Theophilus as representing the type of reader whom he hopes to reach. Nothing is known of this man except from the present passage, and the similar dedication at the beginning of Acts. Some have conjectured from the name "God-loving" that he was an imaginary character, a symbol of that pious, thoughtful minority among the Gentiles who would wish to know more about the Christian message. The name, however, was quite a common one, and there is no reason to doubt that Theophilus was a real person, of honorable position (as is denoted by the title "most excellent") who had already become a Christian and was anxious for further enlightenment. To this man, a friend or patron of his own, Luke dedicates his book:

Inasmuch as many have attempted to draw up a statement concerning the facts which have been accomplished among us, just as they have been transmitted to us by those who were the primary witnesses and servants of the message, it seemed good to me also, after I had traced all things carefully from the start, to write them for you consecutively, honoured Theophilus, that you might know the certainty about those matters in which you were instructed.

Luke here expresses himself in the stilted, conventional style affected in formal dedications, and we cannot but regret that when he was giving us information, now so precious, he did not write in his own clear and natural manner. Yet there are several facts which can be disentangled from the involved language. (1) At the time when Luke wrote, there were a number of writings in circulation, dealing with the origin of the Christian movement. When he speaks of "many" who had written he no doubt uses a word in keeping with the exaggerated style of the passage; but he could not speak as he does unless he knew of at least three or four narratives prior to his own. (2) He makes it plain that these earlier reporters had worked at secondhand. They were not themselves eyewitnesses, but had heard the story from those who were. Their part was simply to put into writing what had so come to them. (3) He admits that he himself is at the third remove from the events. He was not a witness, neither had he heard the story from the immediate witnesses. His information was derived from those written narratives in which their testimony had been put on record. (4) His aim in writing his own book is threefold. (a) The narrative he offers will be fuller than those previous ones. Having acquainted himself with "all things from the start," he will not confine his interest, as others had done, to aspects or episodes of the history. (b) He aims at superior accuracy. Previous writers, he felt, had been wanting in historical instinct. For himself he claims that he has made a real study of the evidence, and has given a narrative that will be found intelligible and trustworthy. (c) He mentions emphatically, as the chief merit of his work, that he writes "in sequence." This does not necessarily mean that the other narratives were thrown together anyhow, without any regard to chronology. A suggestion of this kind, as we shall see presently, would not have been true to fact. The meaning probably is that material gathered from various separate writings is now coördinated, each item receiving its proper place in a fuller narrative. Luke, in fact, has dealt with the early documents very much as the "harmonizers" were afterwards to deal with the Gospels themselves.

The statement of Luke is thus in keeping with the documentary theory of our Gospels. In view of this direct evidence and of all the observations that have gone to confirm it, the theory itself cannot be reasonably doubted. Difficulties arise only when we try to ascertain the nature of the primitive documents and the manner in which our evangelists have used them.

3. *The Primary Gospel*

It would have been quite impossible to attempt any solution of the synoptic problem if all the underlying documents had been lost. Our position would have been much as it is with regard to Livy and other classical historians. That they drew largely on the work of previous chroniclers is certain, but there is no means of even guessing the nature and extent and validity of their sources. But the opinion of scholars is now unanimous that one of the "many" narratives to which Luke refers has been preserved, just in the form in which he used it. Thus we have solid ground to rest on. Knowing how the one source was employed, we can form some judgment as to the other sources. The case resembles that of a jig-saw puzzle, in which the picture begins to fall into shape when there is one portion of it of which we can be certain.

It had long been surmised from the close agreement between the three Gospels that they were in some way dependent on each other. This, as we have seen, had been the conclusion of Augustine in the fifth century. He assumed that Matthew, the Gospel which stands first in order, had been written first, and that the other two, although they also had been directly inspired, were based on Matthew. This priority of Matthew was never questioned until late in the eighteenth century, and was not finally disproved until near the end of the nineteenth. It appeared to be self-evident that Mark was an epitome of Matthew, while in Luke it was expanded and revised. Yet there were some scholars, even a hundred years ago, who perceived that Mark could not be a mere epitome. To be sure it was shorter than Matthew, but they pointed out that where it overlapped with Matthew it was almost always fuller. They observed, too, that in this supposed epitome much that was most valuable in Matthew was left out altogether. Since it was so inadequate, why had this epitome been made at all, and why, if it was thought worth making, had it been preserved? After the middle of the last century, the peculiarities of Mark, as compared with Matthew and Luke, were examined more carefully, with the result that opinion was entirely changed. Instead of being regarded as a late, superfluous Gospel, it came to be accepted as the earliest of the three, and the original on which the others were based. This conclusion is now established, and the effect of it has been to revolutionize all study of the life of Christ. It has come to be recognized, as a first principle, that the accounts in the other Gospels must always be checked by Mark, the primitive record from which they borrowed. The acceptance of Mark's priority has been equally important for the study of the literary problem. One source from which our Gospels are derived is known to us, and here we have a sure point of departure for the whole investigation.

That Mark is the oldest Gospel, and was constantly used by Matthew and Luke, can be proved in a number of ways. There is first the linguistic proof. In style and language Mark is undeniably less polished than Matthew and Luke, and it would be contrary to all example that well-written documents should be so revised as to produce a cruder one. Again, there is the

argument from religious attitude. We know that as time went
on the feeling of the church towards Jesus became ever more
reverential. It was acknowledged that he stood apart from
other men, and no act or sentiment could be attributed to him
which might seem to place him on the ordinary human level.
Mark does not scruple to describe him as sometimes angry or
indignant. He makes him say, "Why callest thou me good?
None is good but God only" (Mark 6:18). He tells us that
at Nazareth "he could do no mighty works" because of the
people's unbelief (Mark 6:5, 6). It is noticeable that in Matthew these admissions of human limitation are toned down.
Jesus "would not" perform miracles. He says "why dost thou
ask me concerning the good?" (Matt. 19:17.) His impulses
of anger and indignation are passed over. So everywhere in
Mark we are brought closer to Jesus as a human figure than
in the other Gospels: the later theological influences have not
yet had time to work. Once more, the literary argument is
decisive in favor of Mark's priority. It can be shown that
while Matthew and Luke constantly differ from each other,
they tend invariably to agree with Mark. When one of them
omits a passage of Mark the other retains it, and this is likewise true of words and phrases. The point is well illustrated
by Dr. E. A. Abbott, who was a great head master before he
became a New Testament critic. He tells how three papers
would sometimes be handed in at an examination which were
suspiciously like each other. Which of the three candidates
had furnished aid to the other two? There was, he always
found, one infallible test. When A and C agreed with one another they also agreed with B. When they differed, one of
them, sometimes it would be A and sometimes C, agreed with
B. Thus it was apparent that B was the boy who sat in the
middle, and the others when in difficulty had looked over his
shoulder. Now this is precisely the test which can be applied
to Matthew and Luke in comparison with Mark; and it yields
its most crucial result when we examine the *order* which they
follow in their narratives. They differ widely from each other

in their arrangement of the various incidents, but either Matthew or Luke never fails to adopt the order which is found in Mark. From this it is evident that they have both gone to Mark for the ground plan on which they work. They take liberties with the plan, and each of them remodels it after his own fashion, but the outline of it is plainly apparent in them both.

There can be little doubt, therefore, that one of the documents to which Luke, in his preface, admits his obligations was the Gospel of Mark. Some critics have argued that what he used was not our present Mark but an earlier form of it. They point to a number of passages in Mark which do not appear in Luke, particularly one considerable section which deals with the wanderings of Jesus after his departure from Galilee (Mark 6:45-8:26). From such omissions, however, it cannot be inferred that Luke had Mark before him in an earlier and shorter version. He was anxious to find room in his own work for a large amount of new material, and condensed and abbreviated wherever he could do so without serious loss. It has been noted that even when he leaves out a passage, he usually shows by some incidental reference that he is acquainted with it. That our present Mark has grown out of an earlier work, is more than probable, as we shall see later; but the expansion had taken place before the other evangelists wrote. There is every indication that they possessed Mark's Gospel in much the same form as we have it now.

Matthew and Luke between them include almost the whole of Mark, but both of them break it up, in order to use it as the framework for a great deal of additional matter. In this rearrangement of Mark, they proceed by different methods. Matthew divides it into five pieces, and between each two he introduces a discourse, made up of words spoken by Jesus in his teaching. Luke's procedure is to break Mark's narrative into two great sections. Up to chapter 9, verse 50, he keeps close to Mark, interweaving with it much that he has borrowed from other sources, but never losing sight of it. Then for nine long chapters (9:51-18:14), he throws Mark aside and works entirely with other material. When he has disposed of this he returns to Mark where he had left off and continues to follow it.

The question has often been raised as to whether Matthew and Luke may have some mutual dependence, apart from their common dependence on Mark. Is it not possible, for instance, that among the "many" writings which he consulted, Luke had access to Matthew's Gospel and adopted some of its suggestions? It is pointed out in support of this theory that in a number of places (about thirty in all) Matthew and Luke agree with each other, while differing from Mark. Might it not appear from this that one of them had looked into the other's work and noted alterations here and there which he approved? But these agreements of Matthew and Luke against Mark can be adequately explained in several ways. (1) There are several places in which Mark is obviously in error, as when he gives the wrong name to the high priest in the time of David (2:26). Two well-informed men would both notice such blunders and correct them. (2) Most of the agreements are purely linguistic. Two writers with a good knowledge of Greek would independently change a harsh or clumsy expression into that which good usage required. (3) Both Matthew and Luke are anxious, wherever they can, to shorten Mark's account so as to make room for their extra material. Without any collusion, they would single out certain passages which lent themselves to abridgment. (4) It must never be forgotten that Matthew and Luke, as we now have them, are not exactly the same as when they were written. Several centuries had passed before the date of our earliest surviving manuscript, and during this time the text had undergone frequent copying and revision. One of the chief temptations of a scribe was to bring one Gospel into harmony with another. As he copied Luke, he would recall a familiar phrase in Matthew, and it would find its way almost unconsciously into the passage he was writing. We know, for example, from the evidence of the best manuscripts, that Luke's version of the Lord's Prayer was considerably different from Matthew's, yet in most of the later texts it is made almost exactly the same. Something of this kind must have happened in more cases than we can now determine.

That Matthew and Luke worked in entire independence may be regarded as certain. If one of them had known the other, he would not have confined his borrowing to points of minute detail. Luke could have taken from Matthew a whole series of memorable sayings of which he makes no use. Matthew would have found in Luke those beautiful parables which illustrate more vividly than anything else the thought and character of Jesus. It is unthinkable that either evangelist should have neglected such treasures as the one could offer to the other. They must have worked in mutual independence, both of them using Mark and supplementing it from other sources.

4. *The Second Source*

The real difficulties begin when we try to ascertain those sources outside of Mark which have gone to the making of the other Gospels. Mark, by a happy chance, is preserved to us, but the rest of the documents ceased to be copied when they had been incorporated in the longer Gospels, and are now completely lost. It is possible, however, to form at least a general conception of the nature of one of them. When we deduct from Matthew and Luke that portion of their contents which is derived from Mark, there is another portion of about two hundred verses (roughly one-sixth of each Gospel) which they have in common. It is a natural assumption that this represents a second source on which the two evangelists have drawn. This assumption is strengthened when we find that the verses in question are all, broadly speaking, of the same character. They are concerned, not so much with the actions of Jesus, as with his sayings, and afford us, when we put them all together, a full conspectus of his teaching. Scholars are now agreed that, along with Mark, the two evangelists made use of some kind of manual which contained the sayings of Jesus. This indeed was possibly the chief reason why a need was felt for the new Gospels. The tradition had hitherto run in two separate channels — the story of Jesus' life and the record of his teaching. It came to be realized that this division was misleading, since the teaching and the life belonged to each other and neither of them could be rightly understood when they were kept separate. Two writers about the same time decided to blend the two streams of tradition and present in a single work "the things which Jesus said and did" (Acts 1:1).

Reference has been made to that fragment of Papias in which it is stated: "Matthew arranged the Discourses [Logia] in the Hebrew language and each one interpreted them as he was able." This early notice came naturally to the minds of many scholars when they had once perceived that Matthew and Luke must have used a collection of Sayings. They concluded that Papias had spoken, not of our present Gospel of Matthew, but of one of its sources, the manual of teaching for which Matthew may, in the first instance, have been responsible. This conjecture appeared so certain that the lost work was usually referred to as the "Logia." The name, however, is misleading, since the interpretation of Papias' words is far from certain. It has now been generally agreed to give up the term Logia, and to indicate the lost source by the neutral symbol "Q." This is convenient, and commits us to no definite theory as to the nature and origin of the document.

At this point, however, a question arises which has bearings of the utmost importance. Are we justified in referring to the lost source, even by a neutral symbol? The name Q seems to be as colorless as it well can be, but it does at least suggest a regular document, similar to the Gospel of Mark. A generation ago scholars worked on this assumption and made many efforts to define the precise extent of Q and to reconstruct it in its original form. They are now arriving at the conviction that it never existed as a definite work. It grew, perhaps, around some primitive nucleus, but passed through a number of versions, and was constantly being added to and modified. Each important community would have its own copy of Q, which it kept revising for itself, and Matthew and Luke apparently had access to two different copies which agreed only partially with each other. An illustration might again be taken from our hymn books. It is impossible to speak of "the hymn book," for each church has a different one, although they coincide, in so far as they all contain a certain number of familiar hymns. Yet each church has made its own collection, and has edited the universal hymns to make them more suitable to its own needs. The symbol Q may be retained for the sake of convenience, but always with the understanding that it need not signify a single, uniform document.

This becomes evident when we compare those passages in Matthew and Luke which are so much alike that they must be regarded as taken from Q. In their use of Mark, the two evangelists stick pretty closely to their original. They put Mark's language into better Greek and omit and transpose, but their aim is to reproduce their source with due fidelity. There is no reason to doubt that this is also their aim when they employ the other source, and the words as we find them may be accepted as those which stood in Q. But here we observe a striking fact. In the Q passages of Matthew and Luke, there is sometimes a closer resemblance than in the passages taken from Mark, while at other times the difference is very considerable. The Beatitudes, for example, are given quite differently in the two Gospels, and in some places the variation is so great that it is doubtful whether the same saying is in question. Only one explanation seems to cover these facts. The difference existed in the documents which Matthew and Luke had before them, and each of them had used his own edition of Q. Those sayings in which the resemblance is very close had apparently passed unchanged into all the editions, and must have been among the earliest to be written down. Others had been circulated by word of mouth for a considerable time before they found their way into written collections, and in this process had assumed very different forms.

A further question arises in the same connection. We can safely assign to Q only those verses, about two hundred in all, which are found in both Matthew and Luke. It has sometimes been inferred that these verses constituted the whole work, and it is not unreasonable to suppose that the evangelists would try to preserve it as fully as they could. Whatever else they were obliged to shorten or omit, they would desire to make room for the whole record of the actual words of Jesus. Yet if they had Q before them in different versions, Matthew's copy would have sayings not found in Luke's, and vice versa. In each Gospel there are many verses peculiar to itself, and it can hardly be doubted that some of these are genuine Q material, although we cannot now identify them. They had place in only one of the two copies employed, and we can safely attribute to Q only those passages which happened to stand in both of them; but this test has no absolute value. For this reason, the reconstruction of Q will never, with our present knowledge, be possible. All that we can attribute to the lost source is that group of sayings which Matthew and Luke have in common; but we must allow for a wide margin of other sayings which may have stood in one collection, though not in the other.

Q was therefore not a fixed book, but a collection which was always more or less fluid. We may conceive of a missionary carrying about with him a notebook of Jesus' Sayings and inserting in it from time to time any new saying that might come to his knowledge. But while Q was thus constantly changing and expanding, it would retain its general character as a manual of the Lord's teaching. To this extent, it was a definite source to which we can give a specific title. At the same time, we have to reckon with the possibility that, before it reached Matthew and Luke, it had in some measure been incorporated in longer works. Those earlier evangelists to whom Luke alludes in his preface may well have made some use of the Q collection, and the two later writers may have known it only at secondhand. This view is favored by some modern critics, but must be regarded as doubtful. The most obvious reason why Matthew and Luke decided to write their Gospels is that they wished to combine the Q record with that of Mark. If this had already been done in a full-length Gospel, they could have had little motive for undertaking their work.

What, then, was the original character of Q? This question loses much of its importance if we assume that Q was never a fixed document; but even when we think of it as nothing more than a loose compilation, several conclusions may be drawn. (1) In the main it consisted of sayings of Jesus. One of the chief tasks of the missionaries was to impress on their converts the new way of life which Jesus had taught, and for this purpose they needed a manual which preserved his instructions in the very words he had used. (2) It cannot have consisted wholly of detached sayings. Again and again we find a saying linked, in both Matthew and Luke, with an incident which gave rise to it. There is at least one passage traceable to Q (the healing of the centurion's servant) which is more narrative than teaching. Prefixed to the collection, there was apparently a brief account of the ministry of John the Baptist and the beginnings of the ministry of Jesus. To some extent the manual of teaching must have contained the rudiments of a history. (3) Very strangely this work, which recounted the beginnings of the Gospel story, had nothing to say about the end. When they come to their account of the Passion, Matthew and Luke are both anxious to add to Mark's narrative, but in neither of them is there anything that seems to be derived from Q. It cannot be supposed that Q placed a subordinate value on what was always the chief theme of Christian preaching. The presumption rather is that the Passion formed a great subject by itself, which was not to be treated incidentally as a mere part of a record. Paul indicates in Galatians (3:1) that he used to begin his message with a vivid account of how Jesus died, describing the event, apparently, with all

its attendant circumstances ("Jesus Christ was depicted before your eyes in his Crucifixion"). This, it may be surmised,
was the practice of all missionaries. The Q manual would aim
only at assisting their memories as to the details of the teaching; for the great central theme of the Passion, they required
no written data. They would not be missionaries at all unless
they had the story by heart. (4) Although it never had a fixed
literary form, the Q document was drawn up in a certain order. It began with John the Baptist's appearance, and perhaps was arranged throughout roughly according to the chronology. But the arrangement, in the main, seems to have been
topical. Again and again both Matthew and Luke join
together a series of detached sayings which deal with the same
subject (e. g., ritual ceremonies, the Sabbath, divorce, forgiveness), and they had apparently found the sayings thus arranged in Q. The collection had been meant for practical
teaching purposes, and was so constructed that the teacher
might have before him all that Jesus had said on various given
subjects. Matthew, as we shall see, was to carry out more
fully this method of arranging the words of Jesus, but the idea
itself is traceable to Q.

This lost source, which we now know only through its use
by Matthew and Luke, was probably the very earliest deposit
of Gospel tradition. Everything appears to show that it had
been long in forming, and the process must have begun almost
as soon as the church was founded. The disciples could rely
on memory for the events of Jesus' life, but words are in their
nature elusive, and it must have been evident from the first
that if the teaching were to be accurately preserved, it must be
set down in writing. There was an urgent motive for preserving it, since the precepts of Jesus were the law of Christian
practice. They needed from the outset to be fixed in such a
manner that the church could appeal to them for guidance in
any case of doubt or difficulty. On several more definite
grounds it appears evident that the work of collecting the Sayings began very early. (1) In most of them the Aramaic origi-

nal is plainly discernible beneath the Greek translation. Not only can they be turned back literally into the language used in Palestine, but it can be shown in some cases that the Greek translator has mistaken the sense of an Aramaic word or idiom. (2) In many of the sayings, the agreement of Matthew and Luke is extremely close, although they are using different versions. This would seem to indicate that there was a nucleus in the collection so old that it had become unalterable. No matter how conditions might change and Christian thought advance, there was this body of teaching which must be accepted as it was, since it belonged to the very beginnings of the religion. (3) Perhaps the strongest argument for the early date of Q is that Mark himself appears to use this document as a source. His primary concern is with the narrative of Jesus' actions, and it is only incidentally that he gives any account of the teaching. But the life and teaching were so much bound up together that neither could be taken quite separately. Just as Q was obliged to note a number of incidents, so Mark could not wholly neglect the Sayings. His record of them is scanty when compared with that of Matthew and Luke, but where he reports some word of Jesus, he appears to make use of Q, in a version different from that employed by either of the others. Here we may observe one of the most curious and significant facts about the Gospels. Matthew and Luke both contain a number of verses which are known as "doublets," *i. e.*, the same saying is repeated in two somewhat different forms. (E. g., "He that hath to him shall be given" is found in Matt. 13:12 and 25:29; also in Luke 8:18 and 19:26. "He that would follow me let him deny himself" occurs in Matt. 10:38 and 16:24; also in Luke 9:23 and 14:27). The old view was that these sayings were repeated by Jesus on various occasions in order to emphasize their importance, but it is now recognized that wherever we meet with a doublet, one of the forms in which it is given corresponds with a verse in Mark. The inference is that the two evangelists found the same saying, reported somewhat differently, both in Mark and Q; unable to decide which version was the more authentic, they have given both. This phenomenon of the doublets is one of the clearest proofs that Matthew and Luke are derived from two main sources. It also proves that Mark himself made use of the Q source, in some variant copy, when he wished to bring into his history some fragment of Jesus' teaching. Not only did he have Q before him, but he must have had it in Greek, for several of his Q quotations agree almost verbally with those of Matthew and Luke. From this it follows that, although Mark is considerably earlier than the other two Gospels, Q must have existed so long before Mark that it had already passed into a Greek translation.

There can be little doubt, therefore, that Q is the most primitive Gospel source, not perhaps in its whole extent, but at least in its chief elements. Through the Q source, we come nearer than anywhere else to a first-hand, one might almost say a contemporary, account of Jesus. A supreme value thus attaches to this source, though unfortunately we cannot single out with any certainty those parts of it which come from the earliest years, when Jesus was still a vivid memory. Yet the very fact that no portion of Q is markedly different from the rest, is itself significant. We can infer from it that the record of Jesus' teaching, as it was drawn up later, was fully in keeping with the primitive tradition. What we have in our Gospels is a faithful transcript of what Jesus actually taught.

In their employment of Q, Matthew and Luke follow two different methods. Matthew tries as far as possible to alternate his two main documents. He gives a section of Mark's narrative and then a part of the teaching as he finds it in Q, and so continues throughout his book. He does not, however, preserve Q's order as he does that of Mark. Before setting to work he has been at pains to sort out the Q material into five groups of kindred sayings, and each of these groups he presents as a discourse, supposed to have been uttered by Jesus at a given time. Luke has been much less ingenious. He tries when possible to connect the Q sayings with various incidents,

and makes room for those which are left over in the nine chapters (9:51-18:14) inserted between the two parts of his Marcan narrative. The question has been much debated as to
whether Matthew or Luke has reported the sayings with
greater fidelity. From all that we can gather, they both ad-
hered closely to the record before them, and the real question
is, "which of them possessed the Q collection in the more authentic form?" Probably their copies were about equal in
value. In the different versions of Jesus' teaching, there were
sayings which had been modified, but all of them preserved
many sayings just as they had been spoken. It is fortunate that
several copies of the source are represented in our Gospels.
By comparison of Matthew and Luke, and of Mark when he
happens to include a Q fragment, we can usually form a pretty
accurate judgment of what Jesus must originally have said.

5. The Lucan Source

It is certain that Matthew and Luke derived much more
from Q than those two hundred verses which they have in
common; but allowing for the Q passages which cannot be
identified, there is still a large portion of the two Gospels,
perhaps a third of each, which must have been taken from
extra sources. Luke himself speaks of "many" previous documents, and by this he must mean more than two. It is Luke,
indeed, who affords the clearest evidence of a third source,
hardly less important than Mark and Q. His Gospel contains
a large amount of material of which the other evangelists
know nothing, and which consists for the most part of parables
and incidents akin to parables (e. g., the stories of Zacchæus
and of Martha and Mary). The parables which every one
knows by heart are almost all to be found in Luke, most of
them clustered together in that middle portion of his Gospel
in which he breaks away from Mark. They are widely different in subject and application, yet they all bear a family likeness which indicates a common source. It may be that this
collection of Parables formed a work by itself, drawn up by

someone who was peculiarly interested in this side of Jesus' teaching. Or perhaps it was included in a longer record which had many of the elements of a regular Gospel. It is a striking feature of Luke's Gospel that, while he repeats a number of episodes which correspond with episodes in Mark, he describes them quite differently and places them in a different context (e.g., the visit of Jesus to Nazareth, and the calling of the disciples). With Mark before him he could hardly on his own initiative have taken such liberties with the narrative. He must have had an authority to which he attached a value equal to that of Mark, and which at times he preferred. According to a recent theory, he used as his framework, not the Gospel of Mark, but another Gospel altogether. Into this he fitted, now an extract from Mark, and now one from Q, always relying in the main on this other document which he believed to be more in keeping with the facts. Some of the phenomena of Luke's Gospel would seem to bear out this theory, but it must always be remembered that Luke, more than any other New Testament writer, was a literary artist, who was able to weave together varied material and give it the same texture and color. Where he seems to be using a single homogeneous source, he may be combining separate documents, rewriting them in his own language and covering the gaps and seams. In any case, it is hazardous to challenge the view that Luke, like Matthew, has taken Mark as the basis of his Gospel. We know for certain that Luke had Mark before him and made constant use of it. Of that other work we know nothing. Its very existence can be affirmed only on the ground of doubtful inference. There may indeed have been a primitive Gospel which ran parallel with Mark, but all the characteristics of Luke can be quite well explained on the theory that he worked, like Matthew, with Mark and Q, supplementing these main documents with others which had come into his possession. Of these the chief one, and the only one of which we can be reasonably certain, was that from which he derived his parables.

6. *The Other Sources*

When we take out from Matthew and Luke all that belongs
to Mark and Q and Luke's special source, there remains about
a third of each Gospel which is still unaccounted for. No attempt to determine its origin can be anything but guesswork.
A modern historian who makes use of a number of documents
is careful at every point to indicate his sources in footnotes.
Without these references even the best informed reader would
usually find it hard to say where any given fact was vouched
for. Matthew and Luke never tell us the sources of their information, and it came to them from documents which have
now been completely lost. In some recent commentaries, every
verse is confidently set down to some particular authority, but
all this, in the nature of things, may be dismissed as utterly
futile.

We may be sure, however, that besides the documents we
can still identify, the evangelists used others, of less importance; and that they also depended, to some extent, on oral
tradition. A modern biographer, writing of some famous man
of fifty or sixty years ago, is always glad to introduce anecdotes which he has gleaned himself and which have not yet
appeared in print; and our evangelists would naturally do likewise. In the Christian communities to which they belonged,
Sayings of Jesus and stories about him would be current,
some of them, perhaps, with little historical foundation. We
need to allow in our Gospels for this hearsay element, which
doubtless accounts for some passages in them which look more
like legend than sober fact. Taken on the whole, however,
there is wonderfully little that we need to deduct from our
Gospels. When we consider that they were written long after
the event and that a religion had now woven itself about the
Person of Jesus, we might have expected that everything in
the history would have become distorted. As it is, we rarely
are conscious of a false note. When the various incidents are
checked by what we know of Palestinian conditions at that
time, they are all lifelike. The stories, even when they appear

most marvelous, may have grown quite naturally out of things that actually happened. All this is because our Gospels, for much the greater part, are based not on vague tradition, but on documents which had been fixed in writing while the events were freshly remembered. The evangelists have kept faithfully to those documents. Again and again they report a Saying of Jesus which they have not understood, or which contradicts another saying, or which runs counter to the belief of their own time. Their chief object in writing is to preserve the record as it has come to them. With our modern methods of collecting and sifting evidence they were unacquainted, but it may confidently be said that there have been few historians, either in ancient or modern times, who have worked with a more genuine desire to tell the truth.

7. *The Primitive Tradition*

Thus far we have attempted to trace back our Gospels to the earliest documents out of which they were compiled. We have seen that they were written in Greek, on the basis of writings which were also in Greek. These in turn, as we can gather from many evidences, were translated from other writings composed in Aramaic. Even here, however, we have not struck the ultimate foundations of the Gospel history. Before anything was written down, there was a time when all teaching about Jesus was by word of mouth, and what we now have in literary form goes back to this oral tradition. The chief effort of many distinguished critics in our own day is to determine the nature of those oral teachings on which the documents rested. It can be shown that what we now read as a continuous narrative is made up, for the greater part, of separate fragments — sayings, anecdotes, scraps of debate or conversation, which have been pieced together. Many theories have been suggested as to how these fragments originated, and were preserved and transmitted. According to one view, they were a sort of by-product of the early Christian preaching. An Apostle would illustrate his thought by some word or action of Jesus which he remembered, and this would be treasured and handed down. Or in their controversy with Jewish unbelievers, the disciples would recall how Jesus himself had dealt with the points at issue, and his answers to scribes and Pharisees would pass into common currency. Or the church would be faced from time to time with difficult moral problems, and some one would call to mind an incident in Jesus' ministry, when he had to meet just that difficulty. All this, however, is conjecture. If it is hard to disentangle the written documents, the task of sifting out the oral tradition is utterly hopeless. All we can be certain of is the broad fact that before the record was put into writing, it had come down, along various channels and in many different pieces, by word of mouth.

One question of real importance has emerged from this recent inquiry into the oral sources of the Gospels. If the history, as we have it, is a mosaic of separate fragments, what becomes of its continuity? Have we any guarantee that the events happened in anything like the sequence in which they now stand, or that we have any knowledge of the course of Jesus' life, although an incident here and there has been preserved? That the true order of many things in the narrative is doubtful, must be admitted. When we compare the Gospels, we frequently find that an action or saying which Mark or Matthew assigns to one place is reported by Luke in quite a different connection. It is evident that the evangelists had often nothing but their own judgment to guide them as to how they should arrange the miscellaneous notices. Yet the main outline of the life of Jesus could not but be remembered — that his youth had been spent at Nazareth, that he had been baptised by John and had come forward with a message of the Kingdom of God, that he had taught in Galilee and had finally gone up to Jerusalem, where he was crucified. With this general scheme in his mind, an intelligent writer would be able to judge from the character of most of the data where they ought to be placed. Now and then he might be uncertain, but usually it would be evident at a glance that one incident must have happened in Galilee, another in the closing days at Jerusalem. It must be presumed, too, that our evangelists had taken some pains to find out the true course of Jesus' life; otherwise they could never have ventured on the task of recording it.

8. *Results*

In concluding this survey of the critical investigation, we have to ask ourselves what its results have been for our estimate of the Gospel history. In some respects they have been negative. It was formerly assumed that the evangelists, under the guidance of the Spirit, were fully informed on all the facts, and that every statement they made must be accepted without question. We are now aware that the information they put together was of different degrees of value. Some of it had come down from the earliest days, some of it had been set on record at a later time and was affected by legend and dogma. Even the most authentic data had been considerably modified as they passed from one narrator to another. Perhaps there is hardly a saying which has come to us in precisely the form that Jesus spoke it. Almost every event is differently described by the three evangelists, and none of them may have given it exactly as it happened. When all this is taken into account, it appears to many minds that the work of Gospel criticism has been purely destructive.

On the other hand, it is the critical investigation which has put the narrative on a solid basis, so that the main facts can no longer be seriously doubted. In old days, when the whole Gospel history had to be accepted by an act of faith, it was always possible to deny everything. How could one tell that those evangelists, who admittedly wrote long afterwards, had any real information about Jesus? Might it not be that the story was a pure invention and that Jesus was an imaginary figure? We now know, as a matter not of faith but of cold historical analysis, that while our account of Jesus was late in assuming its present form, it embodies a far earlier tradition. We know, too, that this tradition was no mere floating legend, handed down by hearsay, but had long been fixed in writing. Its credentials are just as strong as those of any ancient narrative which is treated by general consent as undoubted history.

Again, it has been established by the critical inquiry that the narrative has come down from a great variety of sources. This is a fact of the utmost consequence in its bearing on our knowledge of Jesus. If all the accounts we have of him were traceable to one source, however well informed, we might fairly question them. The man who appears a saint or hero to one devoted follower often makes a different impression on other people. To understand a man in anything but a one-sided fashion, we need to have various judgments of him. We must learn what he was to his intimate friends, to those who worked with him officially, to strangers who spoke with him only at one casual meeting. It might appear, at first sight, the chief defect of our Gospels that they offer no coherent account of Jesus, but only a series of jottings, a mosaic in which a great number of fragments are joined together. Yet this, more than anything else, is what gives the record its value. It embodies the testimony of many witnesses. They were differently related to Jesus, and met him on different occasions, and looked on him with different eyes; but in all these varied accounts he is manifestly the same figure. The things he did are all in keeping with the things he said. Nothing is told about him in any part of the history which conflicts with what we learn in another. The witnesses have given their evidence quite independently, yet they all agree as to the manner of man he was. This is perhaps the strongest proof that in the Gospels we are face to face with a historical figure. It is conceivable (though by no means likely) that a number of people should have combined to worship Jesus, and then set themselves to imagine things about him which might justify their worship. But if so, they would have imagined differently. We should have had perhaps a dozen or twenty portraits, all of them impressive, but showing by their variety that they were merely fanciful. In the Synoptic Gospels we have recollections of Jesus gathered up from many different quarters, and they are all in a marvelous way consistent. This is our surest proof that the portrait set before us is that of an actual man.

CHAPTER III

THE GOSPEL OF MARK

1. *Origin*

The Synoptic Gospels are based on earlier documents and
need to be studied together, in parallel columns, so that their
common material may be at once apparent. Yet each of them
has also to be examined by itself. Although they are so much
alike, each of the three has a purpose and character of its own
and is beset with special problems. In the minds of most
readers of the New Testament, all the Gospels are confused
together, and the result is a composite picture in which it is
impossible to distinguish any clear outlines. So far as the
ordinary reader is concerned, the ancient attempt to merge
the four records in a single anonymous Gospel might just as
well have succeeded. It is part of the task of criticism to make
clear to us that the names Matthew, Mark, Luke, John,
denote separate works. Due account must be taken of all the
information contained in them, but we need also to keep each
Gospel apart and discover what the author has set himself
to do.

The oldest Gospel, and therefore the most valuable from
a historical point of view, is that of Mark. Matthew and Luke
between them repeat almost everything that is told in Mark,
but no critical sifting of the history would have been possible
if Mark had not been preserved to us. Why it has been preserved is something of a problem. It is certain that Matthew
and Luke, from the moment they appeared, were recognised
as far superior to anything that had gone before. The Q
record of the teaching was superseded so completely that it
ceased to be copied, and the very fact that it had existed was

soon forgotten. We should expect that a like fate would have overtaken Mark, and it may be gathered from the evidence of the surviving manuscripts that Mark was far less frequently read than the other two Gospels. Down to our own times, it was never mentioned without a certain disparagement, as a mere summary of what was recorded much more fully and skillfully by Matthew and Luke. Yet in spite of this powerful rivalry, it maintained itself in being, and at last, in a more critical age, came to its own. This survival of Mark can be explained only in one way. There must have been circumstances quite apart from its intrinsic claims which caused this short Gospel to be valued. For the sake of its origin, the church regarded it with peculiar respect; or there was some prominent community which sponsored it and would not allow it to be discarded. Probably both these causes were at work in securing a place for it when, to all appearance, it had become superfluous.

(1) There might seem, at first sight, to be nothing particularly venerable in the origin of this Gospel. It comes to us as the work of "John, surnamed Mark," who is several times referred to in the New Testament, but always as a subordinate person, in attendance on more eminent missionaries (Acts 12:12, 15:37; Col. 4:10; II Tim. 4:11; Philem. 24; I Pet. 5:13). His mother, Mary, belonged to the primitive church at Jerusalem, and in her house it was accustomed to hold its meetings. He was the nephew or cousin of Barnabas (Col. 4:10), and accompanied Paul and Barnabas on their first missionary journey, but deserted them halfway. At the close of the First Epistle of Peter, there is an affectionate mention of "Mark, my son." The only notice of Mark which is more than incidental is not much to his credit. When Paul and Barnabas were about to set out on a second journey, they quarreled and separated because Paul refused to travel again with Mark, who had previously shown such faint-heartedness. At a later time he seems to have recovered the esteem of Paul and of the church at large, but his name for its own sake would

never have secured the survival of the Gospel. No doubt the
true reason why his name carried weight is suggested in a
passage where Papias, writing about 140 A.D., quotes the
testimony of an "elder" who had given him information about
the earlier days of the church:

And the elder spoke as follows: Mark, who had become the interpreter of Peter, wrote accurately but not in order all that he remembered
concerning the Lord's sayings or doings. For he did not hear the Lord
or accompany him, but was later, as I said, a companion of Peter, who
offered his instructions as the occasion required, without attempting to
frame an ordered account of the Lord's sayings. So Mark made no mistake when he wrote some things as he recalled them. For he was intent
on one aim, — not to leave out or falsify anything whatever of the
things he had heard.

It may be gathered from this passage that Mark's Gospel was
believed, from an early time, to contain the reminiscences of
Peter, who had used Mark as his interpreter or reporter (the
precise meaning of the Greek term is obscure). Thus a special
prestige attached to this Gospel as the work, in some sense,
of the Prince of the Apostles.

(2). Not only could it claim an illustrious parentage, but
there is reason to believe that it was the cherished possession
of the church of Rome, which almost from the first occupied
a premier place. It cannot be doubted that Mark wrote for a
Gentile community, for he frequently appends a translation
of Aramaic words which he happens to use, and is at pains to
explain Jewish customs. A number of minute peculiarities appear to show that Rome was the community he had in mind;
and this is further borne out by the passage in I Peter, which
indicates that it was in Rome that Mark had attended the
Apostle. Above all, we have the fact that Mark's Gospel
continued to maintain itself when other early records were
allowed to fall into neglect. The only church which had influence enough to impose its own wishes on all Christian opinion
was that of Rome.

2. *Date*

At what date was the Gospel written? In view of the issues involved, this question is all-important, but unfortunately we have no means of answering it with any precision. According to Irenæus, who wrote about 180 A.D. and collected many traditions which go back much earlier, Mark's Gospel was not composed until after the death of Peter and Paul. If this statement be accepted (and there is no good reason for doubting it), the year 64 A.D. may be taken as the earliest possible date. The evangelist himself makes no allusion to any contemporary event which would enable us to fix the time when he wrote, but it may be there is one allusion of an indirect kind. The year 70 A.D. had witnessed the awful disaster of the fall and destruction of Jerusalem, the city which had been so intimately connected with the life of Jesus. It was the Christian belief that he had himself foretold the calamity, and if the prediction had been fulfilled when Mark wrote his Gospel we should expect that this would somehow be indicated, as it undoubtedly is in Luke 19:41-44. In his thirteenth chapter, Mark does describe the woes which were to fall on the Jewish people, but the terms in which he does so are so vague that we cannot say for certain that he thinks of the final disaster. The crucial verse is 13:14: "But when you see the abomination of desolation standing where he ought not, let him that is in Judæa flee into the mountain." Here there is a reference to the widespread Jewish belief that wickedness would reach its climax when a heathen image, or the Antichrist himself, should be enthroned in the Temple. But instead of mentioning the Temple, Mark uses the indefinite phrase "where he ought not," and perhaps he so expresses himself because at the time he wrote the Temple had ceased to exist. If this may be assumed, the Gospel was subsequent to 70 A.D., though it cannot be placed long after that date, for it was plainly a well-established work when it was employed, some time before the end of the first century, by Matthew and Luke. Indeed it is possible that the great events in Judæa, of which the whole world was talking, had something to do with the origin of the book. In the destruction of the guilty city, the church saw a judgment on the people who had rejected the true Saviour, and the time seemed opportune for a presentation of his life and message. For every reason, a date very shortly after 70 A.D. seems to fit in best with the facts.

3. Sources

From the earliest time, the Gospel was attributed to Mark, and the validity of the title need not be questioned. Mark was not a man of any particular eminence, and his name would never have been chosen without some strong ground. If the object had been merely to commend a work of uncertain origin, it could have been ascribed just as easily to some personal disciple of Jesus as to a quite secondary figure of the later age. There is good reason, too, to credit the statement of Papias that Mark based his account on the reminiscences of Peter. This information must have come to Papias within thirty or forty years after the Gospel was written, when the circumstances of its origin were still remembered. Moreover, the statement is borne out by the character of the Gospel itself. Next to Jesus, the most prominent figure in it is Peter. The story properly begins at the point where Peter becomes acquainted with Jesus. The scenes most fully described are those in which Peter had some part, and especially those which took place at Capernaum, where Jesus was an inmate of Peter's house. It is noticeable, for that part, that whenever we come to incidents at which Peter was not present there is a falling off in the life-like quality of the narrative; we no longer have the impression that we are hearing a story at first-hand. One point in the statement of Papias has often caused difficulty. He says that Mark "did not recount the events in order," and this is unjust to Mark, who is particularly anxious to bring everything into its right sequence. His order is much more in keeping with historical probability than that of any other evangelist. It may be that Papias implies merely that Mark is content to put down the various incidents as they happened, without much effort to make a smooth, continuous story. As compared with the more finished works of Matthew and Luke, his work is not so much a history as a journal or chronicle.

It is only in parts, however, that Mark's Gospel can have been written from the reminiscences of Peter. Much of it is occupied with the story of the Passion, and of those closing scenes Peter could not have spoken as an eyewitness. Moreover, while it is mainly a narrative, the Gospel tells us something of Jesus' teaching, and we have seen reason to believe that in this part of his work Mark was indebted to Q. Whatever it may have been in its original form, the Gospel as we now have it is composite, like the Gospels of Matthew and Luke. Indeed it may fairly be doubted whether Mark was its author in anything but a qualified sense. It is the Gospel "according to Mark," based, that is to say, on the collection of notes which Mark drew up from his memories of Peter's conversation. This contribution of Mark forms the nucleus and the most valuable element in the Gospel, but after it left Mark's hands it underwent a process of editing and expansion. Material was taken in from various quarters for which Peter and his "interpreter" were not responsible.

That the Gospel was composite in its origin, is borne out by the fact that it contains doublets, such as have already been noted in Matthew and Luke. The doublets in those other Gospels are the undoubted sign of a blending of sources, and a similar construction must be placed on them when they occur in Mark. In one considerable section (7-31-8:26) there are several notable instances of reduplication. Jesus, for example, performs a miracle of feeding four thousand people in the same region where a little time before he had fed five thousand. Here it is evident that the evangelist has reproduced two sources, which had reported the same incident in somewhat different terms.

It may thus be inferred that although Mark's Gospel is the oldest, and supplies the basis for the others, it is itself a

combination of several earlier documents. The author did not
conceive of himself as the pioneer in Gospel composition. His
object, like that of Matthew and Luke, was to offer an inclu-
sive record which would supersede the imperfect records
hitherto in use. Besides the reminiscences of Peter and the Q
collection, he appears to have had before him an extended
account of the Passion. Almost half of his Gospel is occupied
with those closing episodes of the life of Jesus, and perhaps
the new thing which he set himself to do was to combine the
Passion story, which had hitherto existed by itself, with a brief
record of the ministry which had led up to it. For this purpose,
he availed himself of Mark's account of Peter's teaching, and
expanded it with the help of other sources. We have to recognize that in Mark there are different strata of material, not
all of the same value. No one can read the Gospel carefully
without feeling this. There are chapters in which all is natural
and lifelike, while in other chapters we find ourselves in the
realm of the marvelous and legendary. One need only instance
the stories of the Transfiguration, the madman of Gadara,
the miraculous feedings of the multitude. It may well be that
some actual incident is behind each one of those miracles, but
the fact, whatever it was, has been transformed by the Christian imagination. The author has supplemented his primary
account from other and less trustworthy sources.

4. *The Ending of Mark*

Whatever may have been the process by which Mark's
Gospel was expanded and modified, there is no reason to
doubt that it was known in its present form by Matthew and
Luke. The Mark which we now possess was that which circulated in the church about the year 80 A.D. This statement,
however, is subject to one qualification. The last twelve verses
of our present Mark (16:9-20) are found in no early manuscript, and even in later manuscripts they appear in several
diverse forms. They were certainly added by some editor in
order to round off a work which was otherwise incomplete.

What became of the original ending of Mark? This is one of the most puzzling questions of New Testament criticism, and no satisfactory answer to it has yet been found. Apart from the spurious verses which now stand in our Bibles, the Gospel ends right in the middle of the story of the Resurrection. "And they went out quickly and fled from the Sepulchre, for they were troubled and were amazed; neither said they anything to any man, for they were afraid." In Greek the end is even more abrupt than it appears in English, for the final word is one like our "indeed" or "however"— inadmissible at the close of a sentence. It is impossible that the author can have meant to end his book in this way. For that part he had already thrown out indications that he would tell of a meeting of the disciples with the risen Christ in Galilee (14:28; 16:7), but at this point he never arrives. It has been maintained by some writers that the ending of the Gospel has been deliberately suppressed, since it contradicted the later belief that the Resurrection appearances took place in the neighborhood of Jerusalem; but an editor who took this liberty would hardly scruple to go further, and substitute something which was more to his mind. This could easily have been done by a few simple changes. The most obvious solution of the problem is to assume that some accident happened to the last sheet of the Gospel, which would be that part of the roll most exposed to wear and tear. The difficulty is that both Matthew and Luke were apparently as ignorant as ourselves with regard to the end of the Gospel. They follow Mark's narrative right on to the point where the break occurs, and have then to fall back on other sources. If we assume an accident, it must have happened very early — at a time when only one manuscript of the Gospel existed; for if there had been a duplicate, the missing page would have been restored in later copies, such as were used by Matthew and Luke. The theory of accident is indeed the most probable one, but how and when can the accident have happened? However it may be explained, the breaking off of Mark in the very middle of one of the

cardinal passages is perhaps the worst disaster that has befallen the New Testament.

5. *Historical Character*

If Mark's Gospel grew out of the reminiscences of Peter,
we can understand how its character was determined for it in
its later and more elaborate form. Peter had recounted the
things he had witnessed while in Jesus' company, and the work
continued to be mainly one of narrative. For the teaching of
Jesus, other documents were available: this Gospel had for its
governing idea the preservation of the history. We are told
how Jesus was baptised by John in the Jordan and began a
work of his own in Galilee. Scenes from the Galilean ministry
are set before us, illustrating its nature and the course it followed. Several chapters are devoted to the wanderings of
Jesus after the Galilean ministry came to an end. Then we
have an account of the journey to Jerusalem, and of the
tragic events which culminated in the Trial and Crucifixion.
The Gospel makes no pretension to be a full biography. It
omits entirely the life of Jesus before he began his ministry,
though from incidental notices we learn something of his
family and antecedents. The author confines himself to those
aspects of Jesus' activity which had to do with his public work
for the Kingdom of God. There is no regular account even of
the ministry. What we have is rather a selection of anecdotes
or tableaux, which in their origin were evidently quite separate. Some attempt has been made to string them together
by conventional phrases: "after that," "a few days after,"
"then it came to pass." The notes of place are as vague as
those of time: "in a certain place," "he went through the
villages," "on the other side of the lake," "he departed
thence." When closely analysed, the Gospel loses the sem-
blance of continuity which is thrown over it by these devices,
and becomes little more than a collection of stray episodes.
Efforts have often been made to discover a plan in the construction of the narrative, but beyond a certain point they

break down. The author does not appear to have formed for himself any clear conception of the motives which determined Jesus' action. For instance, the two turning points of the history were Jesus' abandonment of Galilee when his work there was in full career, and his subsequent decision to go up to Jerusalem. The fact that he took these steps is recorded in quite casual fashion, without any hint that they were momentous, or any suggestion of a reason. But while the narrative is thus loosely coördinated, the events appear to follow each other in proper sequence. The other evangelists have been at far greater pains than Mark to reflect on the history and arrange it skillfully; but almost always the order of Mark is preferable. Modern writers invariably follow him when they try to form a historical picture of the life of Jesus. This is not merely because his Gospel is the primary one, on which the others are based, but because it seems intrinsically to be most in accord with facts. Almost all the incidents can be best explained when they are taken in Mark's order, and even the sayings seem to fit naturally into the context in which he places them. It can hardly be by accident that Mark has thus arranged his material; neither can we credit him with a better historical instinct than his successors, for he does not seem himself to understand why some things in his story should be connected. It can only be concluded that somehow he was in closer touch with the facts than the other writers. Along with the separate anecdotes, he has received some good tradition as to the general course of Jesus' ministry, and he has arranged the various details within this framework.

6. *Purpose*

On the face of it, Mark's Gospel is a simple, straightforward chronicle of events as they happened, put together without much literary skill, but with the vividness and dramatic force which are often most conspicuous in quite artless narratives. Life is always rich and original, and the plain man who describes a real incident, just as he saw it, will obtain effects which the romancer will seek for in vain. Some critics, however, would regard this Gospel in a different light. They hold that while he seems to offer nothing but an unstudied narrative, Mark has written in the interest of certain theological ideas. As a member of the Gentile church, he was imbued with the Pauline doctrines, and has revised the Gospel history in such a manner as to enforce Paul's conception of Jesus as a heavenly being who had come to earth to secure man's redemption by his death. In support of this view, a number of passages are brought forward in which Mark appears to reflect the teaching of Paul; e.g., the well-known verse (10:45): "the Son of man came not to be ministered unto but to minister, and to give his life a ransom for many." The theory has truth in it, in so far as Mark has not written with a purely historical object. He holds definite views about Jesus, whom he regards, as he tells us in his opening verse, as "the Messiah, the Son of God." It is more than likely, too, that he was affected, more than he was himself aware, by Paul's interpretation of some things in the Christian message. Certainly he writes his Gospel not merely to satisfy curiosity about a wonderful figure, but to strengthen the church in its faith in Jesus and his divine mission. This is doubtless the reason why he tells us nothing of that earlier life of Jesus about which we would give so much to know. He is concerned with Jesus as the Messiah who represented the Kingdom of God, and the story has interest for him only from the point where the work for the Kingdom began. Only such incidents are recorded as in some way bear out the claim of Jesus to be the destined Messiah. Here and there, perhaps, some touch is deliberately added to the story in order to call our attention to its deeper significance. The incidents of the Transfiguration, for instance, and of the feeding of the multitude, are plainly meant to carry a symbolical meaning. Jesus is made to appear, even in his earthly life, as he afterwards became — the exalted Lord, who dispenses life to mankind. All this, however, does not imply that the Gospel is a theological work. No history worth reading has ever been written without some object, other than the mere narration of facts. The writer is in sympathy with a country or a cause or a form of government, and wishes to magnify or defend it. That Mark writes his Gospel in the interest of the Christian mission must be granted; but there is nothing to indicate that his work is in any sense controversial. Those passages in which he seems to advocate Paul's doctrines may be matched with others in which he rather takes the side of Paul's opponents. His so-called theology, in fact, is nothing more than that fervent belief in Jesus which he shared with all Christians.

Since he undoubtedly wrote with this religious bias, he may not have produced a history which was strictly judicial and accurate; but he cannot be accused of any willful distortion of the facts. No one, indeed, can read his Gospel without a feeling of his perfect candor and good faith. He wants to tell his story just as he heard it. The events are sometimes marvelous, and he does not try to rationalise them; they are sometimes homely, and he does not invest them with any false dignity. At the time he wrote, the Christian beliefs, especially in Gentile churches, were merging in strange speculations, but from all this Mark holds himself aloof. His task was simply to collect the surviving records of Jesus and to present them in lifelike and attractive colors, and leave them to make their own impression. In the ancient words of Papias, "Mark was intent on one thing only, — to omit or falsify none of the things that he had heard."

CHAPTER IV

THE GOSPEL OF MATTHEW

1. *Importance*

Although it is not the oldest or the most beautiful of the Gospels, Matthew has been by far the most important. As soon as the New Testament books were collected, it was placed at the very beginning. It has been accepted in all times as the authoritative account of the life of Christ, the fundamental document of the Christian religion.

This primacy accorded to Matthew's Gospel is due to several causes. (1) Its arrangement made it admirably suited to the purpose of instruction. In the other Gospels, the material is all mingled together, while Matthew has carefully gathered it into sections, so that it can be easily apprehended and held in the memory. (2) It is in Matthew that we have the fullest and most succinct account of Jesus' teaching. Not only have a great number of the Sayings been preserved but they are grouped with remarkable skill, so as to reinforce and illustrate one another. Of this, the most notable example is the so-called Sermon on the Mount, where Matthew has taken a short discourse, preserved also in Luke (Chap. 6), and filled it out with many other sayings so as to present a connected statement of Jesus' main teaching. As arranged by Matthew, the discourse has always been regarded as the classical exposition of the Christian ethic. (3) Matthew is, in every respect, the most comprehensive Gospel. It aims at setting before us all sides of Jesus' activity and all the various aspects of his teaching. It likewise represents many different phases of Christian opinion. Attempts have been made, as we shall see, to identify it with some particular interest, but apparently the very object of the writer was to do justice, even at the risk of inconsistency, to all interests. Because of this catholicity of outlook, it has always been the most widely accepted Gospel. (4) Matthew's Gospel has commended itself to the church because it is itself ecclesiastical. The more we examine it, the more we realise that the church is constantly in the writer's mind. He is the only evangelist who explicitly mentions the church (16:18; 18:17). He records a number of parables in such a way as to make them apply to the needs and conditions of the church. He regards the teaching of Jesus as the law which must henceforth be valid in the church, as the law of Moses had been in Israel. This preoccupation with the church gives something of a formal, official character to Matthew's Gospel, and it has never endeared itself to devout Christians like the Gospels of Luke and John. But as the church Gospel, it has taken its place in all ages as the standard presentation of the faith.

2. *Authorship and Date*

According to tradition, the author of the Gospel was Matthew, one of the twelve disciples. Nothing of this kind is hinted in the Gospel itself, although it describes how Matthew, a taxgatherer, was called by Jesus as he sat on the official bench, and immediately followed him (9:19). In Mark and Luke (Mark 2:14; Luke 5:27) the name of this taxgatherer is given as Levi, and it has been commonly assumed that the same man was known by both names. More probably there has been some confusion, or the name of Levi was purposely changed in order to connect Matthew with at least one definite incident in the Gospel he was supposed to have written. That Matthew was personally so obscure is a point in favor of the belief that he had something to do with the Gospel; but he cannot have been in any real sense its author. The book, as we now have it, belongs to a time when Matthew must have been long dead; and it was not only written in Greek, but is based on sources which were also in Greek. If there is any truth in the tradition of Matthew's authorship, it must be simply that he had drawn up some brief document which served as the nucleus of the later work. It has been conjectured that he may have been the first to put some of the sayings of Jesus into writing, and that his name thus attached itself to the Q collection, and finally to the Gospel in which it was incorporated. For all this, however, there is no real evidence. It is convenient to speak of Matthew as the author of the Gospel, but we must always bear in mind that it is not the work of a primitive disciple and must be viewed in the light of later conditions.

Where it was written we have no means of ascertaining. From the strongly Jewish character of some of its passages, it has often been assigned to Palestine; but the author works with sources, and the Jewish coloring belongs to the sources, not to the work itself. Moreover there is much in it that suggests the atmosphere of a Gentile, rather than a Jewish, church. A plausible guess would make Antioch its place of origin. The church of Antioch was a meeting ground of both Jewish and Gentile influences; it was also one of the earliest and greatest of churches and a gospel which issued from it would have a standing such as Matthew possessed from the first. But in the entire absence of any testimony it is hazardous to connect the Gospel with any particular place.

The date, likewise, cannot be fixed with any precision, though it can be determined within certain limits. From various indications in the Gospel itself, we can tell that it was written comparatively late. On two occasions the author refers to something which has continued "unto this day" (27:8; 28:15), implying a considerable time that has elapsed since the event. He echoes the disappointment which was felt towards the end of the first century at the long delay of the promised return of Christ (24:48; 25:5). He alludes several times to persecutions suffered for the name of Christ (5:11; 10:18; 25:36, 39), and persecution did not become a serious factor in the life of the church until near the end of the first century. Such indications of date are borne out by the relation in which the Gospel stands to Mark. If Mark was written shortly after 70 A.D., an interval of about twenty years may be allowed for its passing into such general currency that it was used independently in both the other Gospels. So it does not seem probable that Matthew was much before 90 A.D., and it cannot have been long afterwards, for early in the second century it was in general circulation. We cannot be far from the truth in assigning to it a date about 90 or 95 A.D.

3. Sources

Matthew is dependent, as we have seen, on the two main sources, Mark and Q. But about a quarter of its contents is peculiar to the Gospel itself. This material is so diverse in character that it cannot have been taken from any single document. Some of it almost certainly consists of portions of Q which do not appear in Luke, and a difference may here be noted between Matthew and Luke in their use of sources. Both of them are anxious to abbreviate, so as to leave room for their extra material, but where Luke simply omits Matthew condenses. This is apparent in their use of Mark, and they probably dealt with Q in like manner. Not only may it be assumed that Matthew retains a number of Q sayings which Luke omits, but his copy of Q may have been more extended than that of Luke. For some of his additional matter, Matthew was possibly indebted to no written source. He shows more fondness than the other evangelists for stories of a legendary character, which had apparently come to him from floating tradition: e. g., the dream of Pilate's wife (27:24, 25); Pilate's washing of his hands (25:51-53); the earthquake and ghostly apparitions at the death of Jesus (27:62-66). Perhaps in this category may be placed the opening chapters concerning the birth at Bethlehem. Matthew and Luke are hopelessly at variance in this part of their narrative. If either of the accounts is based on a historical document, it can hardly be that of Matthew, which is much the more fanciful and improbable.

4. *Plan*

It was the arrangement of Matthew's Gospel which commended it from the first as the chief handbook of Christian instruction. Here the author has proceeded on two principles. (1) He has kept the narrative and the teaching separate, alternating a section of Mark with one from Q. (2) He has aimed at massing and coördinating his material. This he has done, to some extent, even in his narrative. Instead of distributing the miracles through his book, he brings them together, devoting the greater part of two consecutive chapters to this side of Jesus' activity (8, 9). But it is chiefly in his account of the teaching that he aims at unifying his data. Where Mark and Luke record isolated sayings, spoken by Jesus on various occasions, Matthew describes him as making long discourses, each of them revolving around one main theme. In the Sermon on the Mount, the new righteousness is set forth in its contrast with the old (5-7); in the charge to the disciples, the duties of Christian missionaries are laid down (10); the incident of the little child (18:1, 2) is followed by a discourse in which Jesus describes the type of character which he requires in his followers; his strictures on the Pharisees are collected in another discourse (23) supposed to be spoken when he came into conflict with them at Jerusalem; his apocalyptic teaching occupies the whole of two chapters (24, 25), placed appropriately at the very end of his public ministry. All these discourses can be shown to be nothing else than amalgamations of a large number of separate sayings, ingeniously fitted into each other so as to form a sequence. The Sermon on the Mount, more especially, is so well constructed that it might easily pass for an organic whole, although the comparison with Luke can leave no doubt that it has been artificially put together out of many pieces. By this method of coördination, Matthew certainly gives a weight and impressiveness to Jesus' teaching which would have been missing in a chance medley of detached maxims. At the same time he has sometimes to do violence to the words of Jesus, in order to make them run consecutively. It is never safe to interpret a verse in Matthew in the light of that which precedes or follows it. The connection may seem close and suggestive, but is due, in very many instances, to the ingenuity of the evangelist himself.

Five times, in the course of the Gospel, we come on the phrase "And when Jesus had finished these sayings" (7:28; 11:1; 13:53; 19:1; 26:1). By means of this formula, the author himself marks out the plan and the main divisions of his book. At the beginning and the end there are two sections which stand by themselves, one of them dealing with the birth of Jesus and the other with his death and Resurrection (1-2; 26-28). Enclosed within these, we have the account of his ministry. In dividing it into five parts the author may merely be following what he takes to be the natural articulation of the history; but more likely he wishes to suggest the parallel of the five books of Moses. Christianity, as he conceives it, is the New Law which has replaced the old, and the account of its origin is modeled on the Old Testament story of God's ancient revelation. In each of the five divisions, there is a passage of narrative, derived from Mark, and this is followed by a discourse. This plan, however, is not carried out in a rigid, mechanical fashion. The sayings of Jesus could not all be so manipulated as to find places in a set discourse on a given theme. Most of the parables, for instance, would have had to be omitted if the general scheme had been strictly followed. In one or two of the sections, therefore, the narrative is only a slender framework for the teaching. Jesus is represented as moving from place to place and meeting with friends and enemies, but the interest centers on what he says, and not on what he does.

Looking more particularly at the five divisions of the book, we find that the first deals with the early ministry of Jesus up to the time of the calling of the disciples; the second with the extension of the ministry over Galilee; the third with the rising opposition; the fourth with the departure from Galilee

and the declaration of Messiahship; the fifth with the journey
to Jerusalem and arrival in the city. This fivefold division is
combined with another, according to which the history falls
into two great parts. Up to the time when he acknowledges
himself Messiah at Cæsarea Philippi (16:13 f.), Jesus comes
before us as a Teacher; after that our attention is fixed on
the great work which he is to accomplish by his death. The
episode of the Transfiguration (17:1-12) may be regarded
as the dividing line between the two parts of the book. On the
mountain the disciples behold their Teacher transformed into
a heavenly being; his true nature and significance are for a
moment revealed to them. For the remainder of the book we
are meant to keep this revelation in mind. All that Jesus does
henceforth is in pursuance of his supreme task as the divinely
appointed Messiah.

5. Purpose and Teaching

We thus come to the much-debated question as to the purpose and theological import of Matthew's Gospel. It will be
apparent from our brief survey of its contents that this Gospel
is much more deliberately written than that of Mark. Mark
himself is anxious to convey to his readers certain convictions
about Jesus and his work, but his chief purpose is to gather
up the historical facts and present them vividly in the order
in which they happened. Matthew also is intent on the facts,
and his principal object in writing is to include many things
which Mark had not told, especially those sayings of Jesus
of which Mark had given only a few examples. But, to a much
greater extent than Mark, he looks at the facts in the light
of given beliefs. He is convinced, for instance, that the mission
of Jesus had all been foretold in Old Testament prophecy. In
almost every chapter the phrase is repeated, "that the scripture might be fulfilled." Sometimes Matthew appears to mention a fact for no other reason than that it answered to a
prophecy. Sometimes, under the influence of scripture, he
misunderstands a fact, or is led to modify it so as to make it

correspond more nearly with a supposed prediction. Thus it is evidently one of his outstanding aims, all through the book, to demonstrate that Jesus, as the true Messiah, had brought all the prophecies to fulfillment. Again, he seeks to emphasise the contrast between the teaching of Jesus and the ancient Law. In the Sermon on the Mount, this contrast is explicitly set forth: "It was said to them of old time," "but I say unto you." Perhaps the very setting of the discourse — a series of commandments promulgated from a mountain — is meant to suggest the replacement of the old law by the new. Once more, the idea of the church, as has been noted already, is everywhere prominent. Apart from the two direct references, Matthew is always trying to relate the teaching of Jesus to the needs and circumstances and practice of the church. It is enough to instance the directions on almsgiving, prayer and fasting (6:1-18); the discussion of marriage and divorce (5:27-32); the rules for conduct towards children and brethren (18:10-14; 5:25-26; 7:12; 18:15-22); the injunctions to be faithful under persecution (10:17-36; 16:24-28). This interest in the church is so strong that it leads, in some degree, to a distortion of Jesus' message. The Kingdom which he proclaimed is confused, as it was in the later theology, with the visible church.

These are only a few of the more obvious aspects in which Matthew sets himself to read his own interpretations into the Gospel history, and it has sometimes been held that he wrote in the interests of some ecclesiastical party. According to the usual theory, he was the champion of Jewish Christianity, as against the more liberal teaching of Paul. There are some, indeed, who perceive a direct reference to Paul in the words of 5:19: "Whosoever shall break one of the least of these commandments and shall teach men so, he shall be called the least in the Kingdom of heaven." This view of Matthew as the distinctively Jewish Gospel was suggested by the statement of Papias: "Matthew wrote in the Hebrew language"; but it might seem to be supported by much in the Gospel itself. We think, for example, of the constant appeals to the Old Testament; the declaration that the Law is valid forever (5:17, 18); the limitation of Jesus' mission to "the lost sheep of the house of Israel" (15:24); the demand that while the scribes and Pharisees must not be imitated, men must obey the things that they teach (23:3). Above all, the pervading conception of Christianity as a New Law, an improvement of the Law of Moses but based on the same principles, might seem to reflect the position of those Judaists who condemned Paul for his abandonment of the Law. Yet against this Jewish tendency we have to set another, which is no less characteristic of Matthew's Gospel. Emphasis is laid on sayings and actions of Jesus which proclaim his message as universal. His disciples are to show love to all men without distinction, imitating their Father who is in heaven (5:43 f.). When the Kingdom comes, many will be gathered into it from the east and the west, while "the children of the Kingdom will be cast out" (8:11, 12). The prophecy is quoted "in his name will the Gentiles trust" (12:21), and the parable of the wicked husbandmen (21:33-43) is a clear prediction of the Gentile church which will take the place of rejected Israel. The fiercest woes are denounced on the Pharisees, the official representatives of Judaism, and the warmest eulogy is bestowed on a Gentile centurion. It is declared in the parable of the Last Judgment that "all nations shall be gathered" and obtain reward or punishment according to their deeds (25:32 f.); and the Gospel closes with the Lord's command, "Go ye, therefore, and teach all nations" (28:19, 20).

Thus in Matthew we have an outlook which is narrowly Jewish and another which is universal. It seems to be maintained, on the one hand, that the Kingdom is only for Israel, and on the other, that its destined heirs are the Gentiles. The truth appears to be that Matthew himself is not responsible for either of those views. He makes use of sources which had come to him from various quarters, some of them from the Palestinian church which opposed the Gentile mission, others

from churches in which the influence of Paul was dominant.
But while Matthew works with material which has been given
to him, he makes use of it all impartially. His object is to do
justice to different tendencies which had hitherto been in conflict. In the time of Paul, the broader conception of Christianity had been obliged to fight for its life against a jealous
type of Judaism, and Paul was hardly in a mood to see much
that was valuable in his enemies' contentions. Matthew's Gospel was written at a later time, when the truth on both sides
could be fairly recognized. It stands, not for any partial interpretation of Christianity, but for one in which all sincere opinion could find its place.

This, it would appear, is the governing motive of the Gospel. The church had sprung out of Judaism, but was conscious
that it had a new revelation; and for a long time was doubtful
as to how it should relate itself to the parent religion. There
were many Christians who revered the Law as still binding;
others could not think of it except as a positive hindrance to
the new message. Towards the end of the century, the old
animosities had subsided and the different factions were disposed to draw together. The idea of a united church, broad
enough to include diverging views, had begun to dawn on the
minds of thoughtful men. Matthew's Gospel is meant to lay
the foundation for such a church. The author's intention is
ecclesiastical, but not in the sense that he is concerned only
with externals, like many of the church statesmen who were to
follow him. He wishes to see the different bodies of Christians united by their sharing in a common loyalty to Christ and
his new rule of life, although on many debated questions they
might stand apart from one another. In his carrying out of
this purpose, his method is to preserve the varying traditions
faithfully and to lay them side by side. It cannot be denied
that he is often inconsistent, and to many this has appeared
the chief difficulty about his Gospel, and they have tried by
one device and another to harmonize his statements whenever
they seem in conflict. But the inconsistency is deliberate. The

evangelist has no uniform scheme to offer, and does not feel that this is necessary. He believes that within the one church there is room for all types of disciples — for those who would cling to the Law and for those who have discarded it, for those who see in Jesus the great Teacher, and those who know him as the Son through whom the Father reveals himself (11:25-27). This catholicity of spirit has made Matthew the representative Gospel, and is also our best guarantee that it has preserved the facts with fidelity. Matthew is not a partisan on one side or another, and makes no attempt to keep anything back or to smoothe away contradictions. He puts on record all the different testimonies, assured that they all are necessary towards a full understanding of the life of Christ.

CHAPTER V

The Gospel of Luke

1. *Connection with Acts*

In Luke's Gospel we have the first half of an extended work which is continued in the book of Acts. That the two writings are by the same hand might have been gathered from their many similarities of language and outlook, but it is placed beyond all question by the opening verse of Acts, in which the author refers to his previous work and dedicates the second, like the first, to his friend Theophilus. It may be that he wrote Acts by an afterthought, when he found that his earlier work had proved useful and was well received. More likely, his intention from the first was to tell the whole story of Christianity, and perhaps he had planned to follow the book of Acts with a third volume, recording the death of Paul and the further extension of the church. In the preface to the Gospel he speaks in general terms of "the things which have been fulfilled among us," and this phrase would cover not only the life of Jesus but its whole sequel in the later history.

The close connection of the Gospel with Acts must be borne in mind when we consider its date and authorship. These questions, indeed, cannot be properly discussed until we come to the later work. At present it need only be said that the Gospel, which was certainly written before Acts, may be assigned to a time not far removed from the year 90 A.D. The author is unacquainted with Matthew's work, and may have written a little earlier, but more probably just about the same date. According to tradition, this author was Luke, whom Paul mentions more than once as his companion, describing him in Colossians 4:14 as a physician. That Luke wrote a diary which furnished much of the information contained in Acts, there is little reason to doubt. Did he himself expand the diary into the book, as we have it, or was this done by a later hand? On this question the authorship of the Gospel depends. The man who wrote the Gospel was obviously the man who composed Acts in its finished form: was this Luke himself, or some person whose name is now lost, and who made use of Luke's diary? The problem is one which does not admit of a positive answer, but it cannot be properly discussed except in connection with the book of Acts.

2. *Purpose*

The two works must be taken together before we can form a right estimate of the purpose of Luke's Gospel, as well as of its date and authorship. No doubt it is intended, like the other Gospels, to record the life and teaching of Jesus. A number of documents were current, each of them presenting some aspect of the life; and Luke sets himself to blend them together and mold them into a unified account. He wished, also, as he tells us in his preface, to deal not merely with the later phases of Jesus' life, but with the beginnings, and to offer a narrative that would be at once more accurate and better arranged. This desire to replace the miscellaneous records hitherto existing with something like a real biography is the primary motive of the book; but it is governed also by other motives which do not fully come to light until we take it in connection with the accompanying book of Acts. At the time when Luke wrote, Christianity had become a world-wide movement, and we are shown in Acts how it had spread out gradually from its first center in Jerusalem to the great capital in the West. The object of the Gospel is to trace this mighty movement to its source. Jesus is brought before us as he pursued his work among the villages of Galilee. It passed almost unnoticed, but from that work of Jesus in a remote province, the influences had gone forth which were now changing the life of the world. Again, it is shown in Acts how a religion which was Jewish in origin had broken away from Judaism and identified itself with the Gentiles, and this motive runs also through the Gospel. Jesus in his lifetime had been misunderstood and rejected by his own people. He was born under the Law but had transcended it, insisting on requirements which in their nature were not Jewish, but were equally binding on all men. From this point of view, Luke reports the teaching and the parables, and draws his picture of the life. The descent of Jesus is traced, not merely to David and Abraham, but to Adam. In all his actions, he stands before us in his broadly human character. Though by accident a Jew, he was the representative man and the Saviour of all mankind. Once more, we have to reckon with an apologetic motive, which in Acts is clearly pronounced and which can be distinguished also in the Gospel. At the time when Luke wrote, Christianity was under suspicion as a revolutionary movement, dangerous to the state. Persecutions had broken out against the church and were held to be justified on the ground of its origin. The historian Tacitus, in the first account we have of Christianity in general literature, tells that "this name was given to it from one Christus, who in the reign of Tiberius had been condemned to death by the procurator Pontius Pilate, so that the pestilent superstition was for the moment put down." This, for the Roman world, was the crushing argument against the new religion. The purity of Roman justice must not be challenged, and the fact was certain that Jesus, who had begun this Christian sect, had been duly examined and condemned by a Roman court. Luke intends his Gospel to meet these objections on which the persecutors grounded their case. He records the early history as it had really been, showing that Jesus had spent his life, not in political agitation, but in teaching and healing. He offers a full account of the teaching, and leaves no doubt in the minds of his readers that it was purely moral and religious. He describes the opposition which had led to the death of Jesus, and traces it entirely to the jealousy and bigotry of the Jewish leaders. Pilate, it is true, had assented to the condemnation, but had merely lent his sanction to a judgment contrived and formulated by the Jewish court. So far from being responsible for Jesus' death, the Roman governor had declared his innocence and had vainly tried to acquit him. It is fairly certain that, in the book of Acts, Luke has unduly softened the hostile attitude of the Roman courts to the Christian missionaries, and probably he has done something of the same kind in the Gospel. In his whole account of the trial before Pilate, we have to allow for that apologetic motive with which he writes.

Along with his defence of Christianity against heathen prejudice, Luke has a missionary purpose. Many earnest and intelligent Gentiles in those closing years of the first century had become interested in the new teaching, and Luke wishes his work to find acceptance with this public outside of the church. This is apparent, not only from his anxiety to meet heathen objections, but from the general character of his work. To a much greater extent than the other Gospels, it is a literary product, composed in good Greek and carefully arranged. The author has been at special pains to make his story interesting. To this day, Luke's Gospel, viewed merely as a piece of narrative, is one of the most charming books in the world; and this is not entirely due to the fact that it deals simply and sincerely with a wonderfully moving subject. If his book was to reach the public he had in mind, Luke needed, above all things, to make it readable. People who had hitherto known nothing of Jesus, or had been prejudiced against him, must have the story so told as to attract them and compel them to follow it to the end. Perhaps it is because of this wish to reach the larger Gentile public, that Luke has little concern with theological questions. At the time he wrote, the church was occupied with building up its scheme of doctrine, and the evangelist himself, according to tradition, was the companion of Paul, who was so prominent in all the current controversies. On this ground, the attempt has often been made to discover the Pauline doctrines in his work; indeed the view has often been held, since very early times, that he wrote at Paul's suggestion and under his influence, as an advocate of the special Pauline ideas. Of this no trace can be found in his work. We are left wondering, rather, that such a fervid admirer of Paul is apparently ignorant of Paul's theology, or at least takes no interest in it. The chief reason is doubtless that Luke did not have a theological mind. Like many excellent Christians, he was content to believe in Christ and follow him, without ever trying to answer those baffling questions to which the Christian message gives rise as soon as we try to explain it. But the absence of anything like theology in his writings may also be due, in some measure, to the object with which he wrote. He addresses himself to a Christian public, especially to those who, like Theophilus, were preparing themselves for baptism and sought to "know the certainty of those things in which they had been instructed." But he also has in view a body of readers outside of the church. They are anxious to hear about Christianity, but with its doctrinal differences they have no concern. All that they require to know as yet is its main teaching and, most of all, the message which had been proclaimed by Jesus and exemplified in his life.

3. Plan

We come back, however, to the chief purpose of the Gospel, which is to present an account of Jesus more adequate than those which had hitherto appeared. Luke is not content, like Mark, to deal simply with a few striking events of the ministry. His object is to write a biography, similar to those lives of famous men which were coming into vogue in the classical literature of the time. Like other popular biographers, he wishes by means of typical anecdotes to illustrate the character of Jesus and make him stand before us as a human personality. In Mark the incidents are selected with a view to proving Jesus' Messiahship. Luke wants to throw light on Jesus himself, and to make us realize how men felt towards him. This interest in character may be discerned also in Luke's record of the teaching. He wishes us to regard the sayings, not only as maxims for the conduct of the Christian life, but as revealing Jesus himself in his manner of thinking and his outlook on the world. If Luke was not a theologian, he had a keen eye for human life, and was susceptible in a peculiar degree to nobility and greatness wherever he found them. This is strikingly apparent in his portrait of Paul, and still more so in his picture of Jesus himself.

Planning, as he does, to write a regular history, he begins with the advent of John the Baptist, whose career was the prelude to that of Jesus. He deals more fully than Matthew with all the circumstances of Jesus' birth, and adds an anecdote of his boyhood — the one incident preserved to us in the Gospels of the life of Jesus previous to his baptism. It may be inferred that nearly all authentic memories of the earlier life had been lost. Luke is bent on making his record as full as possible, but for the first thirty years he had been able to discover nothing except that one anecdote about the visit to the Temple. When he comes to the public ministry, he follows in the main the narrative of Mark, but with a number of differences. For instance, he makes Jesus begin his ministry in Nazareth, while Mark puts the mission to Nazareth later, and describes it much less fully. Sometimes he takes his account of an incident from another source than Mark (e. g., the Temptation 4:1-13; the calling of the disciples, 5:1-11; the dispute with the Pharisees, 11:14-23). In two sections of his narrative, a shorter (6:20-8:3) and a much longer one (9:51-18:14) he throws Mark entirely aside, taking him up again when he has disposed of his extra material. Mark had come to him, as to Matthew, without the original ending, and he rounds off the broken narrative of the Resurrection with the story of the two disciples who met the risen Lord on the way to Emmaus.

Luke's treatment of Mark's record is everywhere freer than Matthew's. He does not reproduce it with the same fullness, and sometimes leaves out considerable passages or notices them only by an incidental allusion (e. g., the death of John the Baptist, which is described at length in Mark 6:14-29, is merely referred to in Luke 9:9; the whole section Mark 6:45-8:10 is passed over). More frequently than Matthew, he changes the order of Marcan passages or in some way modifies their substance. This liberty which he allows himself with regard to Mark may be put down partly to his exercise of historical judgment. He tells us in his preface that he has aimed at "accuracy," and evidently considers the information of Mark as in some cases doubtful. Possibly it was on this ground that he cut out Mark's story of the death of John, which in itself bears the stamp of popular legend and conflicts with the historical data as known to us from Josephus. Perhaps, too, he perceived that Mark had sometimes reported in two different forms what was really the same incident, as in the passage on the feeding of the four thousand (Mark 8:1-9). But his chief reason for departing from Mark appears to be not so much critical, as literary. While desiring to present a narrative that would be historically correct, he wanted to bring in new information which he had collected from various sources, and to arrange all his material compactly, in a story that would run on smoothly and naturally and sustain the interest of the reader. To attain this purpose, he does not hesitate, when necessary, to abridge and alter the record of Mark.

The method thus followed by Luke has the effect in one place of seriously confusing the course of the history. We have had occasion several times to mention Luke's "long insertion," where for nine chapters together (9:51-18:14) he abandons Mark and introduces a great mass of varied incident and teaching. During the period covered by these chapters, which in themselves are among the most valuable in the Gospels, he represents Jesus as making his way slowly from Galilee to Jerusalem. The impression is left on us, by this section of Luke, that a great part of Jesus' ministry came after the confession of Messiahship at Caesarea Philippi, though at that point, as we gather from Mark and Matthew, the ministry was virtually closed. All that now remained for Jesus was to go up to Jerusalem as Messiah and abide the consequences as

God might direct. Some writers, guiding themselves by Luke, have held that the Messianic declaration was only the prelude to a period of further ministry, chiefly on the farther side of the Jordan; but there can be little doubt that Luke was influenced purely by literary motives. When he has brought the history of Jesus to the great turning point, he still finds himself with much of his most precious material unused. It has come to him without any definite note of time or place, and he decides to bring it all in together at this point before he proceeds to the story of the Passion. The main drama has for the moment paused, and these chapters constitute a sort of interlude before the curtain is lifted again for the last solemn scenes.

4. Sources

Here we come to the question of Luke's sources, which has been touched on already in connection with our study of the synoptic problem, but needs again to be considered. Of the contents of the Gospel, nearly two-fifths may be assigned to Mark, one fifth to Q, and over two-fifths to other sources. At all three points, however, this estimate needs to be qualified. (1) A number of passages, which agree with Mark, may possibly be borrowed from another document which overlapped with Mark. (2) Since Q itself is lost, we can now assign to it only those passages which Matthew and Luke have in common, and in Luke, as in Matthew, there is doubtless Q material which cannot thus be identified. (3) Of that two-fifths which is peculiar to Luke, a large portion is homogeneous in character, and there is good ground for supposing that Luke had access to a third document, comparable in extent and value to Mark and Q. This view is now so generally held that it is customary to speak of "L" or "Luke's special source." The chief interest in Lucan criticism centers on this third source. We have seen that, according to one recent theory, Luke has built his Gospel, not on Mark, but on this unknown document; but all that can be affirmed with any certainty is that such a document existed, and that Luke drew on it for much of his most precious information. And besides the three main sources, he had access, apparently, to others, briefer and less important. The two opening chapters are, in this connection, particularly worthy of study. They are strikingly different from the rest of the Gospel, and suggest, both by their thought and language, that they may have come from the early Palestinian church. Indeed it is not improbable that the first chapter, occupied as it is with the wonderful circumstances of the birth of John the Baptist, may have originated in the sect which looked to John as its master.

5. *Characteristics*

The Gospel is so composite a work that at first sight it might seem to be little more than a scrapbook in which a great number of miscellaneous extracts are pasted in together. Yet it everywhere bears the impress of an individual mind of singular attractiveness. It has been called with good reason the most beautiful of all books, and for this charm, which all readers have felt in it, we must allow due credit to the evangelist himself.

It is always hard to analyze those qualities which make some books a delight to all generations; but the Gospel of Luke has several characteristics which are at once apparent. For one thing, it is the work of a literary artist. Where another man might have produced a shapeless compilation Luke so handles his diversified sources as to gain striking effects out of their variety. While blending them harmoniously, he preserves with unfailing instinct all that is quaint and vivid in the primitive records. The result is a work of sober history which has yet the color and freshness of a romance. Again, he has a strong dramatic sense and a gift for indicating character in a few graphic touches. His Gospel is everywhere a picture book, full of persons and scenes which stand out unforgettably. This side of his genius appears at its very best in his record of the parables. It may be that he is here indebted to his special source, but the manner in which he tells the parables is so much in keeping with his style in general that it must be his own. To the skill with which Luke has reported them, the parables owe much of the hold which they have taken on the world's imagination. Once more, Luke was endowed, in a rare degree, with tenderness and sympathy. It is he, more than any other of the evangelists, who helps us to understand the compassion of Jesus, his kindness to the weak and erring, the pathos and sorrow of his own life. Here again we need to remember that Luke had access to special sources, from which he borrowed such lovely stories as those of Martha and Mary, Zacchæus, and the sinful woman who wept at the feet of Jesus. But he had a nature which could respond to such stories and preserve their beauty, where a single false touch would have spoiled them. It has often been remarked that women of every type play a great part in his narrative, from the mother of Jesus to the woman who was a sinner. From this it has sometimes been inferred that he had derived much of his information from women (e. g., the daughters of Philip, the evangelist), or that he was anxious to secure a larger place for female ministry in the church of his time. Such theories are pedantic and unnecessary. The prominence which he gives to women is all of a piece with the emotional quality of his genius. It is doubtless in like manner that we must explain another outstanding feature of the Gospel — what has sometimes been called Luke's "socialism." He delights to present Jesus as the friend of the poor and outcast. He quotes with satisfaction many sayings of Jesus in which the poor are commended and the rich condemned. He tells the parable of Lazarus, and suggests that Lazarus was rewarded in the other world and the rich man punished for no other reason than that the one was poor and the other rich. Here again his attitude has been explained by various theories — for instance, that he belonged to some sect which had turned the new religion into a social propaganda, or that he preserved an aspect of Jesus' teaching which the later church was trying to conceal or minimize. But

it must be observed that while Luke makes much of Jesus'
sympathy with the poor, he also brings out, more fully than
the other writers, the faith and goodness which were often
displayed by the rich. He tells of the loyal women who ministered to Jesus of their substance (8:2, 3), of the generous
publican whom Jesus singled out for special favor (19:1-10),
of the wealthy centurion on whom he bestowed his eulogy
(7:1-10). The term "socialism," as applied to Luke's attitude to the poor, conveys a wrong idea. It suggests that he
was a partisan or political theorist, while the truth is simply
that he was a man of warm and generous sympathies. There
is no reason to doubt that Jesus himself had all that compassion for the poor which Luke ascribes to him, and of this we
have abundant testimony in the other Gospels. Luke, however,
gives especial prominence to this aspect of Jesus' teaching because he was attracted to it by his own humane temper.

6. Teaching

Efforts have often been made to discover a theology underlying Luke's presentation of the history, alike in the Gospel
and in Acts. Of this there is no real sign. The theological
ideas often attributed to Luke (for instance the place which
he gives to the conception of the Spirit), are probably to be
set down to his sources more than to his own thinking. He
aims, apparently, at setting forth the Christian message, apart
from any doctrinal construction. Everywhere he lays stress on
two things. (1) The message is from God, and its divine origin was attested by manifest signs — works of power, visions
and voices, marvelous changes in the minds and hearts of men.
(2) It was intended for all men alike. What Luke derived from
his master Paul was this spirit of universalism. He is always
seeking to enforce the worldwide scope of the gospel, not because he writes for a Gentile public, but because he has fully
grasped Paul's great principle that Christ came as the world's
Saviour. In the book of Acts, he was to trace out the expansion of the movement which began from Jerusalem, but his

aim in the Gospel also is to show that Christianity, by its very nature, was universal. Even when Jesus was confining his ministry to Galilee, there was that in his teaching which involved the later mission. We are shown how he rose superior to the Law, how he recognized faith in publicans and Samaritans, how Gentiles were drawn to him, how his sayings, addressed to his own countrymen, yet breathed the fullest spirit of humanity. Paul sets himself to prove the universal sweep of the gospel, by arguments derived from scripture and theological reflection. Luke is content to assure us that it was inherent in the whole character and teaching of Jesus, even while he lived on earth.

CHAPTER VI

THE BOOK OF ACTS

1. *Title and Authorship*

The historical work which opens with Luke's Gospel is continued in the book of Acts. As he begins this second part of his history, the author links it to the first by another reference to his friend Theophilus, but there is no formal dedication. It may be conjectured that the two parts were issued together and that the preface to the Gospel was meant to cover the whole work.

The title "Acts of the Apostles" seems to have been added at a later time and does not rightly describe the contents of the book. It is mainly concerned with only two Apostles, Peter and Paul, and no more than two or three of the others make any appearance at all. Perhaps the title was given when Acts was detached from the Gospel and placed at the beginning of the collected Epistles. In the most ancient manuscripts, it is followed immediately by the Epistles of James, Peter and John, then by the letters of Paul. The early editors may have felt that a work introducing this collection should bear a title in which all the Apostles were included. What the author himself called it, we do not know. Most probably he used a title which embraced both the Gospel and Acts, and which had to be changed when they were separated. The loss of the original title is unfortunate, since it would have given us a clue to the author's own conception of the nature and purpose of his work.

The question of authorship has already been touched on in connection with the Gospel, but before considering the book of Acts it needs to be examined more carefully. With regard to the Gospel, the personality of the author matters compara-

tively little, for we know that in any case he belonged to a
later generation and knew the life of Jesus only through documents. But the value of the book of Acts, as history, depends
very largely on whether the author was acquainted with the
men he writes of, and had taken a personal part in the events.
On this problem a great deal of discussion has centered in
recent years.

The tradition is unanimous that the two books were written
by a companion of Paul, "Luke the physician, the beloved"
(Col. 4:14). Paul, as we know, was subject to sudden attacks
of illness, due apparently to some form of epilepsy, and the
company of a physician in his travels would be valuable to
him. How he had made the friendship of Luke we do not
know, but according to later tradition Luke belonged to Antioch, and the author of Acts would seem to display special
knowledge whenever he writes of Antioch. It may have been
this very fact that gave rise to the later belief, and the direct
New Testament references appear rather to connect him with
Macedonia or the Western part of Asia Minor. His name
suggests that he was a Greek, or like Timothy half Greek, and
when Paul mentions him in Colossians he seems to place him
in a group which he distinguishes from "those who are of the
circumcision." That Luke had something to do with the authorship of Acts is certain, for in a series of passages the first
person plural is used, indicating that the writer was himself
in Paul's company. (E. g., "And after he had seen the vision
we endeavored to go into Macedonia." 16:10). It is true that
in these passages Luke is never mentioned by name, but since
we know that he was one of Paul's companions and that the
church always regarded him as the author of the book, there
is no reason to doubt that he is indicated. Even the fact that
Luke is never named in the book of Acts is evidence that there
was some reason for keeping his personality in the background, and no reason could be more natural than that he
himself was writing and did not care to bring forward his own
name.

The question arises, however, as to whether he was responsible for the whole book or for only those parts of it in which the first person is used. Those "we-sections" are four in number (16:10-17; 20:5-15; 21:1-18; 27:1-28; 16). It is noticeable that in all these sections the writer appears as traveling along with Paul, and the inference has been drawn that these sections formed part of a diary he kept, as travelers have been wont to do in all ages, in which he noted down the places visited and incidents by the way. The theory has therefore been maintained that this diary of Luke fell into the hands of a later writer who recognized its value as a first-hand source of information for the life of Paul. He transcribed it much as it was, retaining the first person for the sake of vividness, but wove what he took from it into his own account of the early days. In this manner, the name of Luke came to be given to the whole book of Acts, and to the Gospel which accompanied it, although Luke was the actual author of only the travel diary. In support of this theory, it is argued that Acts contains inaccuracies and mistakes which would have been impossible to a personal friend of Paul; that in various places it contradicts the evidence of Paul's own Epistles; that it misrepresents Paul's attitude and teaching in several vital respects. On the other hand, it has to be admitted that the "we-sections" are quite of a piece with the rest of the book. All the peculiarities which mark them, alike in thought and language, are found in the book generally and also in the Gospel. By itself, this argument is not conclusive, for when he incorporated the diary the author may have taken care to smooth it out and assimilate it to his own style. But when he preserved the "we," would he not have made a special point of quoting literally? A modern historian who has got hold of a soldier's letter or an old traveler's journal would never think of spoiling its effect by changing its spontaneous phrasing into conventional English; and no one knew better than the author of Acts how to gain a literary effect by making different persons speak in their natural characters. To his happy reproduction of old documents, with all their curious turns of thought and speech, the charm of his work is largely due; and if the language of the diary is in every respect so like his own, we are justified in assuming that he himself wrote it. None of the arguments on the other side is in any way decisive. It may be granted, for instance, that Acts is often inaccurate, that it sometimes conflicts with Paul's own statements and shows imperfect knowledge of his teaching. But in all this there is nothing to raise suspicion. In writing the biography of his dearest friend, a man may fall into many serious errors. Few people, for that part, could render an account of their own doings after the lapse of a dozen years without mixing up the dates and forgetting many of the important facts. It is possible, too, to know a man well and write his life admirably, and yet have little expert knowledge of his special work. The biographer, say, of a musician or philosopher may himself have no turn for music or philosophy, although he can fully appreciate the character of a great man. If Luke shows little understanding of Paul's theology, the reason most probably was that he was not a theologian. Because his mind in this respect differed so greatly from that of his hero, we cannot conclude that he had no personal knowledge of Paul.

There is no sufficient ground, then, for holding that although Luke wrote the diary he was not the author of the whole book. This conclusion would be necessary, only if it could be shown that the book was written at a time so long after the death of Paul that none of his companions could possibly have been alive. To the question of date, we shall turn presently; but if the book can be dated at any time within the first century, there is every indication that Luke was its author. Luke was presumably a young and vigorous man when Paul chose him as a traveling companion and, if he was about thirty when Paul died, in 62 or 64 A.D., he would still have been under seventy when the century ended. The Gospel and Acts were ascribed to him by the general voice of the church as far back as we can trace them, and from all that we know of him he was just the man who may have been their author. He was a member of that Gentile church for which they were written; he was a physician, and therefore a man of good education; he was a friend and admirer of the Apostle Paul. Add to all this the practical certainty that he was the writer of the travel diary, which can be shown by every test to be entirely uniform with the work as a whole.

2. Date

What was the date of the book of Acts? This is a question of peculiar importance, since the date of the Synoptic Gospels must be determined mainly by that of Acts. Luke's Gospel was written earlier than his second work; Luke and Matthew appeared about the same time, and Mark, which is used in both of them, must have been in existence for something like twenty years in order to have become a standard work. It is by this train of reasoning that the date of the Gospels has to be established, and the positive clue is afforded by the book of Acts. Some scholars in recent years have maintained that it must be placed at the very end of the first century or even later, since the author betrays a knowledge of Josephus, whose history did not appear until 94 or 95 A.D. Of this, however, there is no real evidence. Since Luke and Josephus both deal with events in Palestine during the years preceding the fall of Jerusalem, they inevitably have some things in common, but their differences are on the whole much more striking than their agreements. A writer whose subject was the rise of social legislation in Germany would doubtless make a number of references to Bismarck and his policy. Some of them would correspond pretty closely with facts recorded in a given biography of the statesman, but it would not follow that the author had borrowed from that particular book. Information about public events and historical personages is common property. Against a late date for the book of Acts, there is one argument which may be regarded as decisive. From the beginning to the end of the book, the author shows no acquaintance with Paul's

Epistles, and in several places overlooks or contradicts their evidence. We know that before the end of the century the Epistles had passed into general circulation in the church, and a late writer, undertaking to record the life of Paul, would naturally have used them as his chief source of information. Luke's neglect of them can be set down to no other cause than that he wrote before they were commonly known.

On the other hand, there has been an effort on the part of some scholars to place the book of Acts too early. They build chiefly on the abrupt ending of the book, which leaves Paul a prisoner at Rome, awaiting his trial. Every reader has been conscious of a disappointment when he arrives, after a series of thrilling chapters, at the closing verses. After Paul has made his appeal to Caesar, the whole interest is centered on what will happen to him when he appears at Rome, before the emperor's court. But we never learn what happened. Just when the culminating scene is due, the curtain suddenly falls. Of this extraordinary feature of Acts, no explanation has been offered which is entirely satisfying. Some have supposed that Luke intended to follow the Gospel and Acts with a third work; but even if this were so, the account of Paul's trial would naturally have come within the volume which dealt with Paul's career. A more plausible conjecture is that nothing is told us of the trial because it resulted in Paul's condemnation. All through the book Luke has been contending that, while the Jews were hostile to the church, Rome itself had always been friendly. He has set himself to prove from history that in earlier days, when its nature was better known, the new religion had always been recognized as politically harmless. This line of evidence would have been shattered if his book had closed with the admission that, when the chief Apostle was tried before the supreme court of the empire, he had been sentenced to death. Here, perhaps, we have the true reason why Luke left his story unfinished: but still his procedure is strange. He might have shown, without much difficulty, that Paul was condemned on false evidence or under a misapprehension. As it is, he says just enough to suggest that he has something compromising to hide. A theory has therefore been put forward that the book was written when the issue of Paul's trial was still undecided. We are asked to suppose that while Luke attended Paul in Rome, waiting for the event which was indefinitely postponed, he occupied his time with literary work. He wrote the Gospel, then the book of Acts; and when he was compelled to give up his task, was still unable to say what had happened to Paul. Perhaps he hurried his book to a conclusion with some idea that Paul's judges might read it before the approaching trial, and see from it that the accusations were all groundless. The theory is ingenious, but breaks down on the fact that, in an earlier part of the book, the author plainly forecasts the death of Paul. He describes the pathetic scene in which the Apostle bade farewell to the elders of Ephesus at Miletus, and they all wept, "knowing that they would see his face no more" (20:38). Apart from this explicit notice, there is a sense all through the latter part of the book that the great Apostle is now under the shadow of the end. It may be added, too, that when the date of Acts is placed so early, the whole chronology of the Gospels is thrown into hopeless confusion. In his own Gospel, for instance, Luke plainly alludes to the fall of Jerusalem, which happened ten years after Paul's arrival at Rome. The Gospel of Mark is certainly the earliest of the Gospels, but it cannot be assigned to so early a date as this theory would give to the book of Acts. When all the evidence is put together, it may be concluded that the true date of Acts is somewhere about 90 A.D. — nearly thirty years after Paul's death.

3. *Character and Purpose*

Assuming that the book was written towards the close of the first century, we have now to consider its character and purpose. Its title, "the Acts of the Apostles," was given to it, as we have seen, at a later time, and is not fully appropriate. Yet it correctly describes the book, as not so much a regular history as a series of actions or episodes. Of the "Apostles" with whom it deals, three-sixths of the space are devoted to Paul, two-sixths to Peter, one-sixth to all the others together. The real theme, however, is not the doings of the Apostles, but the expansion of Christianity through the energy of the Spirit. In his Gospel, Luke has recorded the earthly life of Jesus, and in Acts he continues the story, showing how Jesus had worked on, after his death, by the Spirit which he had imparted. The movement, which had begun obscurely in Galilee, had spread in ever-wider circles and had at last established itself in the world's capital. This marvelous growth, we are constantly reminded, was due to two things. On the one hand, the message, though it had first been delivered to the Jews, was intrinsically universal. Jesus had appeared as the Saviour of all men, and there was something in his teaching to which all could respond. On the other hand, a divine power was behind the message. The Apostles themselves were ordinary men, pursuing their work in the face of many difficulties, but God was using them as his instruments. He had endued them with a courage and wisdom not their own, and had prepared the way for them, and had seconded their efforts with a mighty hand. So Luke undertakes to show that the best evidence for the truth of the new belief was the story of its actual achievement. In view of the amazing growth of this movement which he had begun, who could doubt that Jesus had come forth from God?

As to this general purpose of the book, there can be little question; but the view has sometimes been held that it had a more specific purpose. There are many indications that Paul had accomplished his great work in spite of much opposition from other Christian teachers. He had perceived that Christianity was a new religion, open to all men on the one condition of faith, while the older disciples held to the Law and were unwilling to admit the Gentiles until they had first conformed to the Law. All through his life, Paul had to contend with a Jewish-Christian party which attacked, not only his teaching, but his motives and character, and tried at times to undermine his work. His Epistles are full of references to this struggle, which was constantly going on within the church itself. It has been held that the book of Acts was written, a generation later, for the purpose of healing this conflict. Jewish and Gentile Christians were at last ready to come together, and Luke, in the interest of peace, revised the earlier history and sought to make out that Paul and the elder Apostles had always been in agreement. He described the Gentile mission as begun by Peter and carried out by Paul, who returned from time to time to Jerusalem to give an account of his progress. Nothing is said in Acts about the quarrel of Paul and Peter, which is described in the second chapter of Galatians. Care is taken to put both the rival Apostles on an equal footing. They both heal a lame man (3:2; 14:8), perform a miracle by way of punishment (5:1; 13:6), are freed from prison supernaturally (5:19; 16:26), and restore life to a person who was supposed to be dead (9:36; 20:9). Peter is represented as making friends with Gentiles (9), while it is constantly impressed on us that Paul, on his missionary tours, was wont to preach first in the Jewish synagogue.

Now it cannot be denied that the author of the book of Acts makes the life of the early church more harmonious than it was, and brings Paul into closer relation to Jerusalem than the facts would seem to justify. But it does not follow that this has been done with a deliberate purpose. We have to allow, in the first place, for the softening influence of time. After every great controversy, there comes a period when things can be seen in better perspective, and one party is willing to do justice to the other. When Acts was written, the church looked proudly back to the heroic age which had gone before, and thought of all the Apostles as great men who had worked together in the common cause. Again, there is good reason to believe that too much has often been made of the differences that existed in the early church. Paul indeed had enemies, but he admits himself that the chief Apostles were on the whole well disposed to him. They were not prepared to go all the way with him, but they acknowledged his zeal and sincerity, and the attitude of an extreme Jewish section did not represent the general opinion. We know from his letters that Paul looked with respect to the mother-church, and never forgot, while he worked among the Gentiles, that he owed a duty to his own countrymen. At the most, therefore, Luke has only overemphasised the admitted facts. Once more, his supposed intention to conceal the true state of matters in the primitive church is due largely to the literary plan of his book. He conceives of Christianity as a movement which began in Jerusalem and was continually expanding. In the working out of this governing idea, he takes care to keep Jerusalem at the center, and thinks of it as uniting and supervising the other churches. This may not be strictly true to facts, but we must never forget that Luke was a literary artist. A great deal, both in the Gospel and Acts, which is sometimes attributed to sinister theological motives is more properly to be explained by his sense of dramatic fitness.

If there is any purpose in his book, other than the obvious one already mentioned, it is that of proving that Christianity was not politically dangerous. We have seen that, in his Gospel, he seeks to make clear to the pagan world that Jesus was not a revolutionary, bent on overturning the Roman government. In the book of Acts he sets himself more explicitly to clear the new religion from the suspicions to which it was commonly exposed. He makes it known that Paul was a Roman citizen, and that Roman officials had again and again protected him. He insists that opposition to the new teaching had come almost wholly from the malice of the Jews, and that this had been acknowledged more than once by the regular magistrates. From Paul's own letters, we can infer that at different times he had come into conflict with the Roman authorities, and at Ephesus, more particularly, had encountered deadly perils for which they must have been responsible. On all this Luke is significantly silent. He closes his book abruptly, as we have seen, at the very point where he would have needed to tell of Paul's condemnation. Everywhere we have traces of the apologetic motive. The author is aware that the state is now hostile to Christianity, and seeks to prove, in the light of past history, that there is no ground for the antagonism.

4. *Arrangement*

All other motives, however, are subsidiary to the main one of setting forth the process by which the church had grown from humble beginnings to a world-wide power. That this is the author's design, is made evident by his arrangement of the book. It falls into six distinct sections, each of them closing with a formula which marks the stage attained and points forward to the one that follows. These sections comprise (1) the origin of the church at Jerusalem (1:2-6:6); (2) the spread of Christianity through Palestine (6:8-9:30); (3) the expansion from Palestine to Antioch in Syria (9:32-12:23); (4) the advance from Syria to Asia Minor (12:25-16:4); (5) the work of Paul in Macedonia and Greece (16:6-19:19); (6) the events that had their issue in the arrival of Paul at Rome (20-28).

This scheme of the book has to be considered before we can fully appreciate the author's purpose or do justice to his manner of executing it. Often it has been complained that his history is patchy and inadequate. He does not inquire into the causes of events or show how they were related to each other. He is wont to hurry over considerable periods, on which we should have liked some detailed information. He does not recount the career, even of his hero, Paul, with anything like completeness. Paul himself, for instance, refers in Romans (15:19) to a mission in Illyria, of which Luke tells us nothing: he deals in Galatians and II Corinthians with critical situations, on which no light is thrown by Acts: in II Corinthians (11:24-28) he enumerates the "deadly perils" which he had undergone up to that time and, out of thirteen which he mentions, Luke seems to be acquainted only with two. In view of these many serious gaps in the narrative, Acts has sometimes been set down as a loose, unreliable survey, or as a mere pamphlet, written in some particular interest. The author's design, however, is not to present the history in full, but merely to single out a number of outstanding incidents which will afford a vivid idea of how Christianity had made its way. If we complain that he has left out so much, we may be sure that his own regret was much keener. He must have had a mass of interesting material, especially on the life of Paul, which he was eager to communicate. But he had to confine himself to the purpose in hand. Out of the many incidents known to him he had to select those which would illustrate most aptly the various stages by which Christianity had expanded from Jerusalem to Rome.

5. Qualities and Defects

When once we realize that this was his task, we cannot but admit that he has performed it admirably. The episodes he selects are all significant ones, each of them marking a real turning point in the history of the church. All of them, too, are interesting in themselves and sometimes intensely dramatic, e.g., the day of Pentecost, the martyrdom of Stephen, the conversion of Paul, the call from Macedonia, the visits to Athens and Corinth, the trial before Agrippa, and the shipwreck on the way to Rome. In Acts, as in the Gospel, Luke reveals himself as a born story-teller. His book is full of unforgettable scenes which have been the delight of hundreds of painters. Indeed the defects of Luke as an historian are due to his very excellences. Like other writers with a keen instinct for dramatic situations, he is tempted to sacrifice accuracy to effect. It is doubtful, for instance, whether Stephen was judicially condemned, or was merely the victim of a popular outbreak. It is still more doubtful whether Paul had any part in his death except that of an onlooker who approved the deed. Luke, however, could not resist the opportunity which the death of Stephen afforded him. Paul, the future Apostle, becomes the chief agent in the official murder of his forerunner. It is more than likely that a number of scenes in the narrative have been heightened in like manner for the sake of effect, and this is true, in a very special degree, of the speeches. The practice of all ancient historians is to convey their own comments and display their literary skill by means of speeches ascribed to their leading characters. The works of Herodotus, Thucydides, Livy, Tacitus, are full of speeches which cannot possibly have come from any authentic report. A considerable part of Acts is likewise made up of speeches, some of which may preserve at least the substance of what was actually said on the given occasions. In others, Luke has apparently gathered up the main elements of certain types of Christian teaching. The speeches of Peter, for instance, as recorded in the early chapters, are of peculiar value for our knowledge of the primitive beliefs; and the long speech attributed to Stephen at his trial is most likely a theological tract, so ancient and valuable that Luke decided to preserve it in this form. Some of the speeches, however, have all the appearance of having been composed by himself, with little to guide him except his own sense of dramatic fitness. The speeches of Paul at Athens (17:22-31), at Miletus (20:17-35), and possibly that before Agrippa (26:2-29), may be assigned to this class. They are masterpieces of eloquence which we should be sorry to miss, but they do not properly belong to history.

Along with an overfondness for striking effects, Luke may be charged with carelessness in matters of detail. A good deal of what has sometimes been set down to willful misrepresentation seems really to be due to nothing else than literary indolence. A good illustration is afforded us in the three accounts of Paul's conversion which are given in the course of the book (9, 22, 26). They all agree in the main facts, but are hopelessly at variance in details. In 9:7, Paul's companions hear a voice, but see nothing and stand speechless. In 22:9, they see a light, but hear no voice. In 28:8, 12, they hear and see nothing, but fall to the ground. Luke could have had no motive for thus contradicting himself, when any one could detect him by simply turning the page. His procedure can be explained in only one way — that he paid little attention to detail, so long as he was right on the essential facts.

Another of his characteristics is his love of the marvelous and supernatural. He delights in angelic appearances, miracles, divine interventions. He records as sober history much that bears the plain mark of legend. This is no doubt partly due to his conception of the new religion as coming from God and attested by signs of divine favor and power. We must remember, too, that the mind of the first century was disposed to look for the miraculous, just as we now assume that everything must arise from natural causes. But Luke's love of the marvelous is peculiar to himself, in so far as his genius was more imaginative than scientific. This must be borne in mind before we dismiss anything in his record as a mere fable, not to be taken seriously. He is anxious, as he himself assures us, to write a true history, but while recounting the facts, he sees them through a certain atmosphere. We must always be careful to distinguish between the thing he records and the halo of marvel or mystery with which he invests it.

Once more, as was noted in the survey of his Gospel, he had a mind which was religious, rather than theological. Although he took little interest in the special Pauline doctrines, he had grasped Paul's message of a salvation offered to all men. He never tried, perhaps, to explain his faith in Christ in intellectual terms, yet he had responded to him with his whole heart, as the true revelation of God. There are two things about Christianity which he keeps always in the forefront, and neither of them is concerned with its strictly theological teaching. On the one hand, he sees in it a message of human brotherhood. He shows that, through the power of this new religion, estranged races and classes have been brought together, and men have learned sympathy with the poor and oppressed and outcast. On the other hand he dwells on the *gladness* which has entered human life through the faith in Christ. One of the characteristic words in Luke's writings is "gladness." Whenever he tells of new converts who were added to the church, he has something to say of the joy which came to them. His Gospel begins with the proclamation of the angel, "Behold I bring you good tidings of great joy which shall be to all peoples"; and here, it may be said, he states the theme which he develops in his two books.

6. *Historical Value*

The book of Acts is our one account of the primitive Christian age, and the question of its value as history is therefore of supreme importance. Paul, it is true, alludes in the course of his Epistles to many of the events described in Acts and, wherever there is conflict between his testimony and that of Acts, the preference must be given to Paul. As himself the chief actor in the events he speaks of, his word has an authority which cannot be questioned. But Paul does not pretend to be a historian. His notices are fragmentary and incidental, and without the help of Acts we should be unable to grasp their significance. All else that we can discover about the primitive church has to be set in the framework of Acts.

As to the historical value of the book, there has been wide difference of opinion. Some writers have made claims for it which are plainly extravagant, and would have surprised the author himself. They have credited him, not only with the most careful research, but with impartial judgment and deep insight into the meaning and bearing of events. They would rank his narrative, in spite of its brevity, with such historical monuments as the works of Thucydides, Tacitus, and Gibbon. It is well to have such overestimates of the book, for too often it has been unduly disparaged. We are told that its author was ignorant and credulous; that he has given us little more than a series of hearsay reports, clumsily put together; that he was unable to distinguish between fact and fable, and that none of his statements can be trusted unless they can be authenticated from other sources. For some of this harsh criticism, Luke has himself to blame. He is too ready to sacrifice accuracy to effect; he is often careless in detail, and the many small errors can be so massed together as to throw serious doubt on the whole narrative. But the adverse criticism is due, for the most part, to the judgment of his work by standards which are not fairly applicable. He did not profess to write a history in the proper sense, and it is unjust to condemn him for his omissions and incoherences. He had no conception of modern historical methods, and was not in a position, even if he had so desired, to verify all his dates and facts, and sift the evidence of his various documents. When we realize what he set himself to do, and compare him, not with the modern investigator, but with historical writers of his own time, we cannot but recognise the high quality of his work. No one can deny that he has given us a story of surpassing interest and beauty, and even when we judge it by purely historical tests it comes out well. The only direct test that can be applied, is that of comparison with Paul's Epistles. At times, no doubt, the data supplied in Acts are in conflict with Paul's evidence, but in general they are in full agreement, so much so that many of the allusions in the Epistles are intelligible only in the light of Acts. This harmony with Paul is the more significant, as the author of Acts does not seem at any point to have consulted the Epistles. Apart from this direct proof of Luke's trustworthiness, it has to be noted that his geography is usually exact, his references to the Jewish and Roman history of the period are borne out by documents and inscriptions, his picture of the church in the first century fits in with all the known conditions. It may be added that his record is almost always intrinsically credible. We know nothing, for instance, of how the church arose in Jerusalem and what were its earliest beliefs; yet the events may well have happened in the way that he describes them, and the later development of Christian thought points back to just such beliefs as he assigns to the primitive disciples. All through the book, we feel ourselves in contact with real personages and genuine incidents. It is not difficult to convict Luke of occasional error, but when we turn from his book to the apocryphal Acts, which were produced in the following century, we are conscious at once of the difference between history and historical romance.

7. *Sources*

The question of Luke's trustworthiness cannot be separated from that of his sources, for in the book of Acts, as in the Gospel, he has followed the method of compilation. This is apparent at once from the heterogeneous nature of the material which he has brought together. He has combined it skillfully and has impressed his own style and mode of thought on all that he has borrowed, but the seams and inconsistencies are still apparent. Statements of fact are mixed up with popular legend. Notices which plainly bear the primitive stamp are filled out with later additions. A constant feature in the earlier chapters is the repetition of what is evidently the same incident, e.g., the Apostles are twice arrested (4:1 f 5:17 f.), two accounts are given of the community of goods (2:44, 45; 4:34-37), the death of Stephen is narrated twice (7:54-58; 7:59-8:1). These parallels are to be explained, like the doublets in the Gospels, by the use of two documents, describing the same events, but in partial conflict with each other. In the case of the Gospels, however, one of the sources employed has come down to us in our Gospel of Mark and, in the light of this known source, we can form conclusions as to those which are lost. All the documents that went to the making of Acts have disappeared, and nothing can be said about them which is not pure conjecture. The difficulty is all the greater, as Luke has evidently recast his documents to a much greater extent than in his Gospel. He was there dealing with actual words of Christ, and with a tradition which was familiar to his readers and which could not be seriously altered. The sources which he used for Acts had nothing sacred about them, and he was free to edit them as he thought best. From the uniformity of the style and the presence of certain governing motives, it may be inferred that he has remolded the original documents, so that it is now hardly possible to distinguish them.

The only source of which we can be reasonably certain is the travel diary, which seems to have begun just at the point where Paul was about to enter on his first mission to Europe (16:10-17). It is only in the four sections of the book in which the pronoun "we" is used, that we can plainly detect the diary; but there is reason to believe that the first person has occasionally been changed into the third, and that the document has been used much more largely than is now apparent. Perhaps its influence extends, in one form or another, over the greater part of the description of Paul's missionary journeys. Along with the diary, kept presumably by himself, Luke would no doubt draw a great deal on oral information. As one of Paul's circle, he would be in close touch with many of the Apostle's comrades, who would tell him of events which had happened when he himself was absent. It has been surmised that his chief authority for some episodes was Philip, the evangelist, or perhaps one of the four daughters of Philip, who were prominent in the church towards the end of the first century. The place which Philip occupies in the history is out of all proportion to his real eminence, and the explanation may well be that the book is partly composed from his reminiscences. The question of sources is particularly difficult with regard to the first twelve chapters, which deal with the period before Paul had begun to take a leading place as an Apostle. To those early chapters of Acts, we owe most of our knowledge of the origin and early history of the church, and the problem of sources is therefore of primary importance. It is now generally held that, for the first part of his work, Luke was dependent in the main on two documents, one of which was associated with the church in Palestine, the other with the church of Antioch. Both the records would seem, from a number of linguistic indications, to have been written in Aramaic. They cannot have consisted of much more than brief notices, for even when Luke has combined them and filled them out with speeches and dubious traditions, he can produce only a scanty narrative. The truth appears to be that very little was known, at the time when he wrote, of the beginnings of the church. He has done his best to make a coherent story, and the few records he has preserved are now of priceless value. But the Christian movement had begun so quietly, and the significance of the early events was so little appreciated, that the memory of those first days had become blurred. Perhaps the chief actors themselves could tell little, a few years afterwards, about doings which were to prove of momentous consequence for the whole future of the church. In the later part of his book, the author is on solid ground. He deals with persons and incidents within his own field of knowledge. He describes the progress of the church in a time when it had come out into the full light of day, and all its undertakings aroused a keen interest. For this later period there was abundant material, and Luke's difficulty was no longer to expand a few meager notices into intelligible history, but to select what was most important. It is hard to say which part of his work he has done with greater skill. He was the earliest of church historians, and has had hundreds of successors, but he is still the most interesting and valuable.

CHAPTER VII

THE EPISTLES OF PAUL

1. *Origin*

For seventeen years after his conversion, Paul confined himself to a limited field. He worked for three years in Damascus, then for fourteen years in Tarsus and Antioch and the region between — the borderland of the two great provinces of Cilicia and Syria. In the year 48 or 49 A.D., he began the larger enterprise which made him the Apostle of the Gentiles. Accompanied first by Barnabas and later by other colleagues, he traveled over Asia Minor, Macedonia and Greece, founding a Christian church in each important center at which he arrived in the course of his journeys. These churches were left to govern themselves after his departure, but they continued to regard him as their overseer, and he tried, as far as he could, to keep in touch with them. From time to time he sent one or another of his assistants to visit them and, whenever they stood in special need of his direction, he communicated with them by letter. It was this accident that Paul, as a traveling missionary, was separated for long intervals from his churches, which brought Christian literature into being. Paul's First Epistle to the Thessalonians is the earliest in date of the New Testament books; and all the Pauline Epistles belong to a period considerably before the Gospels or any of the other writings were in existence. If they had no other merit, they would still be of supreme value as the earliest documents of our religion; but besides their historical claim, they have an intrinsic and much higher one. They come to us directly from the hand of the greatest of the Apostles, and are themselves among the most vital and suggestive books that have ever been written.

2. *Mode of Composition*

It was doubtless the excellence of the Epistles which secured their preservation. Letters are by their nature ephemeral, and are usually thrown away when once they have been read and answered; but it was realized from the first that Paul's were no ordinary letters. He tells us himself that this was admitted, even by his opponents. "For his letters, they say, are weighty and powerful, but his bodily presence is weak and his speech contemptible" (II Cor. 10:10). They professed, that is, to think little of him personally; his appearance was disappointing, and his preaching, to a critical Greek audience, was dull and unattractive. But even those hostile judges had to allow that, when he wrote, he was a different man. Paul was fully aware that in the arts of the orator he was deficient. "When I came among you, brethren, I came not with excellency of speech or of wisdom, declaring unto you the testimony of God" (I Cor. 2:1). Like many other great teachers, he was unable to do justice to himself in public address, and was easily eclipsed by a brilliant speaker like Apollos. Perhaps this was one reason why he took special care with his letters, in which he knew that he could express his mind adequately, in a manner that compelled men to listen.

That the letters were written with care, is quite apparent when we study them. It has sometimes been assumed that they were thrown off on the spur of the moment, and it has seemed wonderful that these casual letters should still keep their place among the chief documents of the Christian faith. We know, for that part, that Paul did not even write them himself, but dictated them to someone who happened to be with him, adding only the signature and a few words of personal greeting. From this, however, it does not follow that the letters were unstudied. For some reason, he found the act of writing irksome, and was better able to think and to express himself when he was not hampered with a pen. This is not surprising when we remember the labor that must have been involved in the use of ancient writing materials. But however they were produced, it is wrong to think of Paul as dashing off his Epistles, just as a busy man today attends to his correspondence when he has nothing better to do. In the first place, the letters were meant to be read aloud at the meeting of the church, and were thus public documents which needed to be written with care, and in language of a certain elevation. Ever and again they contain passages of lofty eloquence, which cannot be fully appreciated until we hear them read out by a finished speaker. Again, while Paul wrote to one particular church, he knew that the letter would be circulated. At the end of Colossians (4:16), he himself directed that neighboring churches should exchange the letters he had sent to them. Conscious, as he was, that what he wrote would be copied out and read by a large public, he would put his best care into the writing. But the chief proof that he did not write these letters hurriedly is given us by the letters themselves. In all of them there is a wealth of profound thinking, such as can hardly be matched in any other writings of the same compass. In Epistles like those to the Romans and Ephesians, he presents a sustained argument which must have been fully worked out before pen was put to paper. Even in point of language, the great passages have evidently been composed with studied art. It can be shown by analysis that every word in these passages has been deliberately chosen, the cadence of each sentence has been molded, as in the work of a great poet, with a view to a given effect. Such writing cannot have been improvised. In these letters, which seem to have the ease and naturalness of familiar conversation, Paul has given us the ripest fruits of his mind.

3. *Epistolary Character*

In view of the "weighty and powerful" character of the letters, it was formerly believed that the epistolary form was little more than a convention. In ancient times, as now, it was a common device to issue as an "open letter" what was really a tract or pamphlet intended for the world at large; and it

was assumed that Paul, wishing to put on record his theological teaching, embodied it in these Epistles. Ostensibly he
wrote a letter to Corinth or Galatia; in reality he addressed
himself to Christians of all times and races. This view is no
longer maintained. With our fuller knowledge of ancient letters (of which many thousands have been recovered from
the old rubbish heaps of Egypt) we can see that Paul followed the model employed in ordinary correspondence. His
Epistles are not of the kind written for publication, but genuine, friendly letters. Not only so, but they deal with actual
situations, and vary in style and contents according to the
readers for whom they were intended. We have come to see,
indeed, that none of the Epistles can be properly understood,
unless we first determine the special object which the writer
had in his mind, and the circumstances and character of the
first readers. The Epistle to Philemon is obviously a private
letter, in which Paul never for a moment loses sight of the
man he is writing to and the request he has to make. The other
Epistles are addressed to churches, not to individuals, but
they are just as truly letters as that one to Philemon. Before
we can apprehend their meaning, we have to put ourselves into
the position of those definite communities to which Paul wrote.

In this connection, it has to be noted that he never writes
for the purpose of vague exhortation. It would have been
quite natural if the Apostle, separated from a church in which
he took a deep interest, had now and then sent it a letter in
which he enlarged in general terms on the aims and duties of
the Christian life. But he seems never to have indulged (as
pastors have often done) in sermons disguised as letters.
Whenever he wrote he had some clear-cut purpose in view.
He had been consulted about a difficulty which had arisen, or
news had come to him that one of his churches was in trouble
or had fallen into error or disorder. He may take occasion
when writing to throw in general exhortations, or to state his
mind on some doctrine or belief; but his immediate object is
always to deal with the given question, and even his more

general counsels have some application to it. To this his Epistles owe much of their vitality. They deal with large principles,
but always in the light of concrete situations.

4. The Extant Letters

The Epistles traditionally ascribed to Paul are fourteen in
number: Romans, I and II Corinthians, Galatians, Ephesians,
Philippians, Colossians, I and II Thessalonians, I and II Timothy, Titus, Philemon, Hebrews. The Pauline authorship of
Hebrews was never taken quite seriously, and is now accepted
by no responsible scholar. Of the others, I and II Timothy and
Titus, (the so-called "Pastoral Epistles") cannot be regarded,
at least in their present form, as the work of Paul. It is maintained by some critics that Ephesians and II Thessalonians
were written by disciples of Paul, not by Paul himself, but the
arguments put forward for this view are by no means conclusive. The "four great Epistles"—Romans, Galatians, I and
II Corinthians — are indubitably by Paul, and there is hardly
less doubt as to I Thessalonians, Philippians, Colossians, and
Philemon. We have thus ten Epistles which, with reasonable
certainty, can be assigned to Paul.

Besides those which we now possess, he must have written
many others indeed he makes reference himself to letters
which have been lost (cf. I Cor. 5:9; II Cor. 2:4 and 7:8;
Col. 3:16). It is possible that fragments of this lost correspondence have found their way into the surviving letters.
We shall see, for instance, that Romans 16, may be a note to
the church at Ephesus; that II Corinthians, 10-13, may be part
of an Epistle written before that to which it is appended; that
a stray leaf of a still earlier letter to Corinth may have been
preserved in II Corinthians (6:14-7:1). The Pastoral Epistles,
as we now have them, can hardly be the work of Paul, but they
may have grown out of notes of his, which can still be detected. When account is taken of all these fragments, there is
a larger body of Paul's correspondence than appears at first
sight, though it is fairly certain that most of the letters he
wrote are now entirely lost.

5. Order of Composition

The surviving Epistles all belong to that period of Paul's life which began with his crossing over into Europe. They cover at the most about ten years of a missionary career which lasted for thirty years. Attempts have often been made to trace out a development of Paul's thought, as reflected in the Epistles, but this, on the face of it, is a somewhat futile task. When he wrote the earliest of these letters, Paul was a mature man, perhaps approaching fifty. He had been thinking out his message for twenty years, and had arrived at strong convictions which he was not likely now to change. At some points, no doubt, he might modify his opinions in the light of later experience. When he wrote First Corinthians, for example, he was still confident that he would himself live to witness the Lord's return. In Second Corinthians and Philippians, we find him reconciled to the prospect that he would die. We know that in the interval he had passed through terrible dangers, which may well have shaken his previous confidence. It is significant, too, that in the earlier letters he contrasts the Gospel with the Jewish Law, while in Colossians and Ephesians he is more concerned with the dangers that threatened from the side of Gentile speculation. He had now become aware of types of false teaching which had not previously come within his horizon, and had readjusted some of his ideas in order to meet them. But the ideas themselves do not change. The Epistles form a single group of writings, representative of Paul's thinking after it had become fully developed.

For this reason, the question of the order of the Epistles is of less consequence than it might otherwise be. If we possessed some writing of Paul which dated from his earlier years as a Christian, a flood of light would be thrown on many problems which now beset his theology. As it is, the Epistles all reflect his thinking in its later phase and, even if we could date them with perfect accuracy, we should gain little new insight into the growth of his mind. At the same time, it is important to place them as nearly as we can in their proper sequence, since they are historical documents of the highest value and their information on Paul's own life and on conditions in the early church must be judged in the light of their date.

Before placing them in what appears to be their order, it is necessary to recall the outstanding events of Paul's career during the period which they cover. It is here that the narrative of the book of Acts comes to our assistance. Sometimes, as we have seen, its evidence is vague and defective, but it does at least provide the framework into which we can fit those writings wherein Paul speaks for himself. We know from Acts that, after the Council of Jerusalem (48 or 49 A.D.), he began a Gentile mission on a wider scale than he had thus far attempted. He traversed again those regions of Asia Minor which he had visited on his first journey, and in due time found himself at Troas, a seaport town near the site of ancient Troy. It was here, where Europe and Asia had first come into memorable contact, that he had his vision of a man of Macedonia calling him. He passed over into Europe and founded a church at Philippi, which was henceforth to be dearer to him than any of his other churches. From Philippi he went to Thessalonica, where he may have remained for several months, and then proceeded, by way of Berea and Athens, to Corinth. At Athens his message had produced little effect, and he reached Corinth in deep discouragement, fearing lest his great effort to plant Christianity in the west was to end in failure. But the mission in Corinth proved highly successful. He worked in the city for nearly two years, and left behind him a large and florishing church. From Corinth he returned, for some reason which we can only guess, on a flying visit to Jerusalem and Antioch, calling on the way at Ephesus, which he fixed on as his next field of missionary work. More than a year must have elapsed before he was free to carry out this purpose, but when once he took up his residence at Ephesus, he remained there for three years (probably from 54-57 A.D.) Little is known of his life during this period, but it is certain that he underwent grave dangers and, towards the end of his stay, his suffering was increased by bad news from the church at Corinth, which had been induced by mischief-makers to throw off his authority. Finally he made his way back to Corinth and remained there for three months, prior to a journey to Jerusalem which was to complete a scheme on which he had long set his heart. For several years, he had been trying to unite his Gentile churches in an effort to collect a sum of money for the relief of the mother church. The collection was now ready, and he traveled to Jerusalem, along with deputies from the various churches, to present the gift. As a renegade from Judaism, he had earned the hatred of the Jewish authorities, and he knew that by venturing back into their stronghold he was putting himself into danger. The event proved worse than his anticipations. He was mobbed in the Temple and arrested, and for two years was kept a prisoner at Cæsarea. Availing himself of his privilege as a Roman citizen, he appealed to the emperor's court and was sent to Rome. Here, after an adventurous voyage, he was detained for three years awaiting his trial. At this point the record breaks off, but there seems to be little doubt that the trial ended disastrously and that he was put to death.

The various Epistles have to be set in their appropriate places, in that latter half of Paul's career which has here been outlined. Some of them indicate for themselves when and where they were written. The Thessalonian letters belong to the time when Paul was just beginning his work at Corinth. The First Epistle to the Corinthians was sent from Ephesus, in the earlier part of Paul's three years' sojourn in that city. He wrote Second Corinthians soon after his departure from Ephesus, when he had crossed to Macedonia and was preparing to visit Corinth for the last time. Romans can be dated more exactly than any of the other Epistles. It was composed during those three months when Paul was waiting at Corinth for the deputies who were to accompany him to Jerusalem with the money which had been collected. The dating of other

Epistles is beset with difficulties. In the case of Galatians, for instance, the question of place and time is peculiarly important, but there is nothing in the Epistle itself which affords any certain clue to the answer. The most probable guess is that it was written at some time during the stay at Ephesus. Philippians, Colossians, Ephesians, and Philemon were all written, as they clearly state, when Paul was in captivity, and we naturally think of his long imprisonment at Rome. This was taken for granted until recent years, but the theory has now gained favor that they may belong to an earlier time, when Paul was a prisoner at Ephesus.

There is thus room for considerable difference of opinion as to the true order of the Epistles; but they may be arranged, at least provisionally, as follows: I Thessalonians, II Thessalonians, Galatians, I Corinthians, II Corinthians, Romans, Colossians, Philemon, Ephesians, Philippians. The Pastoral Epistles, in their present form, were composed long after Paul's death, but the fragmentary notes embodied in them were perhaps written while he was a prisoner at Cæsarea, after his arrest at Jerusalem.

CHAPTER VIII

The First Epistle to the Thessalonians

1. *Historical Importance*

A special interest attaches to this Epistle, not merely as the earliest of Paul's letters, but as the oldest Christian writing which now survives. Collections of Jesus' sayings had been drawn up before it, not to speak of some of the records incorporated in the Gospels and the book of Acts; but these are preserved only as building material in works of later date. I Thessalonians has come down to us in its original form as a separate writing.

The Epistle is interesting and important in another way. At first sight, when we compare it with the greater Epistles of Paul, it seems to have little to say on the deeper significance of the Christian message. Its teaching has more in common with that of the opening chapters of Acts than with that of Romans and Ephesians. The reason is, however, that Paul is writing for a community which had been only a short time in existence, and to which he had so far imparted only the more elementary truths of the Gospel. His other Epistles are addressed to fully instructed converts, with whom he can discuss some of his deeper thoughts; in I Thessalonians he keeps within the limits of his ordinary missionary teaching. The Epistle has thus a vital bearing on one of the great problems of early Christianity. It is sometimes contended that Paul broke away from the primitive Gospel and replaced it with a mystical theological doctrine which had little in common with previous Christianity except in name; and certainly when we turn from the Synoptic Gospels to the Epistle to the Romans, we feel as if we had entered into a quite different world of thought. But Paul was a Christian missionary, as well as a great theologian. When he went to a heathen city to proclaim the Gospel for the first time, he did not perplex his hearers with doctrinal issues which would have been utterly beyond their apprehension. He took his stand on a few simple beliefs, which were the same in all essentials as those held by the church before him. These to the end were the foundations of his faith, although he built on them that imposing body of doctrine which we know as Paulinism. Between Paul and the older Apostles, there was far less difference than has often been supposed.

2. *Occasion of Writing*

I Thessalonians, then, was written to a community which had been Christian for only a few months altogether. We learn from the book of Acts that, after entering Europe, Paul and his companions had passed from Philippi to Thessalonica, the chief city of Macedonia. Owing to its situation, it has always retained its importance, and today, under the name of Salonica, it is one of the commercial centers of the Levant. Paul began his mission by speaking for three successive Sabbaths in the Jewish synagogue, and appears to have continued his work for some time longer among the purely heathen population. During his stay in Thessalonica, he found himself nearly destitute, owing perhaps to the lack of employment in his trade of tent-making, and was supported only, as he afterwards remembered with gratitude, by gifts that reached him from his loyal church at Philippi (Phil. 4:16). This was the one exception that he ever made to his principle of refusing money for his missionary services. His teaching at Thessalonica, as we learn from Acts, turned on the elementary Christian beliefs. Jesus was the Messiah; in pursuance of his Messianic task he had died, but had risen from the dead; all that he was to be and do, had been foretold in Scripture (Acts 17:2, 3). On the Jews to whom he first declared it, the message made little impression, but a large number of proselytes (earnest heathen who had adopted the Jewish faith) were attracted to the new teaching. The Jews were not unnaturally resentful of Paul's success in drawing away so many of their converts, and provoked a riot against him which led to his expulsion from the city. This tumult in Thessalonica is memorable in Christian history as the first in which the cry of civil disloyalty was raised in connection with the new religion. "These all do contrary to the decrees of Caesar, saying that there is another king, one Jesus." For nearly three centuries, this charge was to spell disaster to the church.

Expelled from Thessalonica, Paul had journeyed into Greece, but he could not rid his mind of anxiety for his Thessalonian converts. He had been obliged to leave them before he had seen them fully established in the faith. Moreover, he was aware that the persecution which had fallen on himself would now be directed against his followers. Would the young church have strength to maintain itself? In his anxiety to know what had happened, he was on the point of returning, when he was struck down by one of those seizures to which he was liable. This is doubtless the meaning of his words "Satan hindered me," where he uses the same language as in II Cor. 12:7, when he speaks of his "thorn in the flesh." Unable to go to Thessalonica himself, he sent his colleague, Timothy, to strengthen the church and bring him word of how it was prospering. Timothy had at last come back to him with good news and he wrote this letter, apparently from Corinth where he was now settled, to confirm the effect of Timothy's visit.

3. Contents

The letter itself, when once we understand how it came to be written, presents few difficulties. Paul's object is to assure his converts that he still maintains his interest in them, and rejoices to know that they are standing fast. He takes occasion to remind them of the main Christian truths which he had impressed on them while he was present. He reminds them also how he had worked among them disinterestedly, showing plainly that he was no deceiver or adventurer, but passionately believed what he taught. He congratulates them on their fidelity, and urges them to hold on and go forward. In the two closing chapters, he gives them a series of counsels, suggested most likely by the report which Timothy had brought him. We can gather from these exhortations that, while the Thessalonians had been responsive to the message, they had not fully grasped its moral implications. This was always the chief hindrance to Christianity in an old pagan city. From the ancient point of view, there seemed to be little harm in such vices as self-seeking and sensuality, and Paul is always trying to make clear that they are utterly opposed to the Christian spirit. Even when he writes to mature churches, we find him rebuking those sins, and the young community at Thessalonica was evidently still in need of instruction in the very elements of Christian morals. The other difficulty which Paul had to deal with in this Epistle was one for which he was himself partly responsible. He had declared in his preaching that Christ, who had risen from the dead and ascended to heaven, would presently return and bring in his Kingdom. Those who were still living might look forward to meeting the Lord, and passing with him into the new life. The Thessalonians had understood from these promises that Christians were to be exempt from death and yet, since Paul's departure, several of their number had died. What would happen to those loved friends who had departed? Had they missed their chance of welcoming Christ on his return and sharing in his victory? Paul exhorts his readers to keep their minds at rest. Those who die before Christ's coming will lose nothing; they will even have an advantage over those who survive. At the same time, he offers some wise counsels against too much concern with the mysteries of the hereafter and the unseen. The task of the Christian is to live always as a child of light, constantly faithful and watchful. Whenever the call comes, he will be ready; whatever the future brings, it can mean only good to him. So the Epistle closes with a number of brief maxims in which Paul sums up, in the plainest possible way, the duties of the Christian life. He impresses on his converts that they must live in this manner, and prays that God will "preserve them blameless, spirit and soul and body, unto the coming of our Lord Jesus Christ."

CHAPTER IX

The Second Epistle to the Thessalonians

1. *Relation to the Previous Letter*

Paul's second letter to Thessalonica bears a strong resemblance to the first, and must have been written a very short time afterwards. Paul is still associated with Silvanus and Timothy, whose names he had joined with his own in the previous letter. The Thessalonians are still making a brave stand against bitter opposition, and Paul offers them counsels similar to those he had given already. On one point only he is more explicit than he had previously been. He had advised his readers in the first letter to wait calmly for the Lord's coming, assured that all would be well if they were faithful and obedient in the work that lay to their hand. It would appear that these counsels had been misunderstood or willfully perverted (2:2). The Thessalonians had been confirmed in their belief that the end was immediately near, and Paul now writes to explain more precisely what he had meant to say.

2. *The Apocalyptic Passage*

On the face of it, there seems no reason why Paul should not have written to the same people, after a brief interval, a letter which was largely a repetition of the first; but the similarity of the two Epistles has caused misgiving to many scholars. They hold that the second letter is unauthentic, or rather that it is a revision of the first by a later hand. According to this view, the teaching of I Thessalonians had proved, in the next generation, to be mistaken. The Lord had not returned, as Paul had expected, and his letter was rewritten with the purpose of explaining why the end had been delayed. Much that Paul had said was retained in this new Epistle, but its cen-

tral passage (2:1-12) must be regarded as a later addition.
The revised copy was meant to take the place of I Thessalonians, but the genuine letter was already in circulation and
could not be suppressed. Both the Epistles were finally put
side by side as two different letters which Paul had sent to the
Thessalonians.

Before considering this theory, it will be well to glance at
the debated passage, which is certainly one of the most curious
and puzzling in the New Testament. The Thessalonians are
told that they must not be too much excited about the return
of Christ for, though he will come soon, he cannot appear
until a preliminary drama has played itself out. The evil in
the world must reach its climax under the leadership of a mysterious figure, "the man of sin," who will lay claim to divinity
and enthrone himself in the temple of God. The forces of
evil are already preparing themselves for this final outbreak,
but as yet there is a power that restrains them. A day is near
when this restraining power will be swept away, and the field
will thus be clear for "that wicked one." He will deceive men
by deeds that seem miraculous and compel the world's homage,
but presently the Lord will appear and destroy him, and will
bring in the Kingdom of God.

The passage is to be explained in the light of a belief which
meets us at various times in the New Testament, and which
had come in from Jewish apocalyptic. It was supposed that
the advent of the true Messiah would be preceded by that of
the "Antichrist," a sort of devil's Messiah. Satan, perceiving
that his kingdom was near an end, would gather up all his
power for a final assault on the cause of God. He would incarnate himself in a human figure and seek to obtain the worship
and obedience of men, thus inaugurating a great revolt from
God which would accompany the break-up of the present order. This conception of the Antichrist finds a place in the
apocalyptic discourse in the Gospels, (Mark 13:14; Matt.
24:15). It appears in the First Epistle of John (2:18; 4:3)
and plays a central part, as we shall see, in the book of Reve-

lation. Between Revelation and II Thessalonians there is this striking difference, that in the later book Antichrist is identified with the Roman power, while in the Epistle Rome is conceived as holding him back. This is the most probable explanation of "the Restrainer." The Roman power is regarded as the grand upholder of order. So long as Rome exercises control over the world, the forces of lawlessness will be kept under, but the empire is soon to fall, and its fall will be the signal for universal anarchy. The "man of sin" will be, for the time, triumphant.

To many scholars it has seemed impossible that Paul should have written this fantastic prophecy. It is, indeed, on this ground, more than on any other, that his authorship of II Thessalonians has been called in question. The mind which entertained those wild apocalyptic ideas was surely of quite a different type from that which meets us in the lofty religious teaching of the great Pauline Epistles. Yet we have no real means of judging what Paul might and might not have written. He was a many-sided thinker, and all that we know of his thought is from those few short letters which have been preserved to us. For that part, we do know that along with his spiritual interpretation of the gospel he held apocalyptic beliefs, and that these had been prominent in his teaching at Thessalonica (cf. I Thess. 5:1 f.) He seems, indeed, to have prided himself on his gift of apocalyptic speculation (cf. I Cor. 2:6 f.), and the passage in II Thessalonians may well have been from his hand. If not by himself, it must have been written in his lifetime, for the Temple, which fell in 70 A.D., is assumed to be still standing and there is no anticipation of its fall. We know, moreover, that Paul had a strong belief in Roman government, and the picture of the empire as a barrier, forcing back the tide of anarchy, is characteristic of his thought. It may be added that the passage, in spite of its fanciful prediction, has a grandeur and philosophical depth which are not unworthy of him. In our time we have moved away from the apocalyptic mode of thought, and find it hard to do justice to those who used it as a natural vehicle for their ideas. Given the beliefs that were generally accepted in Paul's day, there is a real meaning in his conception of a "mystery of iniquity," a spirit of lawlessness which is always working beneath the surface, and which, although it is repressed by main force, is ready to break forth and embody itself in some monstrous evil, bent on destroying all that is revered and holy. Under apocalyptic symbols, the passage truly describes what has actually happened, time and again, in periods of social dissolution.

3. *Authenticity and Purpose*

No argument against Pauline authorship can be founded on the apocalyptic chapter, and there is nothing else in the Epistle that marks it as non-Pauline. The language is that of Paul, the ideas are those of the previous Epistle, and it was not unnatural that the writer should repeat them when he was dealing with the same problems and difficulties. Among recent scholars, the tendency has been to accept the Epistle as Paul's, but to doubt whether he wrote it to the Thessalonians. One conjecture is that he addressed it to another church, perhaps that of Berea, which he had founded just after leaving Thessalonica, and which the messenger who carried the Thessalonian letter would visit on his way. The two neighboring churches would exchange their letters, and the Thessalonians might preserve copies of both of them and persuade themselves, in course of time, that Paul had sent them two Epistles. This theory is ingenious, but uncalled for. It is easy to conceive circumstances which would make it necessary for Paul to write a second letter soon after the first, dealing with a new development which he had not foreseen when he wrote before. This is what happens constantly in every one's correspondence. For that part, the new situation is pretty plainly indicated in the closing chapter of the Second Epistle. In I Thessalonians, Paul had warned his readers of one consequence which was likely to follow from their expectation of the immediate return of Christ. "We beseech you, brethren, that ye study to be quiet and to do your own business and to work with your own hands as we commanded you; that ye may walk honestly towards them that are without and that ye may have lack of nothing" (I Thess. 4:11, 12). The Thessalonian church was the first to experience a trouble which has since often happened in times of millennarian excitement. When the end of all things was believed to be at hand, men ceased to be interested in their ordinary work. It seemed a waste of energy to do labor which would go for nothing and to earn money which at any moment might become worthless. The result was that some members of the church were living in idleness, at the expense of their more sober-minded brethren. Through them, Christianity was getting a bad name among the heathen, as a fanatical religion which served as an excuse for indolence. Paul had foreseen this danger, but information had come to him that his warning had been neglected, and he now speaks out much more decidedly than in his previous letter. He reminds his readers how he himself had behaved during his sojourn among them, laboring to support himself, not merely from necessity, but because he wished to set them an example. Now he declares that those who refuse to work for their living are not to be recognized as members of the Christian community. Their idleness may be due to devout enthusiasm, but the religion which causes a man to become a burden on his neighbors cannot be true Christianity. It is well to look earnestly for the return of Christ, but this must not be allowed to excuse a man from attending to his daily work and making an honest livelihood. So Paul lays down the great rule, and gives it a religious sanction; "if a man will not work neither shall he eat" (3:10).

The passage is one of many which illustrate the plain common sense of Paul. He never allows his enthusiasm to get the better of his sound judgment and blind him to everyday duties. His greatness is due largely to the rare blend in his character of high spiritual ardor and practical wisdom. In this passage, too, we have the first clear statement of the great principle that honest work is one of the elements of Christian living. Man's chief duty is to seek after God, but this does not require that he should neglect his common tasks for those which appear more spiritual. The highest kind of religion is that which expresses itself in faithful performance of the appointed work.

CHAPTER X

THE CORINTHIAN LETTERS

1. *Paul's Work at Corinth*

By far the largest part of Paul's correspondence was with
the church at Corinth, which he had founded during his first
visit to Europe. Corinth, owing to its position, had always
been a place of great importance. It lay on the narrow
isthmus which connects the northern and southern halves of
Greece, and was not only the strategic key of the whole country, but the natural center for Greek trade and for much of
the commerce of the Mediterranean. It was a famous seat of
Greek culture, as well as a busy commercial city, and close beside it were held the Isthmian games — one of the historic
festivals which served to unite all the Greek peoples. In ancient times it had sent out a number of colonies which had
since eclipsed the mother city itself, but they still remembered
their debt to it. Corinth was associated with some of the most
doubtful practices of pagan religion, and in Paul's day had a
sinister reputation all over the world as a city of pleasure. He
himself confesses that he had begun his Corinthian mission
"with fear and much trembling" (I Cor. 2:3). It seemed like
madness to come with the gospel of Christ into this center of
heathen materialism and immorality.

From the beginning, however, the work at Corinth had been
highly successful. The city was at least alive, not a mere relic
of bygone greatness like Athens, where Paul had presented his
message immediately before without any response whatever.
After this disappointment, he had perhaps gone to Corinth
for the purpose of sailing for home; but instead of that, he
remained for nearly two years, working under happy conditions and building up a flourishing church. In such a city, how-

ever, the mission was faced with peculiar difficulties. The population was very miscellaneous in character, and converts of every type found their way into the Christian fellowship. In order to keep them together, Paul needed to exercise to the full his gift for becoming all things to all men, and had to make allowance for many things which were little in keeping with the Christian ideal. Corinth, moreover, was a typically Greek city and the members of the church had all the failings, as well as some of the high qualities, which belonged to the Greek temperament. In two ways, more especially, as we can gather from Paul's letters, the Corinthian Christians shared in the characteristics of their race. (1) On the one hand, they had the Greek intelligence and took a keen interest in all that concerned the philosophical side of religion. Paul was able to discuss with them many profound questions which in his ordinary teaching he left untouched. But in spite of this zeal for "knowledge," they were strangely blind to the practical demands of the gospel. They needed to be put in mind of elementary moral duties. Vices were tolerated among these intelligent Christians of which any decent pagan would be ashamed. Deep thinking about the truth was taken as a substitute for the effort to carry it into practice. (2) On the other hand, the Corinthians had all the Greek tendency towards disunion. As far back as history goes, this had been the chief cause of Greek weakness, and had finally brought ruin on the nation. The city-states were always in conflict with each other, and each of the cities was divided against itself. It was the strong individualism of the Greek character which had made it so fruitful in men of genius, but the other side of this quality was a fatal incapacity to unite, even when the highest interests were at stake. The spirit of party, which had destroyed Greece politically, soon began to manifest itself in the Christian church. Even while he remained at Corinth, Paul had difficulty in holding the community together, and as soon as he was gone it broke up into parties, violently opposed to one another, and all chafing against the authority of Paul himself.

It is certain that no other of his churches gave Paul so much trouble as that of Corinth, but it was just this circumstance to which we owe his Corinthian letters, which are the fullest and most interesting of all his writings. In his endeavor to keep this unruly church in order, he was compelled to write to it again and again, and the trouble which arose in it was of so many kinds that he had to deal in the letters with almost all the problems that beset the early Christian mission. Not only so, but the dissensions at Corinth had their issue in personal attacks on Paul, so that he was obliged to defend his own character and action. In these letters, therefore, we get at once our most vivid and diversified pictures of an early Christian community and much of our most valuable information about Paul himself.

2. Paul's Letters to Corinth

As we now have it, the Corinthian correspondence is made up of two long Epistles, so different in character that an interval of at least a year must have elapsed between the first and the second. We know, however, from several express references in these letters, that Paul had written several others to the church at Corinth. In the Epistle which we now call First Corinthians, he mentions an earlier letter which had caused some misunderstanding (I Cor. 5:9). He had warned his readers to hold aloof from immoral persons, and they had pointed out that in a heathen city like Corinth this would isolate them entirely. So he now explains that he had been thinking, not of pagans, who made no pretense to higher moral standards, but of professed Christians who were leading a double life. As there had been a letter before our I Corinthians, so there had been one after it, to which he alludes more than once in the second Epistle. It had given him much pain to write, and after it was dispatched he would fain have recalled it (II Cor. 2:4; 7:8 f.), although, as the event proved, it had a salutary effect. There is reason to believe that while these two letters no longer exist in their entirety, fragments of them both have been preserved. The passage II Corinthians 6:14-7:1 is quite out of place in its present context, but contains just that warning against immoral company which the Corinthians had taken in too sweeping a sense, and it can hardly be doubted that here we have part of the lost letter. A more difficult question arises with regard to the last four chapters of II Corinthians. Anyone who reads the first nine chapters, must feel that with the tenth chapter the mood of the writer unaccountably changes. Up to that point, he has overflowed with kindness and forgiveness. He wants to forget the painful episode which is now over and seeks a full reconciliation with his readers, whom, in spite of all differences, he dearly loves. In the tenth chapter, he suddenly turns on them and reproaches them bitterly for their disloyalty. It is difficult to believe that those chapters 10-13 can belong to the same letter as chapters 1-9. Their only effect would have been to destroy the impression which the writer had hitherto been so anxious to create. Many scholars are now convinced that they formed part of the "painful letter" of which Paul has spoken; and while objections can be urged against this theory, it seems on the whole to offer the most satisfactory solution of a problem which undoubtedly exists. It is not improbable that some of the "painful letter" was destroyed (perhaps at Paul's own request), because of personal references which it was desirable to forget. The rest of the letter was obviously too valuable to lose, and in course of time it came to be added, as a sort of appendix, to the Second Epistle.

It seems apparent, then, that there has been some confusion in the present arrangement of the Corinthian letters, and the suggestion has been made that it extends much further than we now have means of judging. May it not be that our First Corinthians is made up of several letters, written at different times, which have been thrown together? As it stands the Epistle runs to inordinate length and deals with a great number of disconnected subjects, and is possibly to be taken as an amalgam of several different letters. This, however, is only

conjecture, and there is no sufficient reason for breaking up the
Epistle, which can be explained perfectly well as it stands. A
letter, when all is said, is not to be judged by the standards
which are justly applied to a formal treatise. It is not constructed according to a set plan. The writer passes from one
subject to another just as it comes into his mind, and the very
charm of it consists in this casual throwing together of different ideas. We must never forget, too, that under ancient
conditions, Paul had difficulty in transmitting his letters. On
the rare occasions when he had the chance of a messenger he
would try to put as much into his letter as possible, even when
the various themes did not fit very well together.

3. Connection of the Letters

So far as we know, therefore, he wrote four letters to
Corinth. The first was that one of which a fragment seems to
be preserved in II Corinthians 6:14-7:1, dealing with the conduct to be observed towards immoral persons. The second
was the Epistle now known as I Corinthians. It was written
at Ephesus and apparently after Paul had been resident there
for some time, for he refers to the expansion of his work
(16:8, 9) and to great dangers which he had encountered
(15:32). The occasion of the letter was twofold. The Corinthians had written to him, putting a number of questions which
he sets himself to answer, and just about the same time reports
had come to him, through "those of the household of Chloe"
(1:11), which had made him somewhat uneasy as to conditions in the Corinthian church. Possibly the letter from Corinth had been brought by those people (Christian servants of
a wealthy lady who had come to Ephesus on her business),
and what they had told him privately had interested him more
than the letter itself. Some time elapsed before Paul again
wrote to Corinth. What had happened in the meanwhile we
can only gather from his own references, for the book of Acts
tells us nothing. It would appear that those forces of disorder
which Paul had tried to stem by his former Epistle had grown

stronger, and had been encouraged by visiting evangelists, hostile to Paul, who had represented him as a self-seeking adventurer, with no right to call himself an Apostle. The position had become so serious that he interrupted his work at Ephesus to pay a personal visit to Corinth, but the result had been disastrous. The Corinthian church, at the instigation of some particular mischief-maker (II Cor. 2:5 f.), had disowned and insulted him, and he had indignantly left the city. Returning to Ephesus, he had sent his "painful letter." If the last four chapters of II Corinthians are to be accepted as part of it, he bitterly reproached the church for its fickleness and defended his claim to be a true Apostle by a moving and dignified account of all he had suffered in the cause of Christ. At the same time, he presented his ultimatum. The Corinthian church must either submit again to his authority and punish the man who had attacked him, or he would have done with it forever. This letter he sent by his assistant Titus, and was tormented with anxiety as to how it would be received. Finally, he crossed over to Macedonia to intercept Titus on his way home, and fell in with him at Philippi or Thessalonica. To his infinite relief, Titus brought good news. The rebellious church had taken the letter in good part, and had duly censured the man who had offended him. So now he wrote his fourth letter, our II Corinthians. He pours out his heart in gratitude for the reconciliation. He assures the Corinthians that he is now fully satisfied, and that the quarrel will be forgotten, at least on his part, when he pays his next visit in a few weeks' time. He takes occasion to remind them of the collection for the church at Jerusalem, which had been sadly neglected during the recent troubles. The time has come when he must be preparing to travel to Jerusalem with the money, and he wishes everything to be ready before his arrival.

This, so far as we can now ascertain it, is the history of Paul's correspondence with Corinth, and we have now to deal separately with the surviving letters.

CHAPTER XI

The First Epistle to the Corinthians

1. *Value*

From every point of view, I Corinthians is one of the most valuable of the New Testament writings. (1) Historically, it is our chief document for the study of early Christian practices and institutions, and of the conflict of the new religion with paganism. Paul does not write with any historical purpose, but, as he deals one by one with the concrete problems which had arisen in a typical Christian community, he offers us a sort of moving picture of the Christian life of his day. (2) Practically, the Epistle illustrates for us, better than any other writing, how the Christian ethic is to be understood and applied. Jesus himself had taught among the villages of Galilee, and his precepts, if we take them literally, might seem to be valid only for the simple form of society which he had before him. Yet Paul perceives that the rule of life which Jesus had laid down is of universal significance. He takes the principles of the Gospel teaching, and shows how they hold good for the complex civilization of a great city, and for people of every race and condition. The task of Christianity today is to make its message applicable to a new time and a new order of knowledge and culture, and in this task we have still to take our guidance from Paul. (3) Theologically, the Epistle contains some of Paul's deepest reflection. He is directly concerned with matters of practice, but it is characteristic of Paul that he makes every question, in the last resort, a religious one. Scattered through the Epistle, and often in connections where we should least expect them, are passages which are full of profound insight into the meaning of the gospel. Besides these occasional utterances, there is one chapter, the longest and most sustained in all Paul's writings, on the subject of immortality (I Cor. 15). Here we have Paul at his very greatest as a purely religious thinker.

The Epistle has two further claims to rank among the most important of the New Testament books. (1) There are two passages in it which bear directly on the Gospel history — the account of the Last Supper (11:23-26), and that of the Resurrection (15:3-9). This latter passage, more particularly, is of supreme value. It was written only twenty-five years after the event and long before the parallel accounts in the Gospels. Paul expressly tells us that, in what he records of the appearances of the risen Christ, he is in full agreement with the immediate disciples (15:3, 11). Here, therefore, we have the primary passage on the Resurrection. All inquiry into this mysterious subject must start, not from the story as told in the Gospels, but from the evidence of Paul in I Corinthians. (2) In this Epistle we have the most exquisite passage that Paul ever wrote — the hymn to love in the thirteenth chapter. It appears in the middle of a long discussion on the nature and value of spiritual gifts, but Paul had most likely composed it independently. Perhaps it first came to him in one of those moods of ecstatic feeling to which he was liable, but he must also have worked on it carefully, with attention to every word and rhythm. Even in its form it is constructed as a poem, with four strophes of equal length, in which the thought is developed and brought to a climax. To bring out its true character, it ought to be printed in poetic form, in some such way as this:

Though I speak with the tongues of men and of angels
    And have not love
I am become as clanging brass or a tinkling cymbal.
And though I have prophecy and understand all mysteries and all knowl-
    edge
    And have not love
I am nothing.
And though I bestow all my goods to feed the poor,
And though I give my body to be burned

And have not love
It profits me nothing.

Love is long-suffering and kind,
Love envies not, love boasts not, is not arrogant,
Does not act rudely, is not self-seeking, is not ill-tempered, thinks no
      evil,
Rejoices not in wrongdoing but rejoices in the truth,
Bears all things, believes all things, hopes all things, endures all things.

Love never fails;
But whether there be prophecies they shall fail,
Whether there be tongues they shall cease;
Whether there be knowledge it shall vanish away.
For we know in part and we prophesy in part;
But when that which is perfect is come
Then that which is in part shall be done away.

When I was a child
I spoke as a child, I understood as a child, I thought as a child;
But when I became a man
I put away childish things.
For now we see in a mirror darkly
But then face to face.
Now I know in part
But then shall I know even as also I am known.
And now abideth faith, hope, love, these three;
But the greatest of these is love.

Another passage in the Epistle is worthy to be classed as
splendid poetry, the majestic close of the great chapter on
immortality (15:42-58). If it were only for these magnificent
outbursts, the First Epistle to the Corinthians takes its place
as one of the outstanding books, not only in the New Testament, but in the world's literature.

2. *Topics of Discussion*

The Epistle, as we have seen, is very miscellaneous in its
contents. Paul had been consulted by the Corinthians on a
number of their difficulties, and he had heard of others by re-

port. Without any attempt at logical sequence, he takes up
the various subjects brought before him, turning from one to
another with some brief formula (e. g., "Now concerning").
The topics with which he deals are: (1) the party divisions
(1-4); (2) a case of gross immorality (5); (3) lawsuits between Christians (6); (4) marriage and divorce (7); (5)
meats offered to idols (8-10); (6) veiling of women (11:1-
16); (7) observance of the Lord's Supper (11:17-34); (8)
spiritual gifts (12-14); (9) the resurrection (15); (10) personal notices and greetings (16).

It has to be admitted that some of the topics dealt with are
now of little interest. The question, for instance, as to whether
women should be veiled in the public meeting, must be viewed
in the light of ancient sentiment on what was seemly in dress
and behavior, and on these points, more than on any others,
the feeling of one age differs from that of another. Paul's
ideas about such matters were a little old-fashioned, even in
his own day. The discussion of marriage, likewise, is chiefly
interesting historically. Paul is less concerned with the marriage relation itself than with the problems which arose in a
mixed community of Christians and pagans. So far as he deals
with the broader question, he is governed by the belief that
the return of Christ and the end of the present order are close
at hand. He has often been credited with an ascetic aversion
to marriage, but this quite misrepresents his attitude. His
view was simply that in face of the great crisis now imminent,
men and women were better to dispense with ties which would
preoccupy and distract them. The discussion on meats offered
to idols is also bound up with a first-century problem. In a
center of paganism, where animals for sacrifice were constantly required, much of the available meat had first passed
through some temple. The visitor to Pompeii to-day will find
the meat market attached, as a sort of annex, to the temple of
Jupiter. Christians of tender conscience were seriously troubled by the fear that, by eating meat which had been consecrated
to an idol, they might unwittingly contract some moral harm.

Others, who were convinced that an idol was nothing, made light of these scruples, and would use the meat ostentatiously and try to force it on their more scrupulous brethren. Paul deals with this apparently trivial matter in such a way as to give it a permanent significance. He declares that, while obeying his own conscience, a man must also respect the consciences of others. What to you may be morally harmless, may cause your neighbor to lose his moral bearings altogether, and you must be willing to put restraint on yourself for his sake. Liberty is your Christian birthright, but liberty must be held in check by Christian love. The two longest discussions in the Epistle are those on party strife and on the spiritual gifts. Here again Paul lifts the immediate question to a level at which it becomes a permanent one. He shows that, in Christianity, all party divisions ought to be transcended by a common loyalty to Christ. Human leaders have their place, and each of them has something to contribute; but their task is to lead you to the divine master, in whose service all things are yours, to be used as instruments towards your higher welfare. In the same manner, Paul is led to consider profound issues in his discussion of the spiritual gifts. Christian worship in the primitive days was accompanied by enthusiastic outbursts, supposed to arise from the direct impulse of the Spirit. The worshiper would give utterance to strange cries, would fall into trances and see wonderful visions, would sometimes express himself with lyrical fervor or moving eloquence. These gifts, with their suggestion of mystery, were much coveted, and seem to have been regarded in Corinth more especially as the chief evidence of a genuine Christianity. Paul examines the nature of those ecstatic phenomena and concludes that they are of inferior value. The real manifestations of the Spirit are to be found in the normal life of Christian goodness and service. It is in this connection that Paul introduces his hymn in praise of love. Without love, all other gifts are worthless. To have love, much more than to possess genius or eloquence or mysterious powers, is the proof that God's Spirit is working in your heart.

3. The Chapter on Immortality

Paul reserves to the close of the Epistle his great argument on the future life. He had heard that in Corinth there were those who denied the Resurrection (15:12). This cannot mean that they did not believe in immortality, for to a Christian such an attitude was unthinkable. What they doubted was a bodily existence in the hereafter. On this point, there had always been a striking difference between Greek and Jewish thought. For Greek thinkers, the body was the grand impediment to true life, and the soul was conceived as free only when it had been released from its bodily prison. For the Hebrew mind, the very idea of life implied a body. Without a physical organism through which to act, the soul was powerless, and if it continued in being, it could exist only as a ghost or shadow. Immortality, for Hebrew thought, thus involved a resurrection, a reunion of the soul with the body. Paul takes his stand on the Jewish position, but refuses to accept it in its crude traditional form. He concedes that the present body is "of the earth earthy," and that its natural destiny is to corrupt and disappear. Flesh and blood cannot inherit the Kingdom of God. But he holds that in the hereafter, the soul will be clothed in a new, a "spiritual" body — an organism that will correspond with spiritual, as this one with mere animal, life. Elsewhere he calls it a "body of glory" (Phil. 3:21), and seems to regard it as woven out of some infinitely fine material, akin to the nature of light. Apparently he thinks of Christ as having risen, not in the body which was laid in the grave, but in that "body of glory" which he had himself seen, as a great light in heaven, on the way to Damascus. He declares that the Christian after death will inherit a body like that which Christ now wears. Even those who do not die, but survive to the Lord's coming, will undergo a change, their material bodies mysteriously dissolving into the higher, spiritual substance. It is evident, not only from I Corinthians 15 but from a number of other passages in the Epistles, that Paul attached a cardinal value to this belief that life in the hereafter will be life in a body. His interest, no doubt, was to maintain the fact of personal identity. The Greek conception led inevitably to the idea that, while the soul was immortal, it was absorbed after death into a universal soul, in which all individual distinctions were finally lost. Paul insisted that Christians would survive as personal beings, preserving in the future that fellowship with Christ on which they had entered on earth. He accepted the body as the pledge and necessary organ of this separate existence, although he held that a "spiritual body" would take the place of this earthly one.

CHAPTER XII

THE SECOND EPISTLE TO THE CORINTHIANS

1. *The Two Sections*

The main problems connected with II Corinthians have already been indicated. According to the view which, on the whole, appears most probable, the Epistle as we have it is made up of two, the earlier of which is contained in the last four chapters. Many attempts have been made to discover unity in the Epistle just as it stands. It is suggested, for instance, that Paul may have written the first part when he was full of the relief and gratitude which the good news from Corinth had brought him; but when he completed the letter, after a few days' interruption, the glow had passed off, and he now gave vent to the feelings which he had so far suppressed. Or it is pointed out, quite justly, that we do not know the whole circumstances. Paul may have been aware of factors in the Corinthian situation which made it necessary for him to break into indignant remonstrance, although his aim was conciliatory. There can be no doubt, however, that the tone of the last four chapters is entirely different from that of the first nine, and the simplest solution is to take them as a separate letter — part of the "painful letter," which was undoubtedly written when the trouble at Corinth was at its height.

2. *The Personal Defense*

These closing chapters are of surpassing interest, as constituting what may be called Paul's autobiography. Stung by the charges which had been brought against him, he begs that for a little time he may be indulged in "boasting," and may recount for himself, since no one will do it for him, what he has done and endured on behalf of the gospel. It is a wonderful record, and we realize, as we study it, that the author of Acts, with all his exaltation of Paul, has told us hardly anything.

Of the Jews five times I received the forty stripes save one; thrice was I beaten with rods; once was I stoned; thrice I suffered shipwreck; a night and a day I have been on the open sea; in journeyings often, in perils by rivers, in perils from bandits, in peril from my own people, in peril from the heathen, in peril in the city, in peril in the wilderness, in peril on the sea, in peril among false brethren; in weariness and pain, in wakefulness often, in hunger and thirst, in fastings often, in cold and nakedness; and besides these outward troubles the burden that weighs on me daily, anxiety for all the churches. [11:24-28.]

Even more moving than this story of his labors, is the passage that follows, where Paul tells of his spiritual conflict (12:1-11). He had been favored more than other men with "visions and revelations," high experiences of an ecstatic nature. He dwells particularly on one occasion, fourteen years before, when he had felt himself transported and caught up to the third heaven. But lest he might become too proud of these lofty privileges, it had been ordained that after each of them he should suffer terrible agony from a "thorn in the flesh," some form, apparently, of neurotic attack which humiliated him in his own eyes and those of others. He had prayed that this "messenger of Satan" should be driven from him, but the Lord had answered, "my grace is enough for you; my strength is perfected in weakness." So he is prouder now of his weakness than of all his great achievements. It is in his times of helplessness that he is most conscious of a divine presence which lifts him above himself.

As he tells his own story, Paul reproaches the Corinthians for their injustice to him and their submissiveness to those enemies of his whose record could not for a moment compare with his. Who those enemies were, we are not told, though we can gather that they had come from the outside, with letters of introduction from men high in authority, on the strength of which they claimed to be "Apostles in the first degree" (11:5). It is hard to avoid the conclusion that these interlopers were acting for that extreme Jewish party which had been seeking for years to injure Paul's work among the Gentiles. His anger, however, is directed not so much against them as against the Corinthians themselves, who had so easily been won over to renounce their own Apostle.

3. *The Main Letter*

If this is the "painful letter," it is unfortunate that an accident has placed it at the end of the Epistle to which it is really a prelude. Paul writes the main Epistle in a burst of gratitude for the change which has taken place at Corinth, and we can best understand the change after reading that appeal of Paul, which had apparently moved the Corinthians as it moves us still, at a distance of two thousand years. In its own way, the other letter is a document just as revealing as the letter of autobiography. As he had formerly given rein to his indignation, so the Apostle now pours out his heart in a passion of tenderness. Everything else is forgotten and he rejoices to know that he has won back his church and can feel the same to it as he did before. Apart from this self-revelation, the Epistle is chiefly noteworthy for the great section covered by Chapters 3-5, in which personal feeling merges in lofty meditation. As he assures the Corinthians that he had been single-minded in all his work among them, Paul is led to reflect on the nature of his work and the responsibility it laid on him. In the gospel, God had made a new covenant with men, a covenant based not on written enactments, but on a life-giving Spirit. Through the Spirit, which is Christ's gift to us, we enter on a new life, which begins on earth, but will widen out into the eternal life hereafter. Paul breaks away in this passage from his earlier belief that the dead must wait until the general resurrection before they are clothed with the "spiritual body" and so obtain fullness of life. He now holds that the new body is already prepared, and that the believer will enter it as soon as the "earthly tent" is dissolved. It is in this passage, too, that Paul makes his striking declaration as to the manner in which he conceives of Christ:

Wherefore henceforth know we no man after the flesh; even though we have known Christ after the flesh yet now we know him so no more. Wherefore if any man is in Christ he is a new creature; the old things are passed away, behold they are become new. [5:16-17.]

He seems here to affirm, in the most emphatic manner, that he no longer concerns himself with Jesus as he had lived on earth, and looks only to Christ risen and exalted — the Lord of that new life which is now offered to his people. It has sometimes been inferred from the passage that the Christ whom Paul worshipped was not the historical Jesus but an ideal, heavenly being, and that in this manner he changed Christianity into a different religion. This, however, cannot be admitted; for while he makes few direct allusions to the Gospel history, the very spring of Paul's devotion is a passionate loyalty to the personal Jesus. It must never be forgotten, too, that the death of Jesus was part of his earthly life, that it was, indeed, the crowning episode in which everything he had done and taught was gathered up into a focus. In so far as all Paul's teaching centered on the Cross, he was concerned from first to last with the historical life of Christ. The passage in II Corinthians is admittedly very obscure and difficult, but it must be understood in the sense that Paul found in Christ's risen life the grand explanation of what Christ had been. To know Christ "according to the flesh," merely as a historical figure in the past, is to know nothing of him. Paul fixed his mind on Christ exalted and, in the light of that vision, perceived the true meaning of the life and death.

The Epistle is an intensely personal one, and even in those theological chapters Paul never loses sight of his immediate object — to put himself right with the Corinthians and make sure henceforth of their affection and confidence. The theological chapters are indeed the most personal in the Epistle. To clear away all misunderstandings, Paul takes his readers into the innermost secrets of his religious life. Towards the end, however, he turns to a very practical matter, the collection which he had been making for the church at Jerusalem and which the Corinthians for some time past had half forgotten. Since he was to sail from Corinth a few months later, he wished to have everything in order, and took the opportunity offered him in the present letter of giving some final directions. The two matter-of-fact chapters, 8 and 9, are in their way as interesting in their revelation of Paul's character as the outpouring of high thought and emotion that has preceded them. It is always embarrassing to ask for money, and for a proud, sensitive man like Paul, it was particularly difficult — all the more so as he knew that the Corinthians were none too enthusiastic about his scheme. He goes about his task very awkwardly, suggesting one motive and another which might incite his readers to liberality. His effort is to put himself in the place of the ordinary practical man, who never gives to anything without calculating whether it is worth while; but this was not Paul's own way of giving, and he does not know how to proceed. He is plainly aware of the futility of the stock arguments, and is half ashamed of putting them forward. At last he suddenly breaks off and closes with his true appeal: "Thanks be to God for his unspeakable gift" (9:15). Gratitude for what God himself has done is the one motive for giving, and the man who cannot respond to it will be moved by nothing.

This matter of the collection makes a somewhat disappointing finish to a great letter, but perhaps without it the letter would not have been written. When Titus arrived with his good news that all was well at Corinth, Paul decided to send him back immediately to attend to the collection, and wrote the letter that he might take it with him. Shortly afterwards, he went on to Corinth himself. We are told nothing as to how he was received, but there is no reason to doubt that he found himself once more among friends. He made a sojourn of three months at Corinth, and it was during that time that he wrote his Epistle to the Romans, the most elaborate and closely reasoned of all his writings. The character of this Epistle is our best evidence that after a long period of storm and anxiety he was at last enjoying peace of mind.

CHAPTER XIII

THE EPISTLE TO THE GALATIANS

1. *Historical and Religious Value*

The Galatian Epistle, although it covers only a few pages, is one of the fundamental writings of the New Testament. Its importance is threefold. (1) It contains the primary account of the beginnings of the Christian church. In defending his right to be an Apostle, Paul finds himself obliged to review the early years of his Christian career. He indicates the circumstances of the church when he first knew it, and tells of his relations with Peter and other Apostles. All this is done in the barest outline, but the testimony is at first hand, and comes from one who was himself a chief actor in the events which he describes. The first two chapters of Galatians thus constitute the bedrock of early Christian history. Whatever may be the value of the Gospels and of the opening chapters of Acts, they were written comparatively late and their evidence may be called in question. But when we turn to Paul's account in Galatians, we know for certain that we are in direct contact with the facts. It was the recognition of this, about a century ago, which began the whole movement of modern critical investigation. Everything in the primitive tradition had been challenged, and it was asked if we had any data which could be accepted with full confidence, as a point of departure for real inquiry. The answer was found in the brief record in Galatians. Here at least there is firm ground on which the historian can proceed to build. (2) Theologically, this Epistle is the chief key to Paul's interpretation of the Christian message. The legitimacy of his teaching had been attacked and he therefore sets forth, as clearly and succinctly as he can, his governing ideas, and shows how they differ from those of his opponents. In other Epistles (e.g., in Romans) he elaborates those ideas and supplements them, but in Galatians we have the classical statement of the Pauline theology, and it is all the more impressive as it is presented in no cold logical form, but with the energy of passionate conviction. (3) Religiously, the Epistle is of permanent value. It is not too much to say that this letter of Paul is the Christian declaration of independence. Up to this time it had been taken for granted that Christianity was no more than a revised Judaism, but Paul now asserts that it is a new religion, founded on a principle altogether different from that involved in the Jewish Law. Ever since, with its bold affirmation of the distinctive Christian beliefs, the Epistle has worked with a quickening and awakening power. It was through an intense study of Galatians that Luther arrived at the convictions which had their issue in the Reformation. His *Commentary on Galatians* was the manifesto with which he launched his great movement. Most of the later religious revivals have likewise found their inspiration in this Epistle; and there are signs that some of its characteristic ideas are again beginning to vitalize the Christian thinking of our own time.

2. *Date and Destination*

This all-important Epistle is beset with many critical difficulties. We know nothing, except by inference, of the occasion which called it forth. We do not know for certain to whom it was addressed, or at what point in his career Paul wrote it. According to one view, it ought to be ranked as the earliest of all the Epistles, dating from a time before Paul had fairly committed himself to his larger work, and was still a teacher in Antioch. More probably it belongs to the same general period as the other great Epistles, though it must be placed early in the series. Perhaps we shall not be far wrong in assigning it to the first or second year of Paul's stay at Ephesus. We know that during that troubled period of his life, he was burdened with anxiety for his churches, and the storm which was nearly to overwhelm his work at Corinth seems first to have broken out in Galatia.

Who were these Galatians to whom Paul wrote the letter? The name Galatia was properly applied to a region that lay towards the north of Asia Minor. It had been settled three centuries before the time of Paul by wandering Celtic tribes from whom it took its name, "the Country of the Gauls." We learn from the book of Acts that Paul more than once traversed the western border of this country, but no indication is given that he ever went into it to conduct a mission. This silence of Acts means little, for the author does not pretend to give a full account of the work of Paul; but on other grounds it is hard to believe that he evangelised that northern region. His aim, when once his Gentile mission had fairly started, was to make for the great cities of the west, from which the message might find its way most rapidly over the empire. It was to reach those cities that he crossed Asia Minor, after the first experimental journey, by the shortest and quickest routes. Would he have gone out of his way to work in an outlying, sparsely-populated region like Galatia? The view has therefore found favor with many modern scholars that he applies the name "Galatia" to that district to the south which he had visited along with Barnabas on the first missionary journey (Acts 13 and 14). For administrative purposes, the Romans had formed a province which included pretty much the whole of central Asia Minor, and to this whole province had given the name of its largest section, "Galatia." It was Paul's custom to speak of the countries he visited by their official Roman names, and this nomenclature would be specially convenient in the case of a group of cities — Antioch, Lystra, Derbe, Iconium — which were scattered over several territories. A number of considerations seem to confirm this view, that the Galatia of the Epistle was that region in the southern part of Asia Minor where the two missionaries had carried out their first enterprise of preaching to the Gentiles. Paul had again visited it in the course of that second journey which brought him to Europe (Acts 16:1 f.), and in Lystra had found the young disciple, Timothy, who was henceforth to be his most useful assistant. He had paid yet a third visit to those cities when he returned from Jerusalem to take up his work at Ephesus (Acts 18:23).

3. *Occasion of Writing*

Assuming that the Epistle was sent from Ephesus and that it was addressed to South Galatia, it must have been written a short time after that third visit. News had come to Paul at Ephesus that something like a revolution had taken place in the Galatian churches. Hitherto they had been devoted to their Apostle, but had suddenly become estranged from him and had gone over to that narrower type of Christianity to which he was opposed. For some time past there had been a strong party in the mother church which had regarded Paul with suspicion. It was well known that once he had been a persecutor, and now he was notoriously preaching a gospel which disowned the Law and all the sacred traditions of Israel. The antagonism to him had grown so serious that he had gone up to Jerusalem to lay the matter before a council of the church, and in this council, to all appearance, he had been fully vindicated. The leading Apostles had recognised him as a colleague and had consented that he should preach the gospel in his own way, so long as he confined himself to the Gentiles. But the opposition had by no means been silenced. A movement appears to have started for the express purpose of counteracting Paul's mission. The churches he had founded were visited by certain teachers, sent out, it would appear, by the extremists in Jerusalem, who insisted that Paul was no true Apostle, and that Christianity had no meaning apart from the Jewish Law. Paul was naturally bitter against these mischief-makers, but there is no reason to doubt that, though narrow-minded, they were earnest and sincere. They believed that Paul was imperiling the souls of his Gentile converts by his perversion of the Christian message, and that they were doing a real service for God by exposing him. It was their obvious sincerity which made them dangerous, and they were all the more dangerous as they came from Jerusalem, furnished with letters of introduction from revered Apostles. As emissaries from the central church, they were presumably better informed than Paul, whom they described as a self-appointed teacher, an incomer of doubtful antecedents, who had no personal knowledge of Christ, and no right to call himself an Apostle.

These men had penetrated to Galatia, where they made a deep impression. It may be gathered that the whole church in that region had succumbed to their influence. The Gentile converts, whom Paul had left rejoicing in his free Gospel, had now become sedulous in their observance of Jewish customs and festivals, convinced that, apart from this acceptance of the Law, there could be no salvation.

Paul was profoundly disturbed by the news. He saw that not only his Gentile mission, but the whole future of Christianity, was in danger. If the Law was still to be imperative, Christ had died in vain — his gospel had nothing to offer beyond what was given in Judaism. It was under stress of this clear perception of all that was at stake that Paul wrote the Galatian letter. In none of his other Epistles does he display such a passionate earnestness. His thoughts crowd on one another in a torrent. By every means he can think of, — reproach, argument, reminiscence, tender appeal — he tries to convince the Galatians of their error. Two peculiarities, one at the beginning and the other at the end of the letter, bear witness to the excitement under which it was written. In all his other letters Paul begins, in Eastern fashion, with elaborate greetings and congratulations; in this letter he plunges into his theme at once and, without any previous compliments, proceeds to express his disappointment and anger. So, at the close, he makes a striking departure from his usual custom. His letters were always dictated, with only a few final words from his own pen by way of signature. At the end of Galatians, there are eight long verses (6:11-18) written in large letters, as he tells us, by himself. Some foolish theories have been built on this statement: e.g., that he suffered from weak eyes and could hardly see what he was writing, or that he was an unpracticed penman and could write, like a child, only in capitals. To any one who has caught the spirit of the letter, his motive in that closing passage is obvious. When he read over what had been written to his dictation, he was still unsatisfied and, taking the pen into his own hand, added those closing verses in large characters, such as were used in public proclamations. Here, he implied, was his definite judgment, which could be nailed up if necessary for every one to read.

4. *Contents*

The Epistle is written, then, in view of a revolt in one of Paul's churches, that one, most probably, which was the first fruits of his Gentile mission and in which he took a peculiar pride. Throughout the letter, he is dealing with two issues, on the one hand the personal attack, and on the other hand the refusal of the Gospel which he had taught. In his reply the two issues are constantly tangled together, for they could not well be separated. It happens almost always in a great crisis that a cause is on trial along with some particular man. Whole nations wait breathlessly to know the fate of John Hampden or John Brown, for the decision concerning the man will involve the large question on which he had dared to take his stand. So Paul knew that, in defending his own Apostleship, he was defending Christian freedom. Everything turned in this crucial moment on the judgement men were to form of himself.

He begins, therefore, not with the customary formal opening, but with the firm assertion of his personal claim. "Paul an Apostle, not of men nor by men, but by Jesus Christ and God the Father, who raised him from the dead." After a stern rebuke to those who had doubted him, he proceeds to vindicate his full right to be an Apostle. He tells how he had received his call from Christ himself, and was not, as his enemies alleged, a mere interloper who had picked up all that he knew of the gospel at second hand. He owed nothing to men, for he had met the risen Christ, and from him and no other he had received his commission. So he goes on to describe his early years as a Christian, still with the object of proving that he was independent of the other Apostles, and their acknowledged equal. He dwells especially, in the second chapter, on the council held at Jerusalem where the leading Apostles, after a full hearing, had bestowed their sanction on his work and given him the right hand of fellowship. His equality had been so completely granted that he had dared, a little time afterwards, to rebuke Peter himself for trying to impose Jewish customs on the Gentiles. From this account of the historical facts, Paul turns to his message, and vehemently asserts that it is the true gospel (3 and 4). It centers in the hope of salvation by faith alone. Men had failed to attain to righteousness by their own effort, but, through Christ, God had done for them what they could not do themselves, and the one thing needful is to accept by faith this gift of God. Paul argues that, from the very beginning, this had been the divine plan. Long before the Law was given, Abraham had been justified on the ground of faith, and the Law had come in to serve a mere temporary purpose. Now that the need for it was over, the Law had been removed like a scaffolding from a finished building, and the plan which had always been in the mind of God was fully disclosed in the Christian Gospel. In the closing section (5 and 6), Paul defends his teaching from the charges which had been brought against it on ethical grounds. It had been maintained that by separating religion from the Law, he was destroying the sense of moral obligation. Relying on faith alone, men would now feel at liberty to indulge their own wills and passions, and the result would be pure anarchy. In his answer to these criticisms, which have often been urged since in different forms, Paul refuses to abate anything of his claim that Christianity is a religion of freedom.

As servants of Christ, men are to realise that no outward restraints are any longer laid on them, and on no account must they forego this liberty. Yet in place of the old control from without, Christ has given them his Spirit working from within. Those who have put their faith in him are henceforth their own lawgivers. Possessing the spirit, they are set free from their evil nature and can fulfill the will of God as they could never do under the old conditions of slavish obedience. So the Epistle closes with the passage added by Paul's own hand. He repeats, that for the Christian the Jewish Law has become meaningless. Those who are seeking to reimpose it can have nothing in view but unworthy ends of their own. "For neither is circumcision anything nor uncircumcision, but a new creation" (6:15); that is, an inward renewal through faith in Christ. In words of deep pathos Paul makes his final reply to the charges that had been raised against himself. "From henceforth let no man trouble me, for I bear branded on my body the marks of the Lord Jesus" (6:17). He points to the scars left on him by his long warfare in the cause of Christ, and is content that they should speak for him. In face of such evidence, who can doubt that he is a true Apostle on whom Christ himself has set his seal?

5. Temporary and Permanent Elements

The Epistle is written with wonderful vigor, and displays, within a brief compass, all the qualities most characteristic of Paul — his courage, his tenderness, his earnestness and sincerity, his burning devotion to Christ. It also reveals him, here and there, in his less sympathetic character of a rabbinical thinker. In this very letter, in which he declares so emphatically that he is done with the Law, he allows us to see that he was never able to shake off those habits of thought which the study of the Law had ingrained in him. Much of his argument, at least in its outward form, impresses us now as frigid and artificial: e.g., the allegory of the two covenants (4:21-31), and the proof from the history of Abraham that the promise was before the Law (3:15-22). Yet the ideas which he is trying to enforce have a value quite apart from the old-world forms in which he expresses them. He has grasped with the whole force of his being the great truths that Christianity is a religion of liberty, that rites and ceremonies are unnecessary to the true service of God, that salvation is by faith — not by weak efforts of man's own, but by the entire surrender of the soul to God. These truths are bound up with the essential message of Christianity, and they were set forth once for all, with matchless power, in the Epistle to the Galatians.

CHAPTER XIV

THE EPISTLE TO THE ROMANS

1. *Date and Occasion*

Shortly after he had written the Second Epistle to the Corinthians, Paul himself arrived in Corinth on what was to prove his last visit. The date, so far as we can fix it, was towards the end of the year 57 A.D. He had long promised that when he next came to the city, he would stay for some considerable time, and he had now a special reason for carrying out this intention. For several years past he had been working at his scheme of a collection from his Gentile churches on behalf of the poor in Jerusalem, and this enterprise was now in its final stage. The money collected was to be entrusted to delegates, one or two from each church, who would accompany Paul on his voyage and present the gift to the elders at Jerusalem. It had been arranged that he should wait at Corinth until all the delegates had joined him, which could not be until the season of navigation had opened in the spring.

For at least three months, then, Paul stayed at Corinth, with plenty of leisure on his hands, and he occupied himself with preparations for his future work. A vast plan had been forming in his mind — nothing less than to make the Gospel known over the whole Roman Empire, which for that age constituted the world. Obviously there could be no thought of anything like an exhaustive mission, but Paul's design was to establish churches in two or three chief cities of each of the provinces into which the Empire was divided. He was confident that from these centers the truth would radiate, by its own intrinsic power, into the surrounding country. He had also made it his principle not to work in fields where the gospel had been proclaimed already (Rom. 15:20; II Cor. 10:16), and could thus afford to leave large territories untouched. At the time of his sojourn at Corinth, he had arrived at the great turning point in his program. During six or seven years of incessant labor, he had traversed the eastern provinces and could now feel free to devote himself to the west. His natural base in this new enterprise would be Rome, the famous capital which it had been his lifelong ambition to see.

Strictly speaking, his principle of never working in any but new fields excluded him from Rome. At a very early time, the Christian message had found its way to Rome, perhaps through those followers of Stephen who had been compelled after his death to seek refuge in Gentile cities (Acts 11:19). A considerable church, destined before long to become the chief church of all, had established itself in the capital. But although the ground was already occupied, Paul could not but see that, if he was to work effectively in the west, he must begin from Rome and win for himself the sympathy and co-operation of the Roman church. He decided, therefore, to communicate in good time with the Christians in Rome and make sure that they would support him. This was the more necessary, in view of the widespread opposition against which he had to contend. Those Jewish reactionaries who had raised trouble in Galatia and Corinth were sure to do everything in their power to prejudice the Roman church against him, and it would be well for him to get in the first word and let the Romans know the true nature of his gospel. His mission would be hopeless from the outset, if his enemies were to entrench themselves in the capital and spread false rumors about him in the west as they had already done in the east.

2. *Epistolary Character*

During his stay in Corinth, therefore, Paul busied himself with writing his Epistle to the Romans. It is the most ambitious of all his letters — the only one in which he tries to present his thought in systematic fashion, carefully weighing every sentence and word. The view, indeed, has often been taken that Romans must be placed in a different category from the other Epistles, and that it is not so much a letter as a theological treatise. This estimate of it is justified in so far as it deals with general, instead of concrete, problems and has little of the personal note which rings everywhere through the letters to Corinth and Galatia. Yet when we examine it closely, Romans is a true letter. If it is more a conscious literary composition than the other Epistles, the difference may easily be explained on several grounds. (1) Paul was not personally known to the Roman church and could not write to it in the intimate, spontaneous manner in which he addressed his other churches. We all instinctively adopt a more formal tone in a letter intended for strangers than when we write to familiar friends. (2) Paul was particularly anxious to make a good impression on his Roman readers. Not only were they strangers, who would form their judgment of him from this letter, but he could not forget that they represented the church at Rome. It is evident, from many allusions in his writings, that the thought of Rome had strongly affected his imagination. He associated the great city with all that was most august in earthly power. He believed that it had been divinely appointed to maintain order and peace among the contending races. Something of the reverence he felt towards the city attached itself to the church connected with it. He approaches it deferentially and is resolved to give it of his very best. We can perceive, as we study this Epistle, that he has been careful to arrange his thoughts beforehand, that he puts a constant check on his impetuosity so that he may never fall below a dignified level. The result is a letter very different from that which he wrote to the Galatians, though many of the ideas are in substance the same; but none the less he is writing a genuine letter. (3) The aim of the Epistle is not the same as that which he sets before himself elsewhere. His other letters were written in the ordinary course of his missionary work, and deal with definite problems which had been submitted to him and with practical difficulties which had arisen. His object in Ro-

mans is a broader one — to acquaint this church, which had
never known him, with the nature of his teaching. In his other
writings, there is much theological reflection, but it comes in
incidentally. Speaking to those churches which he himself had
founded, he could take for granted a general knowledge of
the doctrines he was accustomed to teach, and needed only to
correct misunderstandings and enforce some truths which were
in danger of being forgotten. In the Roman Epistle, he had to
explain his position from the start and to defend it by reasoned argument. Hence the letter takes on, to a great extent,
the appearance of a theological tract.

3. *Form and Purpose*

The question arises, why Paul thought it necessary to bring
so much of his theological thinking into this Epistle. After
all, his purpose was to introduce himself, and to enlist the
support of the Roman church for his projected mission in the
west. Could he not have done this more effectually by a plain
friendly letter, outlining his plans and wishes, and making a
warm appeal for sympathy? No one could have written such
a letter more tactfully and persuasively than Paul, and if he
had pleaded his cause with the Romans as he had done a short
time before with the Corinthians, he could have gained his object as he did then. Why did he choose to approach them with
a difficult theological argument? A view has sometimes been
put forward that the ostensible purpose of the Epistle is not
the real one. Paul, it is held, had now a presentiment that
he was nearing the end of his life work, and wished before he
died to draw up a summary of his teaching which should be
like his last will and testament. To whom was he to entrust
this authoritative account of his gospel? He decided that no
repository could be more suitable than the church at Rome.
It had taken no part in any of his controversies and could be
relied on to judge him impartially. It was the church of the
capital, and a document addressed to it would carry weight,
and would be widely circulated and preserved for future gen-

erations. So he wrote what purported to be a letter introducing himself to the Roman church, but meant it in reality to be the final statement of how he understood the gospel. Against this view, however, it may be argued that he by no means expounds his whole message in the Epistle to the Romans. He develops only a few of his doctrines, leaving out of account a great deal that was no less essential in his Christianity. Moreover, when he wrote this Epistle, he had no idea that his active work was soon to close, and that nothing now remained for him but to put his convictions on record. As events turned out, he was indeed enjoying his last few months as a free man, but of this he had no suspicion. He believed that his most important work as a missionary was still before him, and wrote the Epistle as a prelude to the new and larger enterprise which he had in view. Once more, and this is the decisive argument, there is no sign that the professed object of the Epistle is not the real one. Paul says explicitly that he writes to the Romans in order to introduce himself, before he comes in person to commence his western mission, and he never loses sight of this purpose. The Epistle is meant directly for the Roman church, not for some imaginary audience which in future days would be interested in the Pauline theology.

Why, then, did his appeal to the Romans take the form which it does in this Epistle? The question can be answered only conjecturally, in view of our ignorance of the given situation. Paul had never visited the Roman church, but, before he wrote, he must have taken pains to inform himself of its circumstances, and there are many indications that he is constantly mindful of them. To a modern reader, the Epistle may seem to be little more than an abstract statement of doctrine, but this is only because we have lost the key. If we only knew something of the Roman church of that day, we should doubtless see new meaning in the Epistle as a whole, and in many passages in it which now appear pointless and academical. Paul has in mind, not only the special problems of the Roman church, but its attitude to himself. He could not help thinking that, by this time, he was known by reputation all over the Christian world, and that his personality and doctrines were being discussed everywhere. Between Rome and the provinces, there was constant coming and going and, wherever he went, he would fall in with travelers who would tell him what the Roman Christians were saying of him. We are to think of him as trying to clear up misunderstandings which had arisen, and which were bound to interfere with those cordial relations which he wished to establish before he paid his visit. Of one thing we may be sure, that Paul knew what he was doing when he wrote just this Epistle to the church at Rome. He had an unequaled gift for adjusting himself to the minds and circumstances of those whom he sought to influence, and when he wrote with such peculiar care to the Roman Christians, he would make it his first endeavor to put himself in contact with them. He would not spend his time on pious generalities, but would deal with matters in which his readers were directly concerned.

4. *Missionary Interest*

In spite of our ignorance of the special situation, we can perceive, at least in a broad way, how the Epistle which Paul wrote was adapted to his purpose. He was going to Rome to start a Christian mission, in countries which had hitherto lain in pure heathenism. He wished to ensure that the Romans would stand behind him in this great venture, and the first thing necessary was to impress on them the universal scope of the Gospel. In Rome, as elsewhere, Christianity had begun as a Jewish movement and, even in the minds of Gentile converts, the idea persisted that it was somehow dependent on Judaism. Paul was known to have broken with the Law, and for this reason even those who admired his Christian zeal were inclined to regard him with some suspicion. They felt that a Christianity which had cut itself off from its Jewish past, and staked everything on faith in Christ, must be in some way incomplete. Paul's object, therefore, is to defend his conception of a gospel free from the Law; and this he does from no personal or controversial motive, but with a purpose in the highest degree practical. He was launching a new mission and desired that the Romans should be with him whole-heartedly: how could he awaken in them the necessary sympathy and enthusiasm? Only in one way; they must be made to feel, as he did himself, that the message of Christ was for all mankind. It had nothing to do with the old racial distinctions, or with outward customs and enactments. It was a new religion, with an inner principle of its own, to which all men alike were able to conform, and those who truly understood it could not choose but impart it to all men. Thus the Epistle is in essence a missionary manifesto. Paul wrote it by way of summons to the Roman church to join with him in his great enterprise. What seems at first sight a labored theological argument is, in reality, an impassioned appeal to all Christian men to recognize their duty as the stewards of a universal message. It is significant that to this day the missionary movement finds its chief support from the Epistle to the Romans. Passages from this letter of Paul are quoted as a matter of course in proof of the church's duty to propagate its message throughout the world. This is not surprising when we realize that the Epistle was written for no other purpose than to kindle the missionary spirit.

5. *Integrity*

Both in style and substance the Epistle is one of the most characteristic of Paul's writings, and only a few whimsical scholars have ever questioned its genuineness. At the same time, it is by no means certain that we now possess the letter in just the form in which Paul wrote it. More than a hundred years ago attention was called to the problem offered by the closing chapter, which consists of a couple of verses introducing the deaconess Phoebe, and then a long series of personal greetings. The men and women to whom Paul sends his remembrances in this sixteenth chapter of Romans are far more numerous than in any other of his Epistles, and the question naturally arises as to how he had so many friends at Rome, which as yet he had never visited. Moreover, when the list of names is examined it is found that several of the persons mentioned were associated with Paul in his work at Ephesus, while almost all of them bear names which are Greek, rather than Roman. It has been suggested, therefore, that the final chapter was a separate note intended for Ephesus, to which Phoebe was about to travel. While introducing her, Paul takes occasion to send his greetings to a number of the cherished friends whom he had left only a few months before. Against this theory it may be argued that Rome was the great center to which people were constantly finding their way. Many of Paul's friends may have settled in Rome and joined themselves to the local church, and he would inevitably think of them as he closed his letter. It may be argued, too, that for the very reason that he was a stranger to Rome, he would make the most of all the connections with it to which he could lay claim. Yet there is much to be said for the view that in Romans 16 we have a separate note to Ephesus. If it was written at the same time as the longer letter, it might easily have come to be appended to it in the copy which was preserved in the archives of the Corinthian church.

The question of the separateness of the sixteenth chapter is bound up with a larger one. It is on record that, in the second century, there were texts of Romans in which the Epistle closed with 14:23, omitting the whole of the fifteenth and sixteenth chapters. In some extant manuscripts, these two chapters are wanting, with the exception of the doxology (16:25-27), which is placed at the end of Chapter 14. Why the Epistle should thus have been shortened, it is hard to explain. There can be no reasonable doubt that Chapter 15 originally belonged to it, for this chapter is the natural continuation of the preceding one, and is so intimately Pauline in character that no one but Paul can have written it. Perhaps the omission came about in some such way as this. The Epistle was early recognized as one

of the most valuable of Christian writings, and all churches
were anxious to have copies of it. As it stood, however, it
was unduly long, and since the concluding portion was of only
personal and local interest, it was left out, and the final doxology was added to round off the work, which now ended too
abruptly. This doxology is quite unlike Paul, both in thought
and language, and may be pretty confidently ascribed to a later
hand; but, when it was once admitted, it was retained as the
formal ending of the whole Epistle. In some manuscripts, it
occurs twice, at the end of Chapter 14 and again at the end of
Chapter 16. That the closing part of the Epistle became subject at an early date to some confusion, is evident from one
curious circumstance. It is Paul's custom to end each of his
letters with a few words of parting benediction, and in Romans
we have no fewer than four of these solemn endings (15:13;
15:33; 16:24; 16:27). Assuming that the sixteenth chapter
is a separate letter to Ephesus, the true close of the Roman
Epistle is 15:33. The previous benediction (15:13) is thrown
in to mark the end, not of the whole Epistle, but of the main
part of it, the rest being of the nature of a postscript bearing
on personal matters. Of the two other benedictions, the first
(16:24) closes the note to Ephesus, while the final one (16:-
25-27) is the formal doxology, added, as we have seen, by a
later hand.

6. *Jews and Gentiles at Rome*

When we turn from the occasion and outward form of the
letter to the letter itself, there is one question which faces us
at the outset. Did Paul address himself to an audience of
Jewish or of Gentile Christians? So much of the Epistle is
occupied with a discussion of the Law and the claims of Judaism that he might seem to be writing, as a Jew, for Jewish
readers. It might fairly be argued that to any others, a great
deal of his argument would be unintelligible. On the other
hand, he refers explicitly to "you Gentiles" (1:51; 1:13; 6:17,
etc.). He dwells on the privilege, vouchsafed to his readers,

of inheriting the promises made to Abraham, although they had no title to be considered his children. He even feels it necessary to plead for due acknowledgment of the claims of Israel on the part of those who were forgetful of their debt (11:13 f.). That he had Gentile readers in mind throughout the Epistle there can be little doubt, and the apparently Jewish cast of his argument may be explained in several ways. (1) He would be aware that, while the Roman church was mainly Gentile, it was saturated with Jewish influences and many of its members were of Jewish stock. (2) The Jewish community at Rome was violently opposed to the Christian movement. A passage in the Roman historian, Suetonius, which contains the very earliest reference to Christianity in general literature, tells that in the year 54 A.D., there was rioting in the Jewish quarter of Rome "on the instigation of one Chrestus." In view of this incessant controversy with their Jewish neighbors, even the Gentile Christians in Rome would be vitally interested in the relation of the gospel to Judaism. Paul would know this, when he devoted so much of his argument to the question of the Law. (3) It has always to be borne in mind that the Epistle was written in view of circumstances which are not fully known to us. Paul was a stranger to Rome, but he had doubtless informed himself of the special difficulties which beset the Roman church. Some conflict was evidently in process, of which we cannot now ascertain the precise nature, but which determined the drift of Paul's thought. This is not mere conjecture, for in Chapter 14 he deals directly with two parties, the "weak" and the "strong," into which the Roman church was evidently divided. It would appear from Paul's references that the "weak," while sincere in their Christian faith, laid store on certain Jewish observances. They avoided particular kinds of food; they made much of stated holy days. Paul's own sympathies were with the "strong," and it is clear that most of his readers belonged to this party; but he pleads for due regard to the conscientious scruples of those who take a different side. From another part of the Epistle (9-11), we can gather that there was a disposition among Gentile members of the church to slight their Jewish brethren, and Paul remonstrates with them. His defense of the claims of Judaism comes strangely from the Apostle who, only a little time before, had written the indictment in Galatians, and the reason for it is no doubt to be sought in the special conditions, now unknown to us, which prevailed at Rome. We may be pretty sure that these conditions, if only we could learn them, would explain much of what is now obscure in the drift of the Epistle.

7. *Theological Argument*

The argument of Romans is highly elaborated, and can here be stated only in bare outline. After greeting the Roman church, Paul tells that he has long desired to visit it, and now at last sees the way open. He had proclaimed the gospel to Greeks and barbarians, and is presently to come as its ambassador to the imperial city. "For I am not ashamed of the gospel of Christ, for it is the power of God to every one who believes, to the Jew first and also to the Greek." Why does it have this universal scope? In the verse by which he answers this question, Paul lays down the theme of the Epistle which follows. "For therein is the righteousness of God revealed, from faith to faith; as it is written: The just shall live by faith." (This is a quotation from the prophet, Habakkuk, and means originally, "the upright man will survive by his steadfastness." Paul takes it in the sense, "he who is righteous by faith will obtain life.")

Paul sets himself to show, therefore, that salvation is by faith, and that this saving faith is made possible by the death of Christ. Proof is offered, in the first place, that all other methods of winning salvation have failed. The Gentiles had cultivated wisdom, with the result that the wisdom in which they trusted had ensnared them and led them into ever deeper corruption (1:18-2:11). The Jews had placed their reliance on the Law, but the Law, while it pointed out the way of life, had given men no power to follow it and had left them more

miserable than before (2:12-3:20). There remains only the
method of faith which Christ has revealed, and which avails
alike for Jew and Gentile (3:21-31). At this point, Paul
develops a thought which he had already thrown out in Galatians, that faith had always been intended by God to be the
one means of salvation. Long before the Law was given,
Abraham had put his faith in God, and on this ground God
had accepted him. The Christian gospel has only brought
fully to light what had always been in the mind of God. A
great chapter follows, in which the nature and effects of the
Christian deliverance are described, and a contrast drawn between the ruin caused by Adam and the restoration achieved
through Christ. Thus far, Paul has thought of salvation on
its negative side, as a rescue from the bondage of sin. He now
proceeds to show that, along with this emancipation, a new
power is given which creates in man a higher life (6-8). It
had been objected to Paul's gospel, as it has often been since,
that by his emphasis on faith he had weakened the moral
law. If we are to trust absolutely in God's grace, why need
we persist in the painful struggle with our evil nature? Paul
answers that the struggle ceases to be necessary. Believing in
Christ we enter on a new kind of life, governed by new motives. The Spirit sent from God takes possession of us, and
creates in us purer desires and a higher moral energy. A vivid
contrast is drawn (and we can hardly doubt that Paul here
transcribes his own experience) between the man who strives
to overcome his baser will with the aid of the Law (7), and
the man who by faith in Christ has received the Spirit (8).
The Epistle culminates in this magnificent eighth chapter, with
its account of that new life in the Spirit whereby the believer
is lifted entirely out of his old self and attains to peace and
freedom.

Who can lay any charge against God's elect? It is God who acquits,
who is he that condemns? It is Christ that died, yea rather that is risen
again, who is even at the right hand of God, who also makes intercession
for us. Who shall separate us from the love of Christ? Shall tribula-

tion or distress or persecution or famine or nakedness or peril or sword? As it is written, For thy sake we are killed all the day long, we are accounted as sheep for the slaughter. Nay in all these things we are more than conquerors through him that loved us. For I am persuaded that neither death nor life, nor angels nor principalities nor powers, nor things present nor things to come, nor height nor depth nor any other creation shall be able to separate us from the love of God which is in Christ Jesus our Lord.

It is in the light of this rapturous passage that we need to look back on that first part of Romans, which it brings to a close. Paul might seem, as we read some of the chapters, to be working out an abstruse argument on the ground of ancient Jewish assumptions, which we can no longer regard as valid. But while his thought is thrown into a logical mold, it is directed throughout by great religious perceptions which can never lose their meaning. Paul is profoundly convinced that everything must come to us by the "grace," that is by the free giving, of God, and that nothing is required of us but "faith," the willingness to receive what God desires to give. The idea is expressed in theological language, but answers to a fact which meets us everywhere in human life. The world of nature, for instance, is all around us, with a wealth of beauty and inspiration which is ours for the taking. Nothing is needed on our part but responsiveness to what is given and by labored effort we only create a self-consciousness which destroys that receptive mood. So with all the great things in life — health, love, happiness, wisdom. They are not to be compelled, but must *come* to us, and all we need to do is to keep our hearts open to high influences which are pressing in upon us always, though we miss them through our blindness and conceit. Applying this principle to religion, Paul declares that salvation is not by works of the Law, but by the grace of God, and that Christ awakens in us the faith which can respond to that grace. Man is justified by faith; there is no other way by which we can attain to that righteousness which God requires.

8. *Second Part of the Epistle*

The second part of Romans consists of Chapters 9-11, in which Paul discusses the destiny of Israel. After the lofty argument of the previous section, this discussion seems to involve an anticlimax, and we wonder why Paul has introduced it and how it connects with what has gone before. No doubt this, like other difficulties, would be cleared up if we knew more of the situation with which Paul was dealing. He was aware, apparently, that the whole question of man's salvation was entangled in the minds of his readers with that of the place of Israel. If the gospel was from God, why had his chosen people failed to respond to it? If he had rejected his own people, what confidence could men have in his promises? It must never be forgotten that, in those early days when Christianity was still in process of freeing itself from Judaism, the whole matter of its relation to the parent religion was of vital consequence. In passing from the new life in the Spirit to the fate of the Jewish people, Paul would not feel that he was making an abrupt transition, any more than Luther did when he connected the highest matters of the faith with questions about the Pope's supremacy.

He points out, then, that the disobedience of Israel has been only partial, and that even for this there has been a great, divine purpose. Refused by the Jews, the gospel has been carried to the Gentiles, and the redemption of the Gentile world will finally react on Israel, so that all men will be saved. God has not broken his promise to his people but is working towards its fulfillment in an ampler and more glorious way. It is in these chapters that Paul sets forth his doctrine of predestination, which came in the later theology to be grievously misunderstood. Paul himself has two interests in upholding this doctrine: (1) to reinforce his conception of grace, by showing that the ground of salvation is not any effort or deserving on the part of man, but is to be sought entirely in God's eternal will; (2) to put the assurance of salvation beyond all possible doubt. Men are to realise that, since God himself has chosen them, they may count on his sustaining them to the end, in spite of their own weakness and unworthiness. It is to be noted that Paul never thinks of Christian men tormenting themselves with fears that they may not be included among the elect. He takes for granted that all who have put their faith in Christ have done so under the leading of God. The very fact that they have become Christian is proof that God has destined them from all eternity to have their place with his elect people.

9. *Closing Chapters*

It is Paul's custom to close his Epistles with a number of moral exhortations, and the last chapters of Romans are of this nature (12, 13, 14, 15). He begins with general counsels for the conduct of life (12); then deals more particularly with the duty of civil obedience (13). It was his constant fear that the church might compromise itself by disloyalty to the appointed government, and this attitude would be especially dangerous in Rome, the capital. So he impresses on his readers the need of good citizenship as a matter, not only of prudence, but of conscience. Political institutions, in so far as they maintain peace and order, are in accordance with God's will, and to assist them in their task is part of our duty to God. In Chapter 14, Paul deals with that conflict between the "weak" and the "strong" which was agitating the church at Rome; then he touches on his own present circumstances and future plans. He is preparing to carry the money he has collected to Jerusalem, and will then be free to commence his mission in the west. He writes this Epistle to the Romans in the hope that soon he will be with them, and will have their encouragement and assistance in the work he has planned.

10. *Nature of the Epistle*

It is noteworthy that in Romans Paul has little to say on mere controversial issues, or in defence of his own rights as an Apostle. Here and there he seems to be anticipating possible attacks that may be made on him, but the Epistle on the whole is marked by its calm, impersonal spirit. Paul's one desire is to make clear to the Romans the nature of the Gospel as he understands it. It is the power of God unto salvation. Its message is for all men alike, and all men have need of it. This detached and positive tone of the letter is no doubt due largely to the circumstances in which it was written. Paul had just emerged victorious from a long period of strain and conflict, and was glad to forget for a time all disputed issues and dwell on the larger aspects of the Christian message. He was writing, also, to a church to which he was a stranger, and was not free to rebuke and expostulate as when he addressed his own communities. If there is controversy in Romans, it is handled indirectly, in allusions to which only the first readers would have the key. But the character of the Epistle is to be explained mainly by the purpose which Paul had in view. It is customary to speak of Romans as his great theological Epistle, and too often it is studied as if it were nothing but a formal exposition of the leading Pauline doctrines. We ought, rather, to regard it as Paul's great missionary Epistle. On the eve of a new extension of his work, more daring than anything he had attempted hitherto, he sets himself to vindicate Christianity as the religion for all mankind. On this ground, he asked the Romans to welcome and support him. He was coming to them and to the strange regions that lay beyond them, confident in his high calling. "For I am not ashamed of the gospel of Christ, for it is the power of God unto salvation."

CHAPTER XV

THE EPISTLES OF THE CAPTIVITY

When Paul wrote the Epistle to the Romans, he intended to start on his western mission as soon as he had made his journey to Jerusalem on the business of the collection. His visit to the west, however, was not to take place for three years, and he was then to go as a prisoner. While in Jerusalem, he was arrested on a charge of causing a riot in the Temple, and after two years' imprisonment at Cæsarea was transferred, on his own appeal, to Rome, where he was to stand his trial before the emperor's court. He remained a prisoner at Rome for at least three years, and was then tried and condemned to death.

Seven Epistles have come down to us which purport to have been written by Paul in prison. Three of them, I and II Timothy, and Titus, cannot be assigned to Paul, at least in their present form. Of the remaining four, the Epistle to the Ephesians has sometimes been denied to him, on grounds which cannot be regarded as decisive. That he wrote Colossians, Philemon, and Philippians there can be no reasonable doubt. These three letters were certainly written from prison, but the question has been much debated in recent years as to when and where he suffered this imprisonment. Formerly it was taken for granted that he was in that Roman prison of which we read in the book of Acts (28:30), but he never definitely says so, and there are some things in the letters which might seem to imply an earlier imprisonment. He speaks, for instance, of various companions who were with him, and we hear of most of them elsewhere in connection with his work at Ephesus. The letters assume, too, that he was in frequent communication with Macedonia and Asia

Minor, and these countries, under ancient conditions of travel, were at a great distance from Rome. The Epistle to Philemon concerns a slave, Onesimus, who had run away from his master at Colossæ, in the interior of Asia Minor; and it is argued that a flight as far as Rome would have been out of the question. A theory has thus found favor with many scholars that the letters date from a captivity which befell Paul during his three years at Ephesus. Colossæ and Philippi were both within easy reach of that city. Almost all the friends whom Paul includes in his greetings were with him at one time or another during his Ephesian period. There is nothing in any of the Epistles which might not apply as well to conditions in Ephesus as in Rome. Against this theory, the main argument is that we are not told of any imprisonment of Paul at Ephesus, while we do know for certain that for several years he was a prisoner at Rome. It has always to be remembered, too, that while Rome was far distant from the east, it was the great center with which all other cities were in constant communication. Messages would travel from Asia Minor to Rome almost as quickly as from one secluded Asian town to another. That Paul should have so many of his old friends near him in his Roman captivity need not surprise us. It was known all over the church that the foremost Apostle was about to stand trial for his life, and the wonder would be if Luke and Timothy and a number of the others had *not* made some effort to be with him. That he was imprisoned at Ephesus, where according to his own testimony he underwent some of his gravest perils, is more than likely. But the danger at Ephesus appears to have taken the form of a sharp crisis, and he would have been imprisoned, as he was at Philippi, with his feet in the stocks, awaiting death or torture at any moment. Under such conditions, he would hardly be in the mood to write letters which are distinguished, above all the others, by their beauty of language and deep theological reflection. The theory that they were sent from a prison at Ephesus cannot, indeed, be put aside; but there is no good reason for abandoning the old tradition that Paul wrote them at Rome, where his captivity was light and time was hanging on his hands. We can well believe that in those dreary years he would welcome the opportunity of still doing some useful work by means of letters.

CHAPTER XVI

THE EPISTLE TO THE COLOSSIANS

1. *Paul's Relations with Colossæ*

While Paul was working at Ephesus, his assistants had been active in the surrounding country. One of them, Epaphras, had carried on a successful mission in the three cities of the Lycus valley — Colossæ, Hierapolis, Laodicæa — about a hundred miles to the East of Ephesus. Paul had never been able to visit this district personally, but was keenly interested in the three sister churches which had been established there, and had formed a warm friendship with one of the Colossian Christians, Philemon, probably a well-to-do merchant who came occasionally to Ephesus on his business affairs. While Paul was a prisoner (presumably at Rome), he had two very different visitors who revived his interest in the Colossian church. One was Onesimus, a slave of Philemon, who had run away after robbing his master, and who had sought refuge, as escaped slaves were wont to do, in the crowded capital. Reduced to desperation, he had sought out Paul and obtained help from him, and had finally attached himself to him as his devoted servant. The other visitor was Epaphras, who had perhaps come to Rome for the express purpose of consulting Paul on a serious difficulty.

2. *The Colossian Heresy*

The church at Colossæ was in danger, owing to the rise of a peculiar type of heretical teaching, in which the Christian beliefs were combined with Jewish and pagan elements. The Colossians were being taught that faith in Christ was not sufficient by itself. In order to be set free from the powers which rule the material world, men must enlist on their side various angelic beings; they must perform certain rites and be initiated into a secret wisdom. Nothing is known of this Colossian heresy except from the vague references of Paul, and it was probably confined to the one locality. But though unimportant in itself, it was the precursor of the great movement known as Gnosticism, which in the following age was to threaten the very existence of the church. The movement had its origin in two main causes. (1) In the first century, when all nations were unified in the Roman empire, there was an effort to complete the political unity by an amalgamation of all religions. It was early recognised that Christianity had much to give, but in the other religions, too, there seemed to be valuable elements. Might it not be possible to combine what was useful in all the types of belief, and so form a new religion which would commend itself to the whole world? (2) Along with this general cause, there was a more specific one. Christianity was above all an ethical religion, and had little to say on the great speculative problems which were supremely interesting to the Greek mind. What was the relation of spirit to matter? How had the world come into being? What was the nature of the soul, and how had it proceeded from the universal soul? In the centers of Greek culture, Christianity was faced with a task which was not dissimilar to that confronting it today. Religious beliefs had in some way to be reconciled with what was then accounted the scientific view of the world.

3. Paul's Criticism of the Heresy

The trouble at Colossæ was a local one, but Paul at once recognised its importance. He had hitherto been concerned chiefly with Jewish opposition to the gospel; now he was called on to answer criticisms of a more sweeping kind, from the side of Gentile speculation. Much of his argument is difficult to follow, owing to our ignorance of the precise nature of the heresy he opposes. The difficulty is all the greater as he makes use of a number of strange expressions, taken, apparently, from the jargon employed by the Colossian teachers. "Let no man disqualify you as he exerts his will in humble-mindedness and angel-worship, making entrance into things which he has visioned" (2:18). Such language, resembling that of a modern psychological textbook, must have been dark enough at the time, and has now become utterly unintelligible. Paul no doubt quotes it ironically, and yet by means of it we are left to make out, as well as we can, the character of those beliefs which he has set himself to refute. None the less, the broad outline of his thought stands out clearly enough, in spite of the murky background. The heretics had maintained that, since man dwells in a material universe, he must offer homage to the cosmic powers as well as to Christ. They had insisted also that spiritual worship must be combined with ritual and magic observances, in which the claims of the visible world were duly honored. Paul answers that, since the whole creation has its center in Christ, the worship directed towards him has made all other worship unnecessary. He declares that the rites of the old ceremonial religion were only shadows of that reality which we now possess in Christ. To piece out Christianity with tatters borrowed from Judaism and Paganism is not to enrich it, but to drag it back to the lower, material plane of worship which it has transcended.

It is in this Epistle that we meet for the first time with a conception which was henceforth to play a central part in all Christian thinking. Paul is content in his earlier writings to hold to the primitive idea of Jesus as the Messiah; but in Colossians he avails himself of a doctrine which had been worked out by the great Jewish thinker, Philo of Alexandria. Philo had contended that within the being of God there is a second divine principle, the Word or Logos, which goes forth from God and effects his work of creation and revelation. This principle is identified in Colossians, as afterwards in Hebrews and the Fourth Gospel, with Christ.

He is the image of the invisible God, the first-born of all creation; for by him were all things created that are in heaven or on earth, —

thrones or dominions or principalities or powers; all things were created by him and for him, and in him all things subsist. [1:15-17.]

In view of pagan criticism, it had now become necessary to attribute a cosmical value to Christ, and Paul seized on a suggestion, which had possibly originated with converts like Apollos, trained in the Alexandrian school. Christ was one with that eternal divine principle, through which all things had come into being.

4. *Ethical Appendix*

The practical section with which the Epistle closes is concerned mainly with the relations that should exist between the various members of a Christian household. Counsels are offered to wives, husbands, children, parents; and the Apostle then dwells, with particular fullness, on the mutual duties of servants and masters. It is not hard to guess why such prominence is given to this subject. Paul's mind had been occupied for some time with the case of the Colossian slave, Onesimus, on whose behalf he was to write a personal letter. Meanwhile he offers a few more general reflections on the bond between master and servant, and the new character it has assumed under the law of Christ.

CHAPTER XVII

THE EPISTLE TO PHILEMON

Colossians thus links itself with the short letter to Philemon, which was written at the same time, to the same destination. Paul's correspondence must have included a large number of private letters, and it is fortunate that at least one of them has been preserved. Without it, we should have had a far poorer conception of some of those qualities in Paul which won for him the loyalty and affection of all who knew him. It is one of the most charming letters ever written — full of kindness and the finest courtesy, with delicate touches of pathos and also of playfulness. Paul's object was to win forgiveness for a slave who had been guilty of one of the worst offences known to ancient law, and his task was a difficult one, even though he was writing to a personal friend. He performs this task with marvelous tact and persuasiveness. Every kind of appeal is brought forward but is never pressed too far.

It has often been objected that, in spite of the beautiful Christian spirit which informs the letter, Paul has nothing to say on the fundamental question of the evil of slavery. Neither in the Epistle to Philemon, nor anywhere else in his writings, does he condemn the system which was the darkest blot on the civilization of the ancient world. To this it may be answered that, by denouncing slavery, he would have accomplished nothing except to bring the new religion into danger, as a movement bent on the subversion of the social order. But it may further be affirmed that, by the attitude he took up in Philemon and Colossians, Paul did more than any other man for the abolition of slavery. He placed the relation of master and slave on a new footing. He declared that as servants of Christ, men become inwardly free, whatever their outward condition. As these new principles sank gradually into the Christian conscience, the institution of slavery became more and more indefensible and finally disappeared of its own accord.

CHAPTER XVIII

THE EPISTLE TO THE EPHESIANS

1. *Destination*

The messenger Tychicus, who was entrusted with the letters
to the Colossians and Philemon, is also mentioned in connection with a third letter (Eph. 6:21). As the opening verse
now stands, this letter was addressed "to the saints who are
in Ephesus," but the words "in Ephesus" do not appear in
the earlier manuscripts. Perhaps they were added to replace
a name which had become obliterated. Perhaps the Epistle was
written as a circular one, with a blank in the opening verse
which the messenger was to fill in before handing a copy to
each of a group of churches. An ingenious theory has been
suggested in recent years, that the letter was originally addressed to the church at Laodicæa, and that this name was
deliberately changed when Laodicæa was denounced in the
book of Revelation (3:14 f.) and fell into bad repute. It is
certain that along with his letter to the Colossians, Paul wrote
another to the neighboring city of Laodicæa (Col. 4:16).
Either it has been lost, or it has survived in our present Epistle to the Ephesians.

2. *Genuineness*

That the letter was not written to Ephesus, may be taken
as certain. It contains no personal greetings, and there are
clear intimations that the writer and his readers were unknown to one another. Since Paul had worked for three years
in Ephesus only a short time before, it cannot have been the
Ephesian church to which he thus felt himself a stranger. A
more important question arises, as to whether Paul wrote
this Epistle at all. The view is held by many modern scholars

that it is the work of one of his disciples, who made use of his master's name, in the manner approved by ancient literary custom. They point out that the style of the letter is involved and diffuse, that the ideas, though Pauline, are more developed than in the other Epistles, and above all that between this Epistle and Colossians there is a suspicious resemblance. Would Paul have repeated himself in this manner? Is it not more probable that some one wrote the later Epistle with Colossians before him, taking up the various ideas and amplifying them with a new purpose and emphasis? The question of the authenticity of Ephesians must be regarded as an open one, but the weight of evidence is decidedly in favor of Paul's authorship. Writing the second letter about the same time as the first, he may well have repeated the same ideas. The difference of style is by no means so great as some critics have made out, and may be accounted for by the fact that through the greater part of the Epistle the writer uses the language of prayer. The thought is in every respect the thought of Paul, even though some of his ideas are carried further. One argument may be taken as almost convincing. The imitator of a great writer, however skillfully he catches the tone and mannerisms of his model, always betrays himself by his inferiority. Now Ephesians is admittedly one of the noblest of New Testament writings. If not by Paul, it must have been written by some one equal to him in genius and religious insight. Can we believe that in the church of Paul's day there was an unknown teacher of this supreme excellence? The natural assumption is surely that an Epistle so like the work of Paul at his very best was written by no other man than Paul himself.

3. Character and Purpose

Ephesians follows much the same line of argument as Colossians, but between the two Epistles there is one conspicuous difference. Colossians is written with a controversial purpose, and nearly every verse in it has some reference to those heretical opinions which Paul was seeking to refute. In Ephesians there is no note of controversy. It may be that the author has some false teaching in view, but, if so, the polemical purpose is never made explicit. We get the impression that in pondering his answer to the Colossian heretics, Paul had arrived at certain great conceptions which he now wished to develop for their own sake. So he decided that, while the theme of Colossians was still fresh in his mind, he would write another letter in which he would leave all controversial issues aside and set forth more fully, in their positive significance, the ideas which possessed him.

More than any other of Paul's writings, Ephesians bears the character of a theological tract, or rather of a religious meditation. For once, the Apostle seems to forget the quarrels and difficulties of his churches and to occupy himself solely with the timeless things of religion. Yet he is never satisfied unless he can give his thought some bearing on his missionary work, and so in this Epistle, while he does not deal with the problems of any particular community, he takes as his main theme the Christian church. For nearly thirty years, he had been engaged in building up a new society in which the old racial and class divisions were to disappear, and men were to be united by a common faith in Christ. Now he sets himself to inquire into the nature and meaning of the church. What was God's purpose in calling this community into being? What was the function assigned to it? What were the duties imposed on those who had entered into its fellowship? These are the questions around which all the thought of the Epistle revolves. Paul tries to discover the ultimate meaning of the work of Christ, in order that he may apprehend more fully the significance of the church.

4. *Theological Argument*

In Colossians he had shown, in answer to the false teachers, that Christ includes and transcends all other powers, so that faith in him is all-sufficient. He had declared that it is God's good pleasure "to reconcile all things to himself by Christ" (Col. 1:20). These words are repeated in a new form in Ephesians, and may be regarded as stating the main conception on which everything in the Epistle is made to turn. "God has revealed to us the mystery of his will, according to the good pleasure which he has purposed in himself: that in his ordering of the fullness of the times he might reunite all things in Christ, things which are in heaven and things on earth, even in him" (1:9, 10). The world as we now see it is the scene of endless discord — strife in nature, division in human society, conflict in the life and will of each individual man. Paul does not enter into the cause of this disunion, but apparently he assumes that at some point, away back in eternity, the creation had been rent by some fatal flaw. The universe which God had created as a harmony had become divided against itself, and ever since God had been planning to reunite it. All the course of the world's history must be understood in view of this "mystery," this secret plan in the divine mind. The whole creation seemed to be utterly at the mercy of powers making for confusion, but God was so ordering all things that in the fullness of time they should be reunited in Christ, who was to be the common center in whom all interests should converge. The innumerable broken strands were to be brought together in Christ, knotted again into one, as they had been at the beginning. In the first three chapters of the Epistle, Paul develops this magnificent conception of an ultimate plan in God's government of the world, a plan which had been hitherto concealed, but had now come to light in Christ. In the second half of the Epistle, this idea is applied, from a different point of view, as the key to the significance of the church. God's purpose is to reconcile all things through Christ, and his instrument in this work of reconciliation is the church. This community of his people is the larger incarnation of Christ, and by means of it he continues his work of creating harmony. Jews and Gentiles have now been brought together; activities formerly in conflict are being directed to a common end; in all their social relations men have come to a new understanding. The church stands for that purpose of worldwide reconciliation for which Christ appeared and, in all their intercourse with one another, Christians must seek to realize this formative idea of the church. As in Colossians, Paul dwells particularly on relations within the family but while his counsels are the same he now grounds them in his great conception. All the everyday duties are to be determined by the knowledge that, as members of the church, men are to give effect in their common life to the eternal purpose of God.

5. Permanent Significance

At first sight, the thought of Ephesians may seem to be little more than an old-world speculation, impressive even now to the imagination, but quite remote from all our modern knowledge and beliefs. Paul thinks of the work of Christ as the key to the whole meaning of the universe. God is seeking to bring a disordered world into harmony, and with this aim he has been directing the infinite movement of things since the beginning. His great design was hidden until Christ came, but now in the light of what Christ has done, we can see how it has determined everything in the past and will fulfill itself in the future. The reconciliation which Christ began in his own Person will spread out through the church in ever-widening circles, and will finally embrace the whole universe. It may be granted that what Paul presents is a sort of mythological picture; yet, at the heart of it, there is a profound truth which still retains its value. Paul believed, with the whole force of his being, that the world exists for a spiritual end, and that this end must somehow be the same as that which is revealed in Christ. The things which Christ stood for — love, truth, goodness — are of absolute worth; nothing which transcends them can ever be conceived; they must in some way represent the purpose of God when he brought the world into being. Rightly to understand the work of Christ is to hold the key

to the meaning of the universe and apprehend the divine plan
which is striving to fulfill itself in all things. Certainly we have
now attained to a scientific knowledge which was utterly beyond the reach of Paul. His conceptions of matter and spirit,
of the nature of the stars, and the forces which control their
motions, belong to a quite obsolete science and, in so far as
his speculations are bound up with it, they have lost their
meaning. But behind the antique mode of thinking, there is a
truth which is still valid. His explanation of the divine purpose in the world means as much to us now, in the fullest light
of our modern outlook, as when he wrote.

6. *Historical Influence*

Historically the Epistle to the Ephesians is of great importance in two different directions. (1) It formulated for the first
time that conception of the church which for many centuries
was to dominate all Christian thought. Already in his earlier
Epistles, Paul had described the church as the "body of
Christ"— the organism in which the life of Christ manifests
itself, as the soul acts through the body. In Ephesians he gives
a mystical value to this conception. He thinks of the church
as in some real way the incarnation of Christ, so that all its
action has a divine efficacy. It was on this assumption that the
church of later days was to base its supernatural claims. As
time went on it degenerated into a political institution, often
pursuing selfish, material ends; but it still exacted absolute
obedience as representing God on earth. Outside of the church,
which was the visible body of Christ, there could be no salvation. (2) Again, this Epistle is like the bridge between primitive Christianity and that more speculative type of religion
which came to prevail after the close of the first century. Ever
and again in Ephesians, emphasis is laid on "knowledge" as
the chief end of the Christian life. It might almost appear as
if the writer was in sympathy with the Gnostic view that the
one means of attaining to true fellowship with God is intellectual enlightenment; to *know* God in the mystery of his

being is to become one with him. But when we look deeper, it becomes evident that the "knowledge" contemplated in Ephesians is not of an intellectual kind. Its real character is set forth in the great prayer which concludes the first part of the Epistle, and gathers up its teaching:

For this cause I bow my knees unto the Father of our Lord Jesus Christ, of whom every family in heaven and earth is named, that he would grant you according to the riches of his glory to be strengthened mightily by his Spirit in the inner man, that Christ may dwell in your hearts by faith, so that ye, being rooted and grounded in love, may be able to comprehend with all saints what is the breadth and length and depth and height and to know the love of Christ which passes knowledge that ye may be filled with all the fulness of God. [3:14-19.]

The highest knowledge is not a matter of intellect. To share, however imperfectly, in the love of Christ is to know Christ, and through knowledge of him to know God.

CHAPTER XIX

The Epistle to the Philippians

1. *Occasion and Purpose*

The three Epistles to the Colossians, Philemon, and the Ephesians form a single group, since they were all written about the same time and are closely related to one another. The fourth Epistle of the Captivity stands apart from them, and has to be studied independently.

Philippi was a city in Macedonia, founded as a Roman "colony," or military settlement, in commemoration of the famous battle in which the murder of Julius Cæsar was avenged. It was the city in which Paul began his mission in Europe, and partly for this reason, but still more because of the loyal, generous character of its members, he had always a peculiar affection for the Philippian church. He showed his trust in it by accepting gifts of money from Philippi, although it was his settled principle to do his missionary work without payment. He could feel that he and the Philippians knew one another thoroughly. Elsewhere he might be suspected of mercenary motives if he took anything, but here there would be no misunderstanding.

It was one of those gifts from Philippi which caused Paul to write the Epistle. Knowing that he was a prisoner and presumably in want, the Philippians had sent him money by the hands of Epaphroditus, one of their number. They had meant apparently that this messenger, besides conveying their gift, should remain with Paul and assist him in any way that might be necessary. Epaphroditus had passed through a serious illness which had left him homesick, all the more so when he heard that the bad news about him had caused anxiety among his friends at Philippi. He was now returning, and Paul gave him this letter to carry with him, thanking the Philippians for all their kindness. He takes occasion, at the same time, to inform them of his own circumstances and to offer them some counsels and encouragements. The Philippian church had been passing through difficult days. It had been subjected to something like a persecution, which Paul, in his generous way, compares to his own trouble, although it probably entailed little more than the petty injustices so often inflicted on Christians by their heathen neighbors. Besides the outward suffering, there had been a good deal of dissension within the church itself, due mainly to personal jealousies and animosities. Moreover, the Jewish enemies of Paul, who had caused such discord in Galatia and Corinth, had not been idle at Philippi, and had caused doubts and misgivings, although they had not shaken the loyalty of Paul's most devoted church. In writing his letter, he is acutely conscious that the Philippians are laboring under a sense of depression, and makes it his chief aim to encourage them. He puts the best face he can on his own situation, assuring them that he hopes soon to be free, and that meanwhile he is in no such dire distress as they had supposed. He tells them that the difficulties which they are themselves suffering will pass over, if only they hold faithfully to their religion and carry out in their daily lives the teaching of Christ. The word most constantly repeated in the Epistle is "joy." Paul declares that his own mood, in spite of all his calamities, is one of joy. He impresses on his readers that, however difficult their task may be, they must not yield to despair. The surest way of overcoming their hardships will be to meet them, not only with a stout heart, but joyfully. On this note, he closes his exhortation: "Rejoice in the Lord always, and again I say, Rejoice" (4:4).

2. *Contents*

The Epistle, then, is a perfectly informal one, such as a brave man writes in a gloomy time to friends whom he trusts and loves. Paul sends his greetings to the Philippians, and tells them what has been happening to him and how he longs to see them again (1:1-26). He offers them his sympathy in their present distress, and advises them to face it in the right spirit (1:27-2:18). He promises that, as soon as possible, he will send them his trusted helper Timothy, and speaks warmly of their own messenger, Epaphroditus, who is now returning (2:19-3:1). Suddenly the tone of the letter changes, and he speaks in bitter terms of those enemies who are trying to undermine his work, and contrasts their conduct with his own (3:2-21). Finally he implores his readers once more to endure bravely and be true to the Gospel, and thanks them for all their kindness to himself (4). These are the topics of the letter, and they are all quite ordinary; but Paul has a wonderful gift of raising whatever he touches to a higher level. Without any pose or effort, he weaves some of his most memorable teaching into the friendly greetings and counsels of this Philippian letter. While he speaks, for instance, of his present sufferings, he dwells on the companionship of Christ, which the believer can rely on, both in life and death (1:20-23). In exhorting his readers to give up their little personal ambitions, he introduces the great passage on the self-forgetfulness of Christ,

who being in the form of God thought it not a prize to be equal with God, but made himself of no reputation and took on him the form of a servant and was made in the likeness of men; and being found in fashion as a man he humbled himself and became obedient to death, even the death of the Cross; wherefore also God hath highly exalted him and given him a name which is above every name. [2:6 ff.]

When he affirms his single-mindedness, in contrast to the hostile teachers, he makes his splendid claim:

Brethren I count not myself to have apprehended, but this one thing I do, — forgetting those things which are behind and reaching forth unto those things which are before, I press toward the mark for the prize of the high calling of God in Christ Jesus. [3:13,14.]

The Epistle, written as might appear for a passing occasion, is full of utterances which have molded the thoughts of men in all ages.

3. *Problems*

With all its simplicity, the Philippian letter has given rise to at least two very difficult problems. One of them concerns that passage on the hostile teachers, which opens so abruptly with the second verse of the third chapter. We know so little about conditions at Philippi that it is impossible to say for certain who those teachers were. Evidently they stood in some manner for Judaism, but were they Jews or Jewish Christians? Did they work within, or outside of, the church? What was their connection with those adversaries of Paul who had caused trouble in Galatia and at Corinth? Apart from the contents of the passage, there is a difficulty as to its connection with the rest of the Epistle. Nothing in the chapters before has prepared us for it, and it seems to introduce an alien and jarring note. The view has been taken by some scholars that it is out of place where it stands, and belongs to some previous letters which Paul had written to the Philippian church. He indicates in Chapter 3:1 that he had sent them at least one letter, and a portion of it may here be preserved. This is quite possible, but an informal letter like Philippians must not be dealt with as if it were a logically constructed treatise. Writing down his ideas just as they came to him, Paul may well have turned sharply from one subject to another.

A much more difficult problem is that which concerns the time and place at which the letter was written. The theory that the Epistles of the Captivity should be assigned to the period when Paul was working at Ephesus can be supported, in the case of Philippians, with arguments of peculiar force. Paul says, for instance, that, if released from his present danger, he will make his way to Philippi (1:27; 2:24), although he had gone to Rome with the intention of starting a mission in the west. The enemies denounced in Chapter 3 are most probably the same Jewish emissaries who called forth the Epistle to

Galatians, and from this it may be argued that Philippians
must belong to the same period. Much can be made, also, of
considerations of time. Epaphroditus had come with a gift;
he had fallen ill and news of his illness had reached Philippi;
reports of anxiety among his friends in Philippi had come back
to him. All these comings and goings would seem to imply that
Paul was in some place easily accessible to Philippi, and
Ephesus would answer this condition much better than Rome.
It is true that Paul makes mention of the "pretorian guard"
(1:13), and of "members of Cæsar's household," and these
references would naturally point to Rome; but there is evidence that the terms employed were sometimes used in connection with the government service in provincial cities, as
well as in the capital. Against the view that the Epistle was
written from Ephesus, it must be noted that Paul had apparently suffered a long imprisonment, during which his prospects
had often changed. Epaphroditus, too, had not come merely
to bring his gift and depart, but to bear Paul company. His
sojourn may have lasted for some months, and thus have
allowed ample time for all the communications of which we
hear in the letter, even when it is assumed that the place of
imprisonment was Rome.

The questions of where and when Philippians was written
are of little moment in themselves, but become of special
interest when we realise that this letter, if it was sent from
Rome, was in all probability the farewell utterance of Paul.
His trial, so long deferred, was now on the point of opening,
and he was weighing his chances of death or deliverance. One
would like to believe that in this letter to the best loved of all
his churches, the great Apostle was speaking his last words.
It gives noble expression to the spirit in which we may be sure
he went forth to his martyrdom.

For I know that this shall turn to my salvation through your prayer
and the supply of the Spirit of Jesus Christ: according to my earnest
expectation and my hope that in nothing I shall be put to shame, but
that with all boldness, as always so now also Christ shall be magnified
in my body, whether it be by life or by death. [1:19, 20.]

CHAPTER XX

The Pastoral Epistles

1. *Historical Setting*

Three Epistles, closely resembling each other in motive and character, have come down to us under the name of Paul. They are addressed, not to churches, but to Paul's missionary assistants, Timothy and Titus. The Apostle writes to these younger colleagues, instructing them as to how they should carry out their work of pastoral oversight, now that they are no longer under his personal direction. In view of their general subject, the letters have been known ever since the eighteenth century as the Pastoral Epistles.

Of the three letters, I Timothy and Titus give no definite indication of the circumstances in which they were written, but in II Timothy we are informed that Paul is in prison, on the eve of his death. He speaks of a "first defence," in which he has been wonderfully delivered, although all the friends who ought to have stood by him have proved false (II Tim. 4:16, 17). Now, however, his case appears hopeless.

I am already being offered and the time of my departure is come. I have fought the good fight, I have finished the course, I have kept the faith. Henceforth there is laid up for me the crown of righteousness. [II Tim. 4:6-8.]

2. *Problem of Paul's Last Days*

These passages give rise to a very difficult question, which has a vital bearing on the place of the Pastoral Epistles. What was the outcome of Paul's trial, when he at last appeared before the supreme court at Rome? The book of Acts, as we have seen, breaks off abruptly before it arrives at the critical episode. From references in ancient Christian literature, we know for certain that Paul was put to death, but nothing is told us of the precise time and circumstances. The probability is that his trial, after his three years' detention at Rome, resulted in his condemnation. If he had been set free and had resumed his mission, some account of his later work would surely have been preserved. According to one tradition, however, he was acquitted at his trial and made his intended journey into Spain, returning after a time to Rome, where he was rearrested, and perished as one of the many victims of Nero's persecution in the year 64 A.D. In our entire ignorance of the facts, it is impossible to say dogmatically that there is no ground for this story. We have seen already that, even in that portion of Paul's career which seems to be fully known to us, there are serious gaps. Nothing, for instance, is recorded of what happened to him during his three years' stay at Ephesus, when he was at the very height of his activity. It is quite conceivable that his life closed with a few obscure years of broken health, on which history is silent.

If the Pastoral Epistles were written by Paul, they would have to be assigned to that dark period between his first trial and his death. This becomes evident when we look carefully into the situation assumed in the letters. The Epistle to Titus is concerned with Christian communities which Paul had founded in Crete, an island which, in the known part of his life, he had seen only from shipboard on his voyage to Rome (Acts 27:8 f.). In I Timothy, we learn that Paul had left Timothy to supervise the work at Ephesus when he himself had proceeded to Macedonia. We know from Acts, however, that when Paul left Ephesus for Macedonia, he had sent Timothy on before him (Acts 19:22). In order to find room in Paul's life for the Pastoral Epistles, the whole scene requires to be set differently, and this can be done only by supposing that, after his trial at Rome, he resumed his missionary work under new conditions.

3. Grounds for Doubting the Epistles

The opinion is now almost unanimous among New Testament scholars that these Epistles, at least in their present form, cannot be by Paul. Arguments from the historical setting cannot, in the absence of full records, be conclusive; but there are further considerations which awaken the gravest doubts. (1) In style and vocabulary, the three Epistles are very similar to one another, but entirely different from all Paul's other writings. A large number of words keep recurring in these letters which he never uses elsewhere. Instead of the vividness and compactness so characteristic of Paul's language, we have strings of monotonous sentences in which the words are often out of all proportion to the matter. (2) The theological teaching is not that of Paul. Where Paul lays stress on the inward fellowship with Christ, this writer is intent on outward performance. He thinks of the Spirit not as a divine power, working in all believers, but as conferred mechanically on the regular officials of the church. Faith, as he regards it, is not so much an attitude of will, as the formal assent to certain doctrines. The difference from Paul's religious teaching is all the more striking as the writer constantly uses the terms and phrases which Paul had himself employed. Evidently he believes that he is thinking just as Paul did, but shows too plainly that he has not understood him. (3) The chief argument that Paul cannot have written the Epistles is to be found in the ecclesiastical order which they presuppose. In the time of Paul, there was no official ministry. Men endowed with the Spirit traveled from place to place, gathering in converts and forming them into little communities of "brethren." When the Pastoral Epistles were written, the church was coming to be regularly organized. We hear of "bishops," "elders," and other officials whose duties were clearly prescribed for them. The traveling missionary is giving place to the local pastor. It seems evident that between the time of Paul and the date of these letters, there had come about the great constitutional change which distinguishes the later church from that of the primitive age.

4. *Genuine Fragments*

It must not be inferred, however, that these Epistles are mere fabrications, with no right whatever to call themselves by the name of Paul. Imbedded in them here and there, are passages which bear the genuine Pauline stamp, and which can be shown, by delicate linguistic tests, to have Paul for their author. This is particularly true of II Timothy, which is in every way the finest and most valuable of the three Epistles. A probable explanation of their origin thus suggests itself. Paul had from time to time sent notes of instruction to his various assistants, and some of these had been preserved and had fallen into the hands of a later teacher. He felt that in themselves they were too brief and unimportant to find a place in the Pauline collection, so he took it upon himself to weave them together and expand them, introducing counsels which would be profitable to the church of his time. It needs to be repeated that in the ancient world the idea of literary property was much less rigid than it is now. With quite a good conscience, a writer could issue as Paul's work these letters which contained only a few fragments of his actual composition.

The Epistles must have been put together at a comparatively early date, when notes which Paul had written were still accessible. They seem to have been known in their present form to Ignatius and Polycarp about the year 116 A.D., and were possibly quoted by Clement of Rome, nearly twenty years earlier. They may therefore be assigned to somewhere about the year 100 A.D., and the ideas represented by them are in full agreement with that date. It was in the closing years of the first century that the new system of church government was firmly establishing itself. It was in those same years that heretical teaching had become a serious menace to the church. The Pastoral Epistles are concerned chiefly with those two issues. The writer is anxious to place the new ecclesiastical system on a sound footing; he is anxious, at the same time, to condemn heretical teaching and to ensure that the church will

vigorously resist it. For these purposes, he makes use of the
Pauline notes which had come into his possession. Paul had
been a great church leader and a champion of the true Christian faith. This unknown disciple of Paul tries to make the
Apostle speak as he would have spoken if he had lived a generation later.

5. *Contents*

In the First Epistle to Timothy, Paul is supposed to write
to his disciple, whom he had left as his substitute at Ephesus.
He warns him against the false teachers who are distorting
the gospel (1), then offers directions as to the conduct of worship (2), and proceeds to discuss the duties incumbent on bishops and deacons (3). He then speaks more definitely of the
manner in which a bishop should resist the false teaching (4),
and in the closing part of the Epistle offers a number of counsels with reference to the various types of people included in
the community — widows, virgins, elders, slaves, rich men.
At the end he reverts to the false doctrines, "profane and vain
babblings and oppositions of pretended knowledge."

The Second Epistle to Timothy is much more of a personal
letter. Paul speaks affectionately of Timothy and his early
Christian upbringing, then he glances back on his own work as
an Apostle (1). He exhorts Timothy to follow his example,
and especially to hold the true faith and withstand those who
would pervert it (2). These false teachers are sternly denounced (3:1-4:5), and Timothy is exhorted once more to be
on his guard against them. Paul then tells of his own circumstances, and leaves his last solemn charge to his successor.

The short Epistle to Titus covers much the same ground as
I Timothy. Titus is reminded of the duties of a bishop, and is
warned against false teachers (1). Counsels are given him with
regard to the various classes within the church (2). True Christian behavior is contrasted with that encouraged by the heretics
and, with a few personal directions, the Epistle closes (3).

6. *Historical and Religious Value*

As documents which illustrate a critical phase in the development of the church, the Epistles have great historical value. They place us near the very origins of the organization which was to stand unchallenged for a thousand years and which, in all essentials, is maintained until this day. They enable us to see how this organization was in large measure the outcome of the early conflict with heresy. The church had begun as a free brotherhood, but, in face of the growing danger from Gnosticism, the early freedom had to be restricted. Each community had to be united and regulated under one strong, dependable man in order to present a solid front to the enemy.

But the Epistles have more than this historical interest. That they are vastly inferior, from a religious point of view, to Paul's genuine writings cannot be denied. Their main defect is that they miss the true connection of Christian faith and Christian living. For Paul, the practical life of the Christian is nothing but the natural expression, the "fruit" as he sometimes calls it, of the inward spiritual life. For this later teacher, two duties are incumbent on the Christian; he must believe certain things and do certain things. There is no attempt to show that there is a vital relation between these two demands. It is simply taken for granted that they are both needed, and that taken together they constitute "godliness," the characteristic mark of the Christian man. Much of the formalism of later Christianity has been due to this separation of faith and life which first meets us, in a pronounced form, in the Pastoral Epistles.

Yet with all their lack of deeper spiritual insight, the Epistles teach a genuine Christianity, in some ways better adapted to the ordinary man than the mystical fervor of Paul.

Let every man that nameth the name of Christ depart from iniquity. Flee youthful lusts, but follow righteousness, faith, charity, peace with them that call on the Lord out of a pure heart. [II Tim. 2:19 f.]

This ideal of the Christian life is enforced in many beautiful and impressive sayings. It is not everyone who is capable of a profound inward religion, but all can hold fast to the faith intrusted to them and aim at a life which will be worthy of the high Christian tradition. The writer of these Epistles was not a prophet or a rarely gifted saint, but a pastor, seeking to form a Christianity which might be the common possession of a miscellaneous church. What he offers is a practical religion within the reach of all, and his wise teaching will never be out of date.

CHAPTER XXI

THE EPISTLE TO THE HEBREWS

1. *Authorship*

No other New Testament writing is beset with so many riddles as the so-called Epistle to the Hebrews. Is it an Epistle? Was it addressed to "Hebrews"? Who was its author? When and where and for what purpose was it written? In what relation does it stand to the other New Testament books? All these questions, and others like them, have been warmly debated, and it does not seem possible to reach a decisive answer with regard to any of them.

The Epistle has been traditionally ascribed to Paul, but this is certainly wrong. It is entirely different in its literary character and its whole manner of thought from any writing of Paul. The characteristic Pauline ideas are absent from it, so much so that the writer does not even seem to be acquainted with the teaching of Paul. That the Apostle did not write it was fully recognized in the early church, and the Christian fathers in the second and third centuries made various guesses as to its authorship. It was ascribed to Barnabas, or Luke, or Clement of Rome, while Origen, the greatest of all the early critics, was driven to the conclusion that "the author is known to God alone." Perhaps the happiest guess was that of Luther, who suggested that the Epistle may have been the work of Apollos, of whom we read in the book of Acts that he was "an Alexandrian, an eloquent man, mighty in the scriptures" (Acts 18:24). The description at all points may well apply to the author of Hebrews; but there must have been a number of men in the early church who would answer to it as well as Apollos. All that can be affirmed is, that Hebrews was written by one of those early teachers, whose name has now disappeared.

2. *Place, Date, Form*

From the greeting at the close, "those of Italy salute you," it may be gathered that the Epistle was either sent from Rome or addressed to Rome. The words most naturally imply that a Roman teacher, removed for the time being to some place outside of Italy, sends the greetings of other Italian Christians along with his own. It is certain that the Epistle was connected in a special manner with Rome, for Clement of Rome, who wrote as early as 96 A.D., quotes from it largely. In view of this use of it by Clement, the date of its origin must fall well within the first century, and many have held that it must have been written before the destruction of the Temple in 70 A.D. They assume, however, that in his allusions to ritual worship, the author has the Temple in mind, while he explicitly says that he refers to the Tabernacle set up by Moses. The Epistle must not be placed too early, since it reflects a type of Christian thinking which belongs to the later part of the century. We cannot be far wrong in dating it somewhere between 80 and 90 A.D.

In its literary form, the work is both a speech and an Epistle. It closes in the usual epistolary style with personal notices and greetings, but it does not open like a letter, and again and again the author represents himself as speaking to an audience. The style throughout is that of an oration, rising at times to magnificent eloquence. It is difficult to account for this double character of the work. Perhaps the best explanation is that a Roman teacher, separated from the company he has been wont to address, wrote a speech which was to be read out in his name, and closed it as he would close a letter with a few personal remembrances.

3. *Readers and Purpose*

To whom, then, does he address himself? This is the most important of all the questions, since it affects our whole understanding of the purpose of the Epistle. It contains no notice of its destination, but at some early time a title was prefixed to it, "to the Hebrews," that is, to a group consisting of Jewish Christians. This, however, was only a guess, based apparently on the fact that the Epistle is full of references to the Old Testament and to Jewish ritual practice. But at the time when Hebrews was written, the Old Testament was the only Bible of the church, and a Christian teacher, whatever audience he addressed, was bound to make use of it and to seek hidden meanings in its prophecies and ordinances. There is nothing in the Epistle to indicate that it was meant particularly for Jewish readers; in some respects, it is less Jewish in character than any other New Testament book. The Greek in which it is written is careful and polished, more akin to classical Greek than to that which was employed by Jewish writers. It contains no reference to the distinction of Jew and Gentile, which for Jewish Christians would be all-important. The author does not even seem to understand what Judaism meant, for he takes for granted that it centered in the sacrificial ritual, while the one thing that really mattered, in the living Judaism of his time, was the keeping of the Law. Up to our own day, however, the Epistle has been interpreted on the ground of its misleading title. The view has been generally accepted that the author wrote for Jewish Christians who were tempted to fall back on their old religion, with its imposing forms of outward worship. Everything in the argument of the Epistle has been forced into line with this false assumption.

It is indeed true that the people addressed were in danger of "drifting away" from their faith (2:1). But it was not into Judaism that they were inclined to lapse; neither was it into sheer unbelief, for the writer expressly says that such apostates were quite outside of the pale (6:4-6). The danger contemplated is simply that of indifference. The people whom the author had in mind were Christians of the third generation (2:3), to whom the message, which had once been so new and wonderful, had become a matter of custom. Under the stress of petty persecution (10:33; 12:4) they had grown discouraged, all the more so as the hope of the Lord's return,

which had sustained the former generation, had now begun to
fail (9:28; 10:35-37). The writer's object is to rekindle in
them something of the early glow, of the marvel and awe
which the gospel had once inspired. He tries to make his readers understand that their religion is not one out of many, but
is the perfect type of worship. They are to be proud of their
Christianity. They are to realize that they have attained at
last to something which all previous ages had been seeking
after. Here we have the true key to the meaning of the Epistle. The author addresses himself to neither Jews nor Gentiles, but to Christians as such. His aim is to prove that what
they possess is the absolute religion. If he does this by means
of a contrast between Christianity and Judaism, this is only
because Judaism alone, of all existing religions, could claim to
have been given by God. If he can show that Christianity has
brought fulfillment to Judaism, he will have demonstrated its
supreme worth. It has carried to fruition what was in the mind
of God from the beginning. In place of types and shadows, it
has put within man's reach the final realities, "the very image
of the things" (10:1).

4. *Religious and Practical Interests*

One thing must be observed before we can enter into full
sympathy with the argument of the Epistle. According to their
outlook and temperament, men differ in their conception of
religion. For some it is an inward fellowship with God, for
some an inspiration to right living, for some the highest exercise of reason. There are others, and the author of Hebrews
was one of them, for whom religion consists above all in *worship*; as they wait upon God in adoration and so realize his
presence, they find their religious longings most fully satisfied.
So in his effort to prove that Christianity is the supreme religion, this writer concentrates on the matter of worship. He
holds that the aim of religion has always been to secure for
men access to God, and in the light of this idea he examines
the ancient forms of religion, as exemplified above all in the

Jewish system. Against that older mode of worship, he sets the new one which has been inaugurated through Christ. If it can be shown that in Christianity we have the perfect worship, there can remain no doubt that the very purpose of all religion has now been fulfilled.

The Epistle, however, is something more than a theological tract, intended to prove a certain thesis. The author himself describes it as a "word of exhortation" or hortatory discourse (13:22), and this is doubtless its main object. Addressed to a group of people who were weakening in their Christian zeal, it is meant to inspire and fortify them, and the theological argument is everywhere subordinate to the practical aim. Again and again, after a passage of abstract discussion, the writer pauses, and turns on his audience with earnest warning or encouragement (2:1-4; 4:1-3; 4:11-16; 6:1-14; 10:19-39). All through the Epistle, the doctrinal interest goes hand in hand with the practical, and towards the close is merged in it entirely. It is only in form that Hebrews is a theological argument. Intrinsically, as the author truly claims, it is a "word of exhortation," and the doctrines are meant only to lend force and significance to the practical appeal.

5. Plan

Of all New Testament books, Hebrews is most consciously a work of literature. Not only does the author study to express himself in rich and forcible language, but he has laid out his work on a regular plan, in which all the parts are clearly articulated. He undertakes to show that the new covenant is "better" than the old, better in the sense that it has brought to fulfillment all that the old covenant had merely foreshadowed. This he does by means of three main contrasts: (1) Christ is higher than the angels, through whom, according to Jewish tradition, the Law was given (1, 2); (2) Christ is higher than Moses, who was the mediator of the Law (3, 4); (3) Christ is the true High Priest, in contrast to the levitical high priests through whom the Law became effectual (5-10). After the superiority of the new covenant has thus been established, the writer dwells on the obligations which it lays on those who have received it. If God's servants in ancient days lived by faith, a far stronger and more living faith is now required of Christians (11). If the Law imposed a solemn responsibility, this is true in far higher degree of those who profess the religion of Christ (12). With a few practical admonitions, the Epistle closes (13).

At first sight, this plan might seem to involve an anticlimax. Surely it might be taken for granted that, if Christ is greater than the angels and greater than Moses, he must be greater than the Jewish high priest; yet the other two contrasts are made preliminary to this third one. For the writer, however, the third contrast is cardinal. Conceiving of worship as the essential thing in religion, he thinks of everything else in God's dealings with men as leading up to the right worship. In a real sense, the angels and Moses had done their work in order to make the high priest possible. The whole plan of God had been so designed from the beginning as to bring about a true mediation between himself and men.

6. Christ as High Priest

In the view of this writer, therefore, the old religion centered in the high priest; and not only so, but the high priest himself existed for the sake of one solemn function which he performed once a year. On the Day of Atonement he offered sacrifice for the sins of the people, and then, carrying the blood of the sacrifice, he passed through the veil into the holy of holies, where he stood for a few minutes in the presence of God. This entrance into the sanctuary was the distinctive act of the high priest. In the person of the one man who was their representative, the whole people renewed that covenant with God which had been broken by the sins of the past year.

In these arrangements of the old religion, the writer of Hebrews sees the types, divinely ordained, which were meant to foreshadow the work of Christ. First of all, he deals with the person of the high priest. By the very nature of his office, a high priest must have a double qualification; he must himself be one of the people whom he represents, and at the same time he must owe his appointment to God (5:1 f.). Christ had this twofold relation to humanity and to God. He became at all points one with men, and yet acted in the name of God — not by right of physical descent, like the levitical priests, but in virtue of his own personality. He was like the legendary Melchizedek, who was the greatest of all priests, although nothing is said of his ancestry. From the person of the high priest, the writer passes to the office. He shows that as Christ was the true High Priest, so he performed the service of which the intercession on the Day of Atonement was only the symbol. First he offered a sacrifice for men's sins — not a mere animal sacrifice, but one of surpassing worth, consisting of himself (9:11-14). Then with the blood of this priceless sacrifice, he entered the sanctuary in heaven, where God dwells in very deed, and entered it to remain forever, interceding for men, not for a moment, once in a year, but continually and without end. The whole argument, as the writer himself is careful to mark out, leads up to this ministry of Christ in the heavenly sanctuary.

Now of the things of which we have spoken the chief point is this: We have a High-Priest who has sat down on the right hand of the Majesty in the heavens, a minister of the sanctuary and of the true tabernacle which the Lord pitched and not men. [8:1, 2.]

The death of Christ is viewed as only the necessary prelude to the crowning act of his entrance through the veil into the holy place in heaven. It was this which made Christ our great High Priest.

7. Defects of the Argument

The argument of Hebrews suffers from the grave weakness that it is based on ritual ideas which have now, in large measure, lost their meaning to us. Here we perceive the inferiority of this writer to Paul, as a religious teacher. Paul often works with old-world beliefs which we cannot now accept, but he is always trying to explain the work of Christ in the light of great religious facts — the love of God, the weakness and sinfulness of men, the eternal value of spiritual things. The writer of Hebrews is content to take the scriptural ordinances as final. He assumes that, since the sacrificial system is ordained in scripture, it must have a divine worth, and he sets himself to prove that the work of Christ had fulfilled the inner purpose of that system. No attempt is made to connect the rites of sacrifice with some eternal spiritual law. The writer is content to know that this method of worship is enjoined in Scripture and must therefore be in accordance with God's holy will. If it can be shown that Christ offered the perfect sacrifice, it must necessarily follow that he gave us the perfect religion. Moving, as it does, within the confines of old ritual conceptions, the Epistle may almost be said to align Christianity with that outworn type of religion against which Jesus himself had made his protest.

8. *Essential Teaching*

But behind the formal argument, there is one thought in this Epistle which makes it one of the most significant of Christian writings. The author declares (and this is the pervading idea in his book) that through Christ we are enabled to grasp the reality of things which have hitherto been known only in their dim reflection. In every chapter we have this contrast presented in various forms — earthly and heavenly, transient and eternal, shadow and substance, visible and invisible, type and fulfillment. Ultimately, the thought goes back to the Platonic conception that this material world is only the reflection of a higher one, an ideal, spiritual world which alone is real. Our task is to lay hold of those eternal things which are only suggested through the things we see. So when he describes how Christ has passed through the veil, and by his priesthood in the heavenly sanctuary has secured for us an immediate access to God, this writer to the Hebrews would have us feel that we belong, as Christians, to the higher, invisible world. Amidst the changes and illusions of time, we have part in the eternal. What Christ has done for us is to bring the unseen realties within our reach, so that they are now closer to us and more real than the things we see.

This underlying thought of the Epistle comes to clear expression in the eleventh chapter, the glorious chapter in praise of faith. For this writer, as for Paul, faith is the essential quality of the Christian; but he understands it in quite a different way from Paul. Faith, as Paul conceives it, is the trust and self-surrender by which we open our hearts to the divine influences. It is that attitude of receptivity in man which answers to the free giving of God. To the author of Hebrews, faith is that power in us whereby we apprehend what is beyond the senses. This is expressly stated in the definition with which the chapter opens. "Now faith is the substance of things hoped for, the proof of things not seen." Its effect, that is to say, is twofold: it makes future things as real as if we now grasped them, and it gives certainty to things which our senses cannot perceive. This meaning of faith is illustrated from one example after another in Old Testament history. It is shown that all the great things ever achieved by men have been due to that faculty which enabled them to work for the future — to believe in truth that seemed to be contradicted by all material fact. The supreme example of this faith is Christ himself, "who for the joy that was set before him endured the Cross, despising the shame, and is set down at the right hand of the throne of God" (12:2). In former times, faith was possible only to rare saints and heroes, and even to them for brief intervals; all the true servants of Christ can now live by it. Christ has entered the higher spiritual world, and through him it has become real to us and we can make it our one interest and desire.

To many readers, the Epistle to the Hebrews has little value apart from this one inspiring chapter, which seems to come like an oasis in the midst of a dreary desert of argument.

But the chapter grows out of the argument, and is an integral part of it. All through his discussion, the writer is seeking to show that through Christ we are brought near to the higher world; in him we have a great High Priest by whom our faith can fasten, like an anchor, on the unseen realities (6:19). Apart also from its main argument, so splendidly brought to a head in the eleventh chapter, the Epistle contains much that is of permanent religious value. One might single out, more especially, the significance which is given to the earthly life of Christ. Paul had made it his resolve "not to know Christ after the flesh" (II Cor. 5:16). Jesus for him was the risen and exalted Lord, whose life on earth had been a period of eclipse, necessary only as the preparation for what was to follow. The writer of Hebrews appreciates the worth of the earthly life, and declares that, by means of it, the son of God became spiritually greater. He could not truly have been our High Priest until he had learned that sympathy with men which came to him through his human suffering. It is only in the Epistle to the Hebrews, outside of the Gospels themselves, that this emphasis is laid on the earthly life of Christ; and for this reason, if for no other, it has a place of permanent value in the literature of Christian devotion.

9. Relations to Earlier and Later Thought

Theologically, the Epistle holds a curious midway position. On the one hand, it anticipates the philosophical mode of thought which was soon to become prevalent in the church. The gospel is brought into relation to the Platonic conception of the ideal, against the visible world. Christ is interpreted in the light of that Alexandrian doctrine of the Word or Logos which is to meet us afterwards in the Fourth Gospel. As the Logos through whom God made the world, Christ is the self-manifestation of God, "the effulgence of his glory and impress of his nature, upholding all things by the word of his power" (1:3). On the other hand, there is much in the Epistle which recalls the most primitive type of Christian thought. The return of Christ as the Judge of the world is expected almost immediately (10:37). The future consummation is described in purely apocalyptic terms (12:22 f.). Satan is regarded as the prince of this world (2:14). The Messiah is an angelic being, exalted above the other angels by a divine decree (1:5 f.). In Paul there is an effort to fuse the earlier type of thought with the later one, but in Hebrews they are simply laid side by side, with the result that the thinking of the Epistle lacks inner cohesion. It is impossible, for instance, to make any consistent doctrine out of the various references to the Person of Christ, though they are bound together in an apparent unity by the use of the vague term "the Son of God." This mingling of quite different types of thought may be due partly to the transitional time at which the Epistle was written. It may also be due to the fact that it is a product of the Roman church. Christianity had passed to Rome, so far as we can gather, directly from Jerusalem, and continued to bear the stamp of primitive apocalyptic belief. When the later philosophical ideas came in, they were simply overlaid on the old conceptions and were never really blended with them. The whole question of the relation of Hebrews to Roman Christianity is one of great historical interest. Even when the Epistle was written, Rome was fast becoming the premier church, and was destined in later times to dominate the Christian world. Hebrews, there can be little doubt, was the first great pronouncement of Roman Christianity. It probably contains the key to much that is perplexing in the later development.

CHAPTER XXII

The Epistle of James

1. *The Catholic Epistles*

Five writings are usually classed together in the New Testament under the title of the Catholic or General Epistles — James, Jude, I and II Peter, I John. The title is given them because they are not addressed to any particular community or person, but seem to be intended for the church at large. In more ways than one this classification is misleading. It is doubtful, for one thing, whether any of the Epistles is in a proper sense "general." I John was almost certainly written for one definite church, though it is never named. James and I Peter are addressed to groups of churches. II Peter and Jude are so problematical that no one can say for whom they were first intended. Again, the common title suggests that these five Epistles form a group by themselves among the New Testament writings, and an idea of this kind leads only to confusion. Each of them has a purpose and character of its own. They are all found, when we come to examine them, to represent different interests and to involve questions of different kinds. It is particularly misleading to include I John in this artificial group of so-called "General Epistles." Its place is undoubtedly with the other writings which make up the Johannine literature, and apart from them it cannot be rightly understood.

2. *Conflicting Estimates of the Epistle of James*

In our English New Testament, the General Epistles are placed near the end of the volume, just before the book of Revelation. The Greek manuscripts put them as a rule, immediately after the Gospels and Acts, and before the writings of

Paul. This was no doubt in recognition of the fact that they bore the names of Apostles who were directly associated with Jesus, and whose authority, therefore, might be considered superior to that of Paul. In keeping with this principle, the first place of all was accorded to the Epistle of James. Its author was assumed to be no other than James, the Lord's own brother.

There is no writing in the New Testament on which critical opinion has varied so widely as on this Epistle. According to one view, it is the very earliest of the New Testament books; according to another, it is one of the latest. Some writers have acclaimed it as nearer than any other book to the genuine teaching of Jesus, while some have maintained that it is not Christian at all, but a Jewish tract to which a few superficial touches have been added, so as to adapt it to Christian use. Others would deny that it is distinctively Jewish. They argue from a number of its phrases and turns of thought that it was originally the work of a Greek ethical teacher.

3. *Authorship*

The Epistle opens with the words "James, a servant of God and of the Lord Jesus Christ, to the twelve tribes who are of the Dispersion, greeting." This is the only place in which the writer makes any reference to himself, and it has been suggested that the verse was prefixed at a later time to a work that had come down without any note of its authorship. This may be, but the second verse seems to be linked to the first by a play on words: "count it all joy" — where the Greek word for "joy" is similar to that for "greeting." This would also indicate that the Epistle was Greek from the first, and not, as some have supposed, the translation of a Jewish tract. The name "James" was a very common one, so much so that it was borne by at least four men who appear in the New Testament, and in the minds of many readers they are frequently confused with one another. The Pope himself fell into error in this connection in a public pronouncement some years ago. The

James of the Epistle, it has always been assumed, was that brother of Jesus who in the early days became head of the church at Jerusalem. From all the accounts we have of him, he was a man of stern integrity, a born leader and administrator, who stood firmly for the Jewish Law; and this Epistle seems to have been written by such a man. But the name by itself gives little clue to the identity of the author. All we can learn from it is that the Epistle purports to be by a Christian teacher called James.

4. Destination and Date

It is addressed "to the twelve tribes of the Dispersion," and these words have sometimes been taken quite literally, as implying that the letter was meant especially for readers of Jewish origin. More likely, however, the writer is using a symbolic form of words which meets us at various times in the New Testament. The church claimed to be the true Israel, and it was made up of a number of dispersed communities, centers of light in a dark world. The "twelve tribes" cannot be understood in any literal sense, for the old tribal divisions of Israel had disappeared many centuries before. Nothing more is implied than that the new Israel corresponds to the old, and that the Epistle is meant for the church in its totality.

No indication is given as to the date of the Epistle or the place where it was written. In view of its apparent conflict with the teaching of Paul, it cannot be put too late, for early in the second century Paul had become a revered figure, from whose opinions no Christian teacher would care to dissent, even in appearance. Yet an early date is equally out of the question. The controversial issues are not those of the primitive age; the denunciations of wealth would have been uncalled for when there were no rich men in the church; the occasionally ornate language points to a time when Christian writers were adopting the Greek culture. Some date about the year 100 A.D. would seem to answer best to all the conditions. As to the place of origin, nothing can be affirmed except that the Epistle was written somewhere in the Gentile world. This may be gathered from the author's full command of the Greek language and his familiarity with classical ideas and phrases. Here we have probably to find the explanation of the curious mixture in the Epistle of purely Jewish with Hellenistic ideas. The author, though his outlook was widely different from that of Paul, had been trained in a similar environment. While he was a Jew, trained in the traditions of the fathers, he had mingled freely from his earliest days with Gentiles and had fallen unconsciously into Gentile modes of thought.

5. *Christian Origin*

We come now to the central difficulty of the Epistle. Although it holds a prominent place in the New Testament, it seems to contain little that stamps it as a distinctively Christian work. The name of Christ occurs only twice, and then in a quite formal and incidental manner (1:1; 2:1). Christian beliefs are indicated only in a few stray expressions (e.g., 5:7; 5:14), and for the most part the teaching is limited to general maxims of morality, to which many parallels can be found in Jewish literature. May it not be that a little textbook of Jewish ethic had come into the author's hands, and that he merely revised it, with a few additions and modifications, to adapt it to Christian use? A good deal may be said for this theory; and an interesting suggestion has lately been made that the opening verse originally ran, "Jacob to the twelve patriarchs." A favorite device in Jewish ethical treatises was to represent Jacob, the progenitor of the race, as offering counsels on his deathbed to each of his twelve sons. But when we examine the Epistle in detail, we cannot fail to be struck with its essentially Christian character. For many people in our day, as in ancient times, the only criterion of whether a book or discourse is truly Christian is its use of certain phrases, traditionally connected with the faith. Judged by this standard, the Epistle undoubtedly falls short; but when we look, not merely for pious words, but for evidences of the

Christian spirit, it is fully in line with Jesus' own teaching. In not a few respects, James comes nearer to the type of thought which meets us in the Synoptic Gospels than any other of the early writers. With theological ideas he has little concern, but again and again he echoes, almost literally, the language of the Sermon on the Mount. To such a writer, however much he may have borrowed from the Jewish literature with which he was familiar, it is difficult to deny the name of Christian.

Not only must the Epistle be regarded as a Christian book, but it enables us, better than any other writing, to trace one leading development of Christian thought. The gospel, as proclaimed by Jesus, was rich and many-sided, and as time went on, it came to be explained in a number of different ways. Men like Paul and John laid hold of the more spiritual elements in the message; there were others who saw in it chiefly a new and purer ethic, which it was the duty of Christians to put into action. In the second century, we find a number of these teachers who lay all the stress on the moral demands of Christianity, and they have had many successors in later times, not least in our own. James is the precursor of these Christian moralists. He is interested in the Gospel, not on its mystical or philosophical sides, but as a practical guide to everyday living. He tends to be contemptuous of mere religious thinking and devotional piety; what he insists on is Christian action.

Pure religion and undefiled before God and the Father is this, — to visit the fatherless and widows in their affliction and to keep oneself unspotted from the world. [1:27.]

6. Contents

The Epistle consists, then, of a series of moral instructions, arranged without any obvious sequence. Three or four main themes keep recurring — patience under trial, the value of practice as opposed to mere theory, justice and respect to the poor, the danger of evil speech, the need for humbleness and sincerity. Around these main themes various maxims are

woven, one reflection giving rise to another. To draw up anything like an ordered summary of the Epistle would be impossible, and yet it does not leave on the mind that confused
impression which is usually all that remains from a string of
proverbs or disconnected thoughts. Although we know nothing
of the writer, he stands before us, after we read his book, as
a well-defined personality, a man with prejudices and limitations, but sagacious, warm-hearted and transparently honest.
With all his plain common sense, he has a gift of imagination
and a moral earnestness which save his wisdom from ever
sinking into mere platitude.

7. *Distinctive Teaching*

Most of the teaching is of the kind familiar to us from the
precepts in the Synoptic Gospels and the moral exhortations
in the writings of Paul, but in two respects the author takes
up a pronounced attitude of his own. (1) He is strongly
biased against the rich, and denounces them again and again
in no measured terms. It is true that in the Gospels also, particularly in the Gospel of Luke, we meet with strictures on
wealth; but it is there condemned on the ground that a man
who has too large a stake in this world will have little care
for the Kingdom of God. James appears to regard wealth in
itself as an evil.

Do not rich men oppress you and drag you before the judgment seats?
Do they not blaspheme that worthy name by which you are called?
[2:6, 7.]

Go to now ye rich men; your riches are corrupted, your gold and
silver are cankered, and the rust of them shall be a witness against you
and shall eat your flesh as it were fire. Ye have heaped treasure for the
last days. Ye have lived in pleasure on the earth and been wanton; ye
have nourished your hearts in a day of slaughter. [5:1-6.]

It has been conjectured that the writer belonged to some
peculiar sect of the early church in which poverty for its own
sake was made a virtue. More likely we should see in his
vehement language only the resentment of an honest man who

worked among the poor and was bitterly aware of the injustice they had often to suffer. So many examples of the abuse of wealth had come before him that he had come to think of wealth itself as an evil.

(2) The other puzzling element in the Epistle is its disparagement of faith as compared with works.

What does it profit, my brethren, though a man say he has faith and have not works? Can faith save him? As the body without the spirit is dead, so faith without works is dead also.

This whole passage (2:14-26) reads like a direct attack on Paul's great doctrine of Justification by Faith, and in this sense it has often been regarded. It is pointed out that the writer takes the very example of Abraham, on which Paul bases his doctrine, and turns it against Paul.

Was not Abraham our father justified by works when he offered his son Isaac on the altar? See how faith wrought with his works, and by works was faith made perfect. [2:21-23.]

One thing, however, is certain, that the man who wrote this passage cannot have read Paul or understood what Paul's doctrine really meant. If the passage is directed against Pauline teaching, it contemplates some perversion of it for which the Apostle was not himself responsible. With all that James says as to the need of worthy practice, Paul would have been the first to agree. He also demanded an active faith, one that expressed itself in a Christian life and was not an empty profession.

It was in view of this passage on faith that Luther made his famous criticism of James as "that Epistle of straw." This contemptuous judgment has often been repeated in various forms, but is certainly unjust to a writing that must always rank high in the ethical literature of Christianity. James is no mere moralist, but a brother in spirit to the old Hebrew prophets; he has more than a touch of the ethical feeling which marks the utterances of Jesus himself. Where he falls short is in separating morality from its spring in an inward religious life. He speaks of a "law of liberty" (1:25; 2:12), and from this it has sometimes been inferred that he had arrived at Paul's conception of a moral freedom attainable through Christ. But his idea appears to be simply that in place of the old Law, Christians are subject to a new and more generous one. It is a "law of liberty," but is still a law, imposed on us from without. There is no good reason to doubt that the author of the Epistle is a Christian, but he does not intrinsically go beyond the requirements of Jewish morality. Conceiving of the new message as a "law," and not as a power which creates a new life, he misses what is deepest, both in the Christian religion and the Christian ethic.

CHAPTER XXIII

THE FIRST EPISTLE OF PETER

1. *Peter in Christian History*

Peter comes before us in the Gospels as the foremost of Jesus' disciples, and it was through him, more than any other man, that the cause of Jesus was preserved after the Crucifixion. For some years, and these the most critical in its whole history, the church looked up to him as its leader. Nothing is more perplexing than the complete disappearance of this "prince of the Apostles" from the later record. He last comes before us at Antioch, when Paul "withstood him to his face because he was worthy of blame" (Gal. 2:11); though he is casually mentioned some years afterwards, showing that he was still alive (I Cor. 9:5). From all that we can gather, it may be surmised that Peter was the victim of a moral tragedy, such as has befallen not a few of the great leaders in history. After a period of noble service in the cause of progress and freedom, he took a false step and allowed himself to be captured by the forces of reaction. Henceforth there was no place for him. The movement he had begun still went forward, but it now found its leaders in men like Paul, who had courage to follow the light.

2. *The Two Epistles*

But while Peter disappears, two Epistles have come down to us under his name. The second, as we shall see, is of very dubious value; but the first, however it originated, is one of the most beautiful writings in the New Testament, not philosophical or profound, but full of the purest spirit of Christian devotion. Can it be accepted as the work of Peter? This is a question which cannot be answered until we have looked at its nature and contents.

3. Destination of the First Epistle

It takes the form of a circular letter, addressed "to the elect sojourners of the Dispersion, in Pontus, Galatia, Cappadocia, Asia, and Bithynia" (1:1) — all of them territories in the northern half of Asia Minor, and including at least part of the missionary field of Paul. Some have inferred from the word "dispersion" that the Epistle was intended for Jewish Christians, but there is nothing in it that points to Jews more than Gentiles, and we may be fairly certain that the writer, like James in his opening verse, is using a symbolic language. The Christians are conceived as the true Israel, scattered in little companies throughout a world in which they are like exiles. According to 5:13, the Epistle was written from "Babylon," and this also has been taken in a literal sense. In the first century, the ancient Babylon was still a considerable city, with a large Jewish population. There was also a Roman garrison town in Egypt, near the site of the modern Cairo, which bore the name Babylon, and some have supposed that this was the place in question. But there is little reason to doubt that Babylon is used as a figurative name for Rome, just as it certainly is in the book of Revelation (Rev. 14:8).

4. Contents and Purpose

The Epistle is divided into three main parts. (1) The writer reminds his readers of the great hope which has come to them through Christ, and exhorts them to live worthily of it (1:1-2:10). (2) He offers directions for conduct in various relations of life, and especially for patience under suffering (2:11-4:6). (3) He passes to exhortations which bear more definitely on personal Christianity, and here again lays emphasis on the need of patience in time of persecution (4:7-5:14). The character of the whole Epistle is hortatory, and any theology it may contain is incidental to its practical purpose.

There are many references throughout to trials which the readers are undergoing, and the nature of these trials is made

quite explicit in the closing section. A storm of persecution
had broken on the churches in Asia Minor, and the main purpose of the letter is to make them aware that other churches
are mindful of them, and to encourage them to bear up bravely. The writer assures them that this trial is meant for the
testing of their faith, and that it will soon pass over, and will
have as its result a larger peace and happiness. Above all, he
calls to their remembrance the example of Christ, who underwent the extremity of suffering and bore it patiently.

For Christ also suffered for us, leaving us an example that ye should
follow in his steps; who did no sin, neither was guile found in his mouth;
who when he was reviled, reviled not again, when he suffered he threatened not, but committed himself to him that judgeth righteously; who
his own self bore our sins in his own body on the tree, that we being
dead to sins should live unto righteousness, by whose stripes ye were
healed. [2:21-24; cf. 3:17, 18.]

The watchword of the whole Epistle is *hope*. At the very
beginning Christianity is defined as a "living hope" (1:3), and
this idea is repeated again and again, and applied in many directions. Amidst the evils of the present, the readers are
pointed forward to a glorious future, the thought of which is
to sustain them and put gladness and enthusiasm into their
service of God. The very mark of a Christian is that he has
become a new man through the hope which has been kindled
in him by the message of Christ. It might almost be said that
hope plays the same part in I Peter as faith does in the writings of Paul.

5. Date and Authorship

All the problems of the Epistle have to be considered in
view of the fact that it was called forth by a persecution. This
can hardly have been one of those sudden outbreaks of mob
violence to which the church was always liable, and of which
we have various examples in the book of Acts. These excite-
ments were by their nature of brief duration, and were confined to some one locality. What is contemplated in the Epistle

is an organized persecution, affecting a wide region and carried out for a long period together, under official sanction. The church is being subjected to a "fiery trial" (4:12). The sufferings endured by Christians in Asia Minor are shared by their "brethren throughout the world" (5:9). The name "Christian" by itself is sufficient ground for condemnation (4:16). Such conditions as are here assumed did not arise before the year 64 A.D., when the Christians of Rome were massacred by the orders of Nero; and it is very doubtful whether even this massacre entailed any serious consequences for Christians outside of Rome. There was nothing like an organized persecution, effective in the provinces as well as the capital, until the year 96 A.D., in the reign of Domitian. To this date, the Epistle is most probably to be assigned. If this be so, its author cannot have been Peter, who perished, according to the general tradition, in Nero's massacre, and who in any case can hardly have survived until near the end of the century. Apart from considerations of date, the authorship of Peter is more than doubtful on at least two grounds. (1) The Epistle is written in excellent Greek, of which Peter, the Galilæan, who for most of his life had never been outside of Palestine, would not have been capable. To this it may be answered that, while Peter supplied the ideas, he may have employed some better scholar to put them into good language. This may possibly be the meaning of the verse (5:12), "I write to you through Silvanus the faithful brother." These words would most naturally be taken as meaning that Silvanus had written the letter to dictation; but they may imply that he had some active part in composing it. (2) A more serious argument can be based on the thought of the Epistle, which is saturated with Pauline influence. The writer must not only have been acquainted with Paul's ideas, but must have studied several of his Epistles, the language of which he repeatedly borrows. It is difficult to conceive of Peter, the elder Apostle, thus making himself Paul's pupil, especially since we know that he had finally ranged himself in opposition to Paul.

How the letter came to be attributed to Peter, we do not know. Perhaps when it was first sent out, it bore some official title which was afterwards believed to designate Peter and was changed into his personal name. Certainly it cannot have been written deliberately under a false name, for it was sent for a definite purpose to Christians in the East, who would be well aware that Peter had been long dead. Neither is there anything in the letter which a later teacher might wish to enforce by means of Peter's authority. The author of the Pastoral Epistles, in his desire to counteract a dangerous heresy, had a good reason for writing in the name of Paul; but no similar reason could exist in the case of this purely hortatory Epistle. The attribution to Peter must have been due to some misunderstanding, but how it arose we cannot now discover.

6. *Connection with Rome*

Whoever wrote it, the Epistle seems to have been written from Rome, and for this reason its association with the name of Peter is highly significant. No historical question has been more warmly debated than that of Peter's residence at Rome. From an early time, the Roman church based its claim to primacy on the ground that it represented Peter, to whom Christ himself had committed the oversight of the church. It thus became customary with Protestant writers, from the Reformation onward, to deny that Peter had ever been at Rome; but the tradition on this point is ancient and general. Perhaps the strongest of all the evidences that Peter was in some way connected with Rome is afforded by this Epistle. Even if he did not write it, the fact remains that it was ascribed to him, and this account of its authorship was not challenged. At a time when the facts about Peter must have been generally known, he was credited with a letter which had been sent out from Rome.

7. *The Spirits in Prison*

The Epistle is one of exhortation, and contains little of

strictly theological teaching. There is one passage, however, which stands alone in the New Testament and has given rise to much discussion — the famous passage on the descent of Christ to the world of the dead.

He was put to death in the flesh but made alive in the Spirit: by which also he went and preached to the spirits in prison who formerly were disobedient, when once the long-suffering of God waited in the days of Noah. [3:18-10.]

The same idea is repeated in 4:6,

For this cause the gospel was preached also to those that are dead, that they may be judged according to men in the flesh but live according to God in the Spirit.

The belief is here set forth that after his death Jesus, restored to life by the Spirit, appeared in the lower world, where the disobedient of past ages were imprisoned, and proclaimed his message to them, so that they also might have their chance of the new life. What was the origin of this belief, which was afterwards embodied in one of the clauses of the Apostles' Creed ("He descended into hell"), and has powerfully affected the Christian imagination in all ages? We are probably to assign it to several distinct causes. There was first the problem as to what had happened to Christ in the mysterious interval between his death and Resurrection. Like other men he must have passed into the abode of the dead, but there, too, he must have been different from others — a messenger from God. Again, there was the influence of the widespread myth of some demigod or hero, — Orpheus, Odysseus, Æneas — who had been privileged to descend alive into the lower world. Once more, and this must have been the chief motive at work, the belief grew up out of a religious interest. The church maintained that salvation was through Christ alone, but the question at once presented itself, as it has done ever since, "What of those who lived before Christ's coming"? Had they missed the offered salvation through no fault of their own, but from the mere accident that they had been born too soon? To answer this difficulty, there arose the doctrine that, as Christ had proclaimed his gospel to the living, so he had made it known to the dead. We are not to suppose that this belief originated with the author of I Peter: indeed he states it as one with which his readers are already familiar, and perhaps an allusion to it may be traced in Ephesians 4:9:

Now that he ascended, what is it but he also descended first into the lower parts of the earth?

But it is in I Peter that the belief first comes before us in explicit terms as part of the Christian faith.

CHAPTER XXIV

The Epistle of Jude and the Second Epistle of Peter

1. *Relation of the Two Epistles*

The name of Peter is attached to a second letter, much inferior in every respect to the first. It is pretty certainly a work of late origin, and was admitted into the New Testament only after long hesitation. In some Eastern churches it was never recognized, and there are Protestant scholars who hold that it ought even now to be removed from our Bibles. This, however, would be difficult, and not altogether desirable. Although it is the least valuable of the New Testament writings, the Epistle has merits of its own, and at least from a historical point of view is well worth preserving.

The problems of the Epistle depend in large measure on its relation to the short Epistle of Jude, and the two documents are so closely connected that they need to be considered together. There can be little doubt that Jude is the earlier of the two. Second Peter, in fact, is a revision of the Epistle of Jude, with additions to make it suitable to a new time and a different circle of readers.

2. *Jude's Epistle*

Jude is addressed "to those who are sanctified by God and preserved in Jesus Christ" (verse 1), but, though no particular church is mentioned, the author has probably some definite group in view. His work, while thrown into epistolary form, is more properly a pamphlet or polemical tract, occupied entirely with the heretical teachings which were finding their way into the church. The author beseeches his readers to hold fast to the accepted beliefs, and warns them against men who profess to be Christian and yet deny the true God and the Lord Jesus Christ (verse 4). Of the doctrine and morality of these

men, he draws a very dark picture, and threatens them with
the doom which had overtaken the wicked angels and the worst
sinners of Old Testament story. From various details in the
description, it is apparent that the heresy in question was of
the Gnostic type. It dealt in a secret wisdom expressed in
mysterious language (verse 16). It divided men into two
classes, the "material" and the "spiritual" (verse 19). It held
that the true God was different from the Creator, and that
Jesus was a man, united for the time being with the divine
Christ (verse 4). These were all characteristic beliefs of Gnosticism. It is evident, too, that the heretics belonged to that
wing of the Gnostic movement which adopted a loose attitude
toward morality. All experience has shown that when men
begin to think in some morbid way of the bodily life, they run
either to an extreme asceticism or to an utter disregard of the
moral obligations. They show contempt of the body, either by
maltreating it, or by giving free reign to all its appetites; and
which of the two attitudes they adopt is largely a matter of
chance. Gnosticism generally was of the ascetic type, but there
were also sects which set all moral laws at defiance, and it is
these which Jude has specially in mind. He does not argue
with the false teachers, but contents himself with denouncing
them, in language of striking vigor and eloquence.

3. Authorship of Jude

He calls himself "Judas the brother of James," and this
would seem to indicate that the James to whom he was related
was a man of high standing in the church, so that it was a
distinction to be his brother. Naturally we think of James of
Jerusalem. In this case, however, Jude would also be the
brother of Jesus, and he says nothing of this infinitely higher
relationship. Possibly he is silent from motives of reverence,
but it may be that the word "brother" has been interpolated,
and that the name originally stood "Judas the son of James."
In this case he would be merely a teacher who bore the name
of Judas, the commonest of all Jewish names, and whose father

had a name almost equally common. That he was not one of the primitive Apostles, may be inferred with certainty from various indications. (1) The description of the heretics is modeled, at least in part, on that which is found in the Pastoral Epistles. These Epistles themselves were written, as we have seen, a generation after the death of Paul. (2) The "Apostles of the Lord" are mentioned reverently as men of a former age who had foretold what is happening now (17, 18). (3) The true Christian faith is regarded as something old and well established, the "faith which was once for all delivered to the saints" (verse 3). (4) The type of Gnosticism attacked in the Epistle is one which came into existence considerably after Apostolic times.

4. *Value of Jude*

An interesting feature of this short writing is its use of Jewish apocalyptic books as if they were on the same level as the Old Testament Scriptures (verses 6, 9, 14, 15). Paul himself, on several occasions, makes similar quotations from apocalyptic literature, which appear to have been much prized and studied in the early church. Perhaps it was the value placed by Christians on this literature which created a prejudice against it in the minds of the Jews. After the second century, Judaism entirely disowned the books which had played so great a part in its development, and we owe their preservation to the church.

As a polemical pamphlet, directed against a form of doctrine which has now quite lost its meaning to us, the Epistle of Jude contains little that is of permanent religious value. Yet an exception must be made in favor of the concluding doxology, which is perhaps the most beautiful of all utterances of this kind in the New Testament.

Now unto him that is able to keep you from falling and to present you faultless before the presence of his glory with exceeding joy, to the only wise God, our Saviour, be glory and majesty, dominion and power both now and ever. Amen.

5. *Purpose of Second Peter*

The author of II Peter claims in no doubtful terms to be Peter, the Apostle. Not only does he state this emphatically in the opening verse, but in the course of the Epistle, he recalls the Transfiguration which he had himself witnessed (1:17, 18), and the prediction of Jesus as to the death in store for him (1:14). He makes mention of his previous Epistle (3:1), and alludes to Paul as his "beloved brother" (3:15). Thus we have no choice but to regard II Peter either as a genuine writing of the Apostle, or as a later work which was deliberately composed in his name.

Before trying to judge between these alternatives, it will be well to glance at the contents and purpose of the Epistle. The three chapters roughly correspond to three divisions of the thought. (1) The readers are exhorted to hold fast the faith they have received. (2) They are warned against false teachers who are seeking to mislead them. This chapter is closely similar to the Epistle of Jude, reproducing not only its ideas, but some of its actual words. One writer has plainly borrowed from the other, and all the indications seem to make it certain that priority is on the side of Jude. (3) It is affirmed, in the face of doubters, that the return of Christ and the end of the present world are close at hand. Since the great crisis may come on them at any moment, men cannot be too earnest in the Christian life.

In a broad sense, the motive of the Epistle is doubtless the same as that of the companion Epistle of Jude. The danger from heresy has become still graver than when Jude wrote, and his warnings are repeated with a new emphasis. But this general aim of combating heresy is conjoined with a more definite one which finds expression in the third chapter. The hope of the return of Christ had been vital for the primitive church, and now it was fading out. This was partly the result of the long delay in its fulfillment.

Where is the promise of his coming? For since the fathers fell asleep

all things continue as they were from the beginning of the creation?
[3:4.]

The decay of the primitive hope was also due partly to the
Gnostic teachings, which rationalized and too often evapo-
rated the beliefs on which Christianity was built. The Epistle
seems to be written with the special aim of reviving the old
confidence in the visible and immediate return of Christ. It is
easy to see that the testimony of Peter would carry a peculiar
weight when one of the original Christian doctrines was in
question.

6. Arguments against Authenticity

The evidences that Peter did not write the Epistle are over-
whelming, and none but the most conservative critics would
now defend its authenticity. (1) No reference to it can be
discovered before the very end of the second century, and it is
then mentioned with the gravest misgivings. For a long time
the church refused to admit it into the New Testament. (2) It
is manifestly based on the Epistle of Jude, which itself, as we
have seen, is a late work, dating from a time when Peter had
long disappeared from the scene. (3) The Second Epistle of
Peter is wholly different from the First in style and character,
and cannot be by the same author. Probably the First Epistle
is not by Peter, but no one can doubt that it has the better
claim to be the work of an Apostle. (4) Reference is made
(3:2) to the death of the "fathers," that is, the founders of
the church. Here the author himself inadvertently confesses
that he belongs to a later generation. (5) The Epistles of
Paul are placed in the same rank as "the other scriptures"
(3:16). This means that the idea of a New Testament of
equal value with the Old has now taken shape; and this did
not happen until far on in the second century.

The Epistle, therefore, cannot be accepted as a primitive
writing, much less as the work of Peter. Its true date cannot
be fixed with any certainty, but it may be assigned to some time
about 150 A.D., and it did not succeed in establishing itself

until the days when critical examination of the sacred writings was forbidden.

Several New Testament books are ascribed to authors who cannot have written them, but in all other cases this can be explained, either by the natural error of later editors, or by the recognized practice of the time. In II Peter alone we have to do with deliberate invention. The orthodox church and Gnosticism were in deadly conflict, and neither side was particularly scrupulous about its weapons. We know that the Gnostics produced a whole library of works to which they attached venerable Christian names, and the church was tempted to retaliate occasionally with the same device. Since Peter stood out as the first of the Apostles, his name was specially liable to misuse on the part of both orthodox and Gnostic controversialists. There still survive, at least in fragments, a Gospel of Peter, an Apocalypse of Peter, and the Acts of Peter. The Second Epistle must be assigned to the same group of spurious writings, though on its own merits it is far superior to the others, and for this reason found its way into the New Testament. It contains a number of impressive passages which give it real religious value, and it serves, better than any other writing, to link the New Testament with the literature of the succeeding age.

CHAPTER XXV

THE JOHANNINE LITERATURE

1. *Writings Ascribed to John*

Five New Testament writings are assigned by Christian tradition to the Apostle John — the Fourth Gospel, the book of Revelation, the First, Second, and Third Epistles of John. By far the most important of these writings is the Fourth Gospel, which is not only a work of supreme religious genius, but has had an incalculable influence on all subsequent Christian thought.

The study of this group of writings is beset with questions of extraordinary difficulty. There are two outstanding problems in the New Testament, the Synoptic and the Johannine; and it cannot be said that either of them is anywhere near a solution. Hundreds of the acutest minds have been concentrated on them for the last century; for they are not only fascinating from a purely literary point of view but are concerned with the fundamental records of the life of Christ. The Johannine problem is perhaps more baffling than the other. It becomes ever more intricate as we explore it, and at best we must be satisfied with certain broad conclusions which need to be accepted with due reserve.

2. *Connection of the Writings*

Before considering the problem it will be well to take a brief survey of the Johannine literature as a whole. It consists, in the first place, of three Epistles, one of them of some length, the others mere personal notes. From the close similarities of thought and language, it may be assumed that these are all by the same author. Then there is the Gospel, which certainly reflects the same type of thought as the Epistles.

Does it come from the same hand? A number of minor differences in teaching can be detected, and on this ground some scholars would give it a different authorship. But the differences are slight, in comparison with the large agreements. Above all, the First Epistle is in its way as fine a work as the Gospel. It is so strongly marked with genius and originality that it cannot easily be regarded as a mere imitation, and the natural presumption is that the man who wrote the Gospel also wrote the Epistle. As for the book of Revelation, Christian scholars have recognized from a very early time that it is entirely different in character from the other writings. The difference has sometimes been accounted for on the ground that in writing an apocalypse the author was obliged to throw his thought into another mold. But the thought itself is of a different texture and quality. The two books stand for types of Christian belief which are at opposite poles, and we cannot imagine the same man passing from one to the other. At the same time, the Fourth Gospel and the book of Revelation present not a few curious points of contact, in view of which it seems more than likely that, while written by different authors, they originated about the same time and in the same surroundings.

3. Place of Origin

What was this place of origin? In the case of Revelation the answer is certain. The book is addressed to the churches of Asia by a writer who himself belonged to the Asian community. His home was probably in Ephesus, the chief city of the province of Asia and the seat of the premier church. In view of the affinities of the other writings with Revelation, there is a strong probability that they also had their origin in the neighborhood of Ephesus, but of this there is no definite proof, and some critics are disposed, for various reasons, to assign them to Antioch. The earliest tradition, however, connects them with Ephesus, and it is borne out by almost all the characteristics of the writings themselves. They certainly proceed from the Hellenistic church, although there are many evidences that the writer was himself a Jew, well acquainted with Jewish ideas and customs and faithful to the Jewish outlook, even when thinking and writing as a Hellenist.

CHAPTER XXVI

THE FOURTH GOSPEL

1. *Traditional View*

Until the beginning of the last century, the Fourth Gospel was universally accepted as the work of John, the Apostle, the son of Zebedee. It was believed that during the troubles which had led to the fall of Jerusalem, he had migrated to Asia Minor, and that in Ephesus, when he was well over eighty years old and was the last survivor of the original band of disciples, he had written his reminiscences of the life of Jesus. A supreme value was thus placed on the Gospel as the record of a personal disciple, and of one who seemed to be designated in the Gospel itself as "the disciple whom Jesus loved." There are indications that this view of the authorship was called in question by an obscure sect in the second century, the so-called "Alogi," or "rejectors of the Logos"; but from the time of Irenæus (180 A.D.) to the nineteenth century, it was never seriously challenged.

2. *Evidence of the Appendix*

It has to be noted, however, that the Gospel itself is anonymous. It indeed closes with a chapter in which the "beloved disciple" takes a prominent place and the express statement is added, "This is the disciple who testifies these things and wrote these things, and we know that his testimony is true" (21:24). But this verse, as is evident from the wording, was added by some one else than the evangelist himself. The Gospel proper has ended with 20:31, and the final chapter is in the nature of an appendix, written in the name of some group of men who attest the value and authenticity of the work. In our time, a posthumous book is furnished with an introduction by the responsible editor; in the Fourth Gospel, the editors put in their word at the end. When we examine their testimony, however, there is one remarkable point which awakens our suspicion. They seem to be sure that the Gospel is by the beloved disciple, but are unwilling to say for certain who that disciple is. All that they do is to give a list of the disciples who were present with Jesus beside the lake (21:2), leaving us to guess for ourselves which of them was the disciple whom Jesus loved. Even in their list of seven, they include "two other disciples" who are not specified. From this it would appear as if those first editors were in some doubt, and did not care to commit themselves. Possibly they wish us to select from their list John, the son of Zebedee, but they leave the choice open. They are even at pains to throw in those two dark figures who make all identification impossible.

3. Modern Theories

It only began to be realized a century ago that the Gospel which had always been associated with the name of John was, in fact, anonymous. Since then the doubt as to its traditional authorship has been steadily growing, although the old view has so much in its favor that it has never ceased to maintain itself. No sooner has it seemed to be finally disposed of than there is a return to it in some new form. We have to reckon today, not with one or two theories of the origin of the Gospel, but with a large number — all of which have their advocates among reputable scholars. The chief theories may be indicated at the outset. (1) The evangelist was John, the Apostle, the son of Zebedee. (2) John, the Apostle, was only in a secondary sense the author. His teaching was worked up in literary form by one of his disciples, so that what we have is the Gospel "according to John," though not by John himself. (3) The author was not the Apostle but another John altogether, possibly "John the elder," who was prominent in the Asian church in the beginning of the second century. (4) The author is entirely unknown, and the church from the earliest time could only make guesses as to his identity. (5) The Gospel as we have it is a composite work, in which we can trace at least two, and perhaps a number, of hands. Some advocates of this view would grant that the Apostle John was responsible for the nucleus of the work, in the same way that Matthew may have drawn up the first short collection of Sayings which was finally expanded into our present Gospel of Matthew. Others would deny that John had any connection with the Gospel at all.

4. *Date*

On one point the modern research into the Johannine problem has tended increasingly towards agreement. Fifty years ago the view was commonly held by radical scholars that the Gospel was a work of late origin, reflecting the theological ideas which grew up towards the middle or end of the second century. This view can no longer be maintained. References to the Gospel can be discovered in the literature of about 150 A.D., and it seems to have been known in Gnostic circles as early as 130 A.D., and must then have been for some time in circulation. On the other hand, it can hardly have been written before the close of the first century, for the author shows acquaintance with the Gospel of Luke, which has to be dated about 90 A.D. It must, therefore, be assigned to some date between 95 and 115 A.D., and most probably belongs to the first decade of the second century. All the peculiarities of its teaching are found, on closer examination, to fit in with its origin about that time.

It is obvious that the farther back we can push the date of the Gospel, the more possible becomes the Johannine authorship. Assuming that John at the time of his companionship with Jesus was a very young man, it is conceivable that he survived until 100 A.D., and wrote the Gospel in his extreme old age. Yet it has sometimes been too readily assumed that, if its early date can be proved, the Gospel must necessarily be by John. The two questions are entirely separate and must not be confused.

In this connection, one fact is significant. Although in the second-century literature we have proof that the Gospel was in existence, it is never explicitly assigned to the Apostle until the time of Irenæus (about 180 A.D.). Indeed the very references which convince us of its early date appear to show that it was regarded somewhat doubtfully, and did not enjoy the same authority as the other Gospels. As already mentioned, there was at least one group in the church which refused to accept it. Such hesitation would have been impossible if the church had been fully aware that this Gospel was not a record at second hand, like Mark or Luke, but had come directly from one of the personal disciples.

5. Early Testimonies

A strong case, however, can be built up for the Johannine authorship; indeed the evidence might seem at first sight irresistible. Irenæus tells us that in his youth he was a pupil in Asia Minor of the aged Polycarp, and can well remember how the old man used to speak of his intercourse with John, the beloved disciple, from whose own lips he had heard the truth about Christ. A letter has come down to us written about that same time by Polycrates, the Bishop of Ephesus, to the Bishop of Rome, in which he asserts the lofty claims of the Ephesian church. One of them is that it had been the home of John, "who reclined on the bosom of the Lord." Evidence from such a quarter cannot be waved aside, for a bishop may be assumed to speak with good knowledge about things that happened in his own church only two generations before. Besides these direct testimonies, we have various stories, handed down in tradition but all of early origin, concerning John's life at Ephesus. There is a beautiful tale, for instance, of how the old Apostle was captured by robbers among the hills, and by his gentleness won over one of the wild men to be a Christian. A story of a different kind describes his horror when he met by chance with the heretic, Cerinthus. If there is truth in those various testimonies that John in his old age lived in Ephesus, there is no good reason to doubt that he wrote, or at least inspired, the Ephesian Gospel which bears his name.

At this point, however, we have to take into consideration a passage by Papias, that early Father whose references to the Synoptic Gospels have been quoted already, and who wrote about 140 A.D. Although the work of Papias has itself been lost, the passage in question is given verbatim by the church historian Eusebius, and is of primary importance for the discussion of the Johannine problem. After telling how in his younger days he had carefully collected all information about the early church which had come down by word of mouth, Papias goes on:

> If any one chanced to arrive who had been a follower of the elders, I would enquire as to the sayings of the elders, — as to what Andrew or Peter said, or Philip or Thomas or James or John or Matthew, or any other of the Lord's disciples; also as to what Aristion and the elder John, the Lord's disciples, say.

This passage has been the subject of endless discussion, but one point seems to stand out clearly. There were two Johns, one of them the Apostle, who was dead when Papias made his enquiries; another, who was living, and who for some reason was also called "the Lord's disciple." May it not be that the whole tradition as to John's residence at Ephesus grew out of the fact that the other John, known as "the elder," had lived in that city? It is possible that this second John, who was evidently much revered in the church and was ranked in a special sense as a "disciple of the Lord," came in course of time to be confused with the Apostle.

That John, the Apostle, was connected with Ephesus becomes more than ever doubtful, in view of the silence of Ignatius. Seven letters have come down to us, written in 116 A.D., by this Father while traveling as a captive through Asia Minor to fight with wild beasts in the Colosseum at Rome. One of the letters is to Ephesus, and the writer is at pains to compliment the Ephesian church on its proud traditions. He makes much of its association with Paul, but of John he says nothing.

This is almost inexplicable if that Apostle had died at Ephesus only a few years before, the most glorious figure in the whole Christian world. On the other hand, we know positively from the book of Revelation that there was a leader in the Asian church called John. "I, John, your brother and comrade, was in the isle of Patmos" (Rev. 1 :9). Here, and several times in the book, the writer gives his name as John, but never signifies that he was an Apostle. On the contrary, he calls himself a "prophet" (22 :9), and thinks of the "Apostles of the Lamb" as the great pioneers whose names are inscribed on the foundations of the heavenly city (21 :4). May it not have been this John who was so venerated in later days by the Ephesian church?

6. *Death of James and John*

In recent years, the attention of scholars has been directed to one possibility which would at once be fatal to the tradition that John, the Apostle, was the author of the Fourth Gospel. Papias, according to an ancient church writer, made a statement in his lost work to the effect that "James and his brother John were put to death by the Jews." This is second- or third-hand testimony, and in itself has little value; but it seems to be corroborated by the well-known passage in the Gospels where Jesus says to the sons of Zebedee, "Ye shall drink of the cup that I drink of and be baptised with the baptism that I am baptised withal" (Mark 10 :39). The natural meaning of these words is undoubtedly that both brothers were to be martyred, and we know from the book of Acts that this was the fate of James (Acts 12 :2). It is possible, in view of the notice in Papias, that John had suffered likewise, dying in Palestine long before the date of our Fourth Gospel. The evidence, however, is altogether too vague to admit of a positive conclusion. Thus far we have considered the external testimonies as to the authorship of the Gospel, and on the whole they balance each other. On the one side, we have a generally accepted tradition, dating back at least to the year 180 A.D., that John the

Apostle lived at Ephesus and there composed his Gospel. Unless there was some ground for this belief, we cannot fully explain how it grew up so early and in the very neighborhood where it might have been most easily disproved. On the other hand, the ancient writers who would most naturally have spoken of John's residence at Ephesus, seem to know nothing about it. Moreover, the tradition can be in some measure accounted for by a possible confusion of John, the Apostle, with another John.

7. The Beloved Disciple

The real decision on the Johannine question must ultimately turn on the internal evidence. Reference has been made already to that closing chapter, added by the first editors, in which it is distinctly stated that the beloved disciple wrote the Gospel; but we have seen that the editors are vague as to the identity of this disciple, who appears in the Gospel itself a number of times but who is never named. For the Synoptic writers, the disciple whom Jesus loved is undoubtedly Peter; but in the Fourth Gospel he is some other, who is sharply contrasted with Peter. Again and again, we are given to understand that Peter was secondary to the beloved disciple, and could approach Jesus only through his agency. The question of his identity will concern us later, but meanwhile it is necessary to look at one reference to him which in the present connection is the crucial one. In the chapter describing the death of Jesus, the evangelist says that the beloved disciple was standing near the Cross, and shortly afterwards he tells how Jesus' side was pierced and out of the wound flowed blood and water. To the truth of this incident, a solemn attestation is added, "He that saw it has borne witness; and that one knows that he speaks the truth, that you also may believe" (19:35). In the appendix to the Gospel, the language of this verse is repeated (21:-24), and the eyewitness at the Cross is identified with the beloved disciple. There is at least a possibility that the editors knew nothing of the authorship of the Gospel, and merely deduced their theory from the mysterious verse. They took it to mean that the eyewitness at the Cross was the beloved disciple, and that it was he who had "borne his testimony" in the Gospel before them.

There is reason to conclude, when the verse is carefully examined, that the editors were mistaken in their interpretation. It is not stated that the eyewitness was the disciple, and the Greek words appear to indicate two persons, both of them distinct from the evangelist himself. We might translate: "The man who saw it told my informant, and that informant can guarantee the man's truthfulness." In other words, the evangelist is anxious to impress on us that he is not reporting idle hearsay, but has learned from a direct source this particular incident, in which he perceives a deep significance. But however the verse is to be explained, it is not meant to tell us anything about the authorship of the Gospel. We can infer from it nothing more than that some one saw with his own eyes this mysterious incident and bore witness to it afterwards.

The evidence of the appendix, therefore, is very doubtful. Those early editors believed that the Gospel was written by the beloved disciple, but most probably had no other ground for this belief than a verse which they had not rightly understood. Assuming that the beloved disciple was the evangelist, they most likely identified him with John, but on this point they do not venture to make any definite statement. So from the closing chapter, which appears at first sight to make the authorship of the Gospel quite explicit, we really gather nothing more than that it was a problem from the first. It had come, we cannot tell how, into the hands of those editors, and they recognised its supreme value. They felt that no one could have written it but one who stood closer to Jesus than any other. But to this chosen disciple they were unable to attach a name.

8. *Internal Evidence for the Tradition*

The appendix, therefore, does not afford any certain guidance, and we are thrown back on the Gospel itself. It nowhere offers a clue to its authorship, but some of its features might seem to imply a close acquaintance with the life of Jesus. (1) Where the other Gospels are vague, this one is often precise in matters of detail, giving names to minor personages and exact notes of times and localities (e. g., "the servant's name was Malchus," 18:10; "six days before the Passover he came to Bethany," 12:1; "these things were done in Bethabara beyond Jordan," 1:28). This, however, means little, for the tendency of tradition is to grow more circumstantial as time goes on. One has only to think how a floating anecdote becomes attached, in the course of time, to some particular man, or how the guide who conducts you over a battlefield or historic building is able to point to the very spots where each of the famous incidents took place. (2) Much more important is the geographical knowledge which the Gospel displays, often unconsciously. There is every sign that the author was well acquainted with Palestine. In this respect, he seems to be superior to the Synoptic writers, and some of his data, which were formerly called in question, have been signally confirmed by modern exploration. But this familiarity with the country in which Jesus had worked does not by any means imply that he had gone over the scenes in Jesus' company. (3) On a number of points, the Fourth Gospel is nearer than the others to historical facts. This is particularly true in its account of the Passion. Where the Synoptic Gospels place the death of Jesus on Passover day, John makes it happen on the day before, and all considerations make it practically certain that this was the true date. In like manner, it is John alone who mentions Annas, the ex-high priest, in connection with the trial (18:13), and from all that we know of Jewish history at that time it is more than likely that this sinister politician was behind the whole plot against Jesus. So in other respects, the Fourth Gospel shows a real knowledge of the facts, and this is the strongest argument in favor of the traditional authorship. Most scholars would now admit that whoever wrote the book had access to some good sources of information; but here again there is no ground for concluding that he was no other than the Apostle John.

9. *Negative Evidence*

On the other hand, the negative evidence is exceedingly strong, so strong that even conservative critics would now claim for John only some indirect part in the authorship. (1) The writer views the life of Jesus in the light of theological conceptions. Certainly we can well conceive of John in his old age as pondering over the wonderful things he had witnessed and discerning in them, as he could not do at the time, a deep spiritual significance. But the light in which they are viewed is that of Hellenistic theology. Would John, to whom Paul refers in Galatians as one of the "pillars" (Gal. 2:9) of Jewish Christianity, have turned in his old age to those foreign speculations? At the time of the council of Jerusalem, when he looked so doubtfully on Paul's teaching, he must have been a man considerably over forty, and the complete change in his whole mental attitude is difficult to conceive.

(2) The life of Jesus is viewed in a manner which would hardly have been possible to an immediate disciple. In parts of the Gospel of Mark we probably have the reminiscences of Peter, and the story is vivid and realistic, full of graphic and life-like touches. This is what we should expect from one who had actually known Jesus; but in the Fourth Gospel, the humanity of Jesus falls into the background, the history is everywhere subordinated to abstract, theological ideas. It is almost impossible to believe that a personal disciple could thus have merged the actual figure of Jesus in the conception of a divine being, answering to the requirement of Alexandrian philosophy.

(3) When compared to the Synoptics, the Fourth Gospel is for the most part remote from the actual conditions. It knows

nothing of the party divisions in the time of Jesus, and speaks of his opponents vaguely as "the Jews." It scarcely mentions the Kingdom of God, which was undoubtedly the main theme of Jesus' teaching, and makes him speak almost exclusively of his own Person. We should never have learned from it that Jesus' favorite method of teaching was by parables; the one or two parables ascribed to him (e. g., the Good Shepherd, the Vine and the Branches) are not parables in the true sense, but mystical allegories. It may be added that the history, as we know it from Mark, is dislocated in the Fourth Gospel. The main scene of the ministry is transposed from Galilee to Judæa; important incidents are put into a new setting or omitted altogether. In several points, as we have seen, John seems to be working on a better tradition; but it can hardly admit of doubt that the Synoptic story, taken as a whole, is more true to life. How does it happen that the personal disciple has misunderstood the facts, while men of the second generation, like Mark and Luke, have given them correctly? The natural answer is surely that the Fourth evangelist cannot have been a personal disciple, but was further removed from the facts than the other writers.

(4) While he differs from the Synoptists, the Fourth evangelist is dependent on them. This is perhaps the crucial argument against the Johannine authorship. The writer speaks of countless acts of Jesus which he has left unrecorded (20:30); yet most of his material, while it is often presented in a much modified form, is taken from the Synoptic Gospels. Is it conceivable that one of the original disciples who would have so much to tell that was entirely new, would content himself with repeating what had been told already in documents compiled by men who had no direct knowledge of Jesus? It is not as if those other evangelists had recorded everything, so that nothing was left to a later writer, however well informed, but to traverse the same ground. Admittedly they had touched only on a few episodes, and these not always the most important. The Fourth evangelist had a clear field open to him, and if he

borrowed from his predecessors, the reason can only have been that he had little material except that which they gave him. All that he had to contribute, apart from a few extra data of unequal value, was his new interpretation of facts already known.

10. *John the Elder*

It is difficult, then, to regard the Gospel as the work of a personal disciple, and the view has been held by some scholars that the author was not the Apostle, but that other John, who went by the name of "John the elder." A confusion between the later and the earlier teacher may indeed explain much that is perplexing in the Johannine tradition; but, from the mere fact that the two Johns came to be identified, we cannot infer that if one of them did not write the Gospel, it must have been the other. One argument for this position has often been deduced from the two short Epistles, Second and Third John. There is every reason to believe that they are by the author of the Gospel, and he expressly designates himself in both of them as "the elder." This, however, seems to have been the common title, about the beginning of the second century, of all teachers who had some direct relation to the primitive church; and there is no ground for assuming that the "elder" who wrote the Epistles was the elder John. A much better case can be made out for the view that this elder John was the author of Revelation. The man who received those visions in the isle of Patmos distinctly calls himself John, and we know from other sources that John, the elder, lived about that time in Asia, and that he was strongly in sympathy with the apocalyptic mode of thought. But if he wrote the book of Revelation, his authorship of the Gospel seems to be excluded. The two works are so entirely different in character that it is hardly possible to think of them as written by the same man.

11. *Composite Authorship*

Of late years, a new mode of approach to the Johannine problem has been adopted by many scholars. Formerly it was

taken for granted that the Fourth Gospel, more than any other
New Testament book, was a unity. It was compared, in a famous simile, to that seamless robe of Christ of which it tells us,
woven of one piece throughout. This view of it has now been
challenged, and some of the foremost critics of our time are
agreed that the Gospel is a composite work. They point to
many inconsistencies in its thought, to awkward transitions in
the narrative, to repetitions and misplaced comments, to passages which break the continuity and cannot well be explained
as the Gospel now stands. Jesus, for instance, resumes his
teaching (12:42), after we have been expressly told a few
verses previously that his public ministry had now closed; in
14:31 he says, "Arise and let us go hence," and yet continues
his discourse through another three long chapters. The trouble
with the theory is that, when we once begin to break up the
Gospel, it becomes so very composite that it falls to pieces; no
one is able to explain how such an intricate mosaic could have
been put together at all. Moreover it insists that the book
should conform to logical standards which were quite alien to
the writer's mind. But while the theory as a whole cannot be
accepted, it has served to draw attention to some facts which
had previously been overlooked. There can be little doubt, for
one thing, that the Gospel, as we now have it, has undergone a
process of editing, perhaps at the hands of those men who
added the closing chapter. Verses have been inserted and
others, it may be, omitted; statements have been changed occasionally from their original form so that they are now in conflict with the teaching as a whole. It is more than likely, too,
that there has been some dislocation in the arrangement of
passages. This may have happened by accident, or perhaps
the author had written his work disconnectedly and left it without a final revision — some of it possibly in loose leaves, which
the editors had to find a place for as best they could. But when
all this has been taken into account two things appear to stand
out as indubitable — that the Gospel, in spite of minor inconsistencies, is a homogeneous work, and that it everywhere

bears the stamp of the highest genius. It cannot have come into existence by some haphazard process of compilation or collaboration. Only one man in the course of centuries is capable of such thought as we find in the Fourth Gospel, and we cannot imagine that a group of men, all of them of that magnitude, were teaching at the same time in the church at Ephesus.

12. *Results of the Inquiry*

Surveying the investigation as a whole, we have to admit that all the results which have yet been obtained are inconclusive. The author of the Gospel was a religious thinker of the first rank, next to Paul the greatest and most original mind of the early church, but we cannot even form a guess as to his identity. It may appear strange that a man so outstanding should be quite unknown, but we have to remember that the period of fifty years after the death of Paul is the most obscure in all Christian history. Scarcely a name has come down to us out of that period, and there may well have been teachers of the highest gifts of whom no record was preserved. It seems evident, too, that the evangelist took pains to leave his work anonymous. Perhaps he felt that it would carry more weight if it were wrapt in a certain mystery and conveyed the witness of the Spirit rather than that of some particular man. Since even the earliest editors could offer only conjectures as to the author, there is little chance of our discovering his secret now. One thing is certain, that this unknown genius had penetrated in a marvelous manner into the inmost mind of Jesus. The early editors were not far wrong when they put forth the Gospel as written by the Beloved Disciple. They could not give him a name, but they felt, as the whole church has felt ever since, that here we have a record of the life of Christ by that follower of his who was spiritually closest to him and understood him best.

13. *Plan of the Gospel*

The aim of the Synoptic Gospels is to recount the events of
Jesus' ministry in the order in which they happened, and so
present something like a consecutive history. The Fourth
Evangelist also writes the life of Jesus, but his interest is not
historical. It might almost be said that for him Jesus is a
static figure, and that the progress is on the part of men in
their attitude to Jesus. The true Light has come into the
world; how will the world receive him? How will men be attracted or repelled by him, and so manifest themselves in their
real characters? So apart from the Prologue, which is introductory, and the twenty-first chapter, which is a later supplement, the Gospel falls into three great sections, approximately
of the same length. (1) In Chapters 1-6, we are told how
Jesus appeared, and men began to take sides for and against
him. Those who were of the light were drawn towards him;
those who were of the darkness held aloof. (2) In Chapters
7-12, the children of darkness become ever more hostile and
definitely reject him, while his own people advance to a stronger faith. (3) In Chapters 13-20, the love and the hatred both
reach their climax. First we have the meeting at the Supper,
in which Jesus is alone with his chosen disciples and takes them
into his fullest confidence. Then he goes forth to be crucified
by the hostile world.

14. *Discourse and Narrative*

Like Matthew and Luke, the Gospel contains a large element of discourse, interwoven with the narrative; indeed by
far the greater part of the Gospel consists of things spoken
by Jesus. When we look more closely, however, we find that
the Johannine discourses are related to the narrative in a different way from those of the Synoptic writers. In Matthew
more especially, the connection is artificial. What the evangelist gives us is simply a large number of sayings which had
come to him in detached form, and which he has arranged in
groups according to subject. These combinations of sayings

are introduced as discourses at convenient places in the narrative. In the Fourth Gospel the incidents and the discourses have a real correspondence with each other. Jesus feeds the five thousand, and then expounds the miracle in its inward significance (6); he heals a blind man and is thus led to speak of himself as the Light of the world (9); the Supper discourses have all a direct bearing on the solemn occasion on which they were uttered. In the narrative portion of his work, as well as in the discourses, the evangelist differs from the Synoptists. Instead of trying like them to bring in all that was remembered of the life of Jesus, he is content to select a few incidents, with which he deals elaborately. It has been calculated that in the whole Gospel we have the record of only eigtheen or nineteen days altogether. Not only so, but the events selected are those which carry a spiritual meaning along with their literal one. It is sometimes asserted that the evangelist resolves the life of Jesus into a sort of allegory, valuing the facts only as a vehicle for some purely religious truth. This is by no means his intention. The great thesis of his Gospel is that Jesus was not the Word merely, but the Word made Flesh; and the reality of the incidents is all-important to him. Yet his aim is always to present the life of Jesus, not only as it was while he dwelt on earth, but as it still is, in the inward experience of the believer. The outward events are made, as it were, transparent, so that we may see through the earthly fact to its inward and eternal meaning.

15. *The Gospel and Its Time*

The Fourth Gospel, therefore, is at once a record of the life of Christ and an interpretation. This was recognized as early as 200 A.D., by Clement of Alexandria, when he said: "After the other evangelists had written down the facts of the history, John wrote a spiritual Gospel." But to understand the manner in which he interpreted the life, we must keep in mind the conditions of the church in those years just after the close of the first century.

Since the death of Paul, there had been several developments of far-reaching consequence. (1) The Christian movement had now identified itself fully with the Gentile world. All his lifetime Paul had been engaged in his great conflict with Judaism, and his victory had been so complete that the meaning of his struggle was forgotten. It was assumed as self-evident that the gospel and the Law were wholly separate. Few Christians, indeed, had any distinct idea of what was implied in the Law. (2) The conception of a Catholic church had now taken root. In the earlier time each community had stood by itself, with its own beliefs and customs. This independence had been jealously guarded as one of the most valuable of Christian privileges. Now it had become evident that if the church was to survive in face of all the hostile forces, it must be united. It must arrive at a common type of government and worship and doctrine. The separate communities must learn to merge themselves in a Catholic or universal church. (3) The heresies which were already springing up in the later days of Paul had made alarming progress, and were all included in what is known as the Gnostic movement. Broadly speaking, Gnosticism was the attempt to transform Christianity into a speculative system. It sought to give depth and permanence to the religion by dissolving the historical facts and regarding Christ simply as a divine principle, or the revealer of a secret wisdom by which men could attain to a higher life. (4) Christian thought had now become Hellenized — that is to say it worked with Greek, instead of Jewish, ideas. Not only did the Gospel appeal more directly to the Gentiles when it was thus expressed in their own terms of thought, but there was much in its message which became more intelligible. The ideas taken over from Greek philosophy were in many ways more adequate to the purpose of Jesus than those which had come to him through Judaism.

The Fourth Evangelist writes for that later time in which so many new interests had arisen and the mode of conceiving the Christian message had so radically changed. It has com-

monly been held that his work was that of an innovator, that
he took the Apostolic teaching as it had hitherto been understood and boldly transformed it into something entirely different. There is truth in this view, in so far as he belonged to his
own age and was in sympathy with its new outlook. But he
was much more a conservative than an innovator. He saw
that Christianity, under the later influences, was in danger of
losing itself in mystical and philosophical speculation, and his
aim was to anchor it again to the primitive tradition. That is
why his work takes the form of a Gospel, a record of the life
of Christ. He feels profoundly that everything vital in the
Christian message was given in Jesus, and that it can never go
beyond him. Other teachers were intent on the new philoso-
phies, which seemed to offer a profounder knowledge; John
falls back on the historical revelation, and is convinced that
the one thing necessary is to understand it better. Accepting
all that has come to him through the later thought, he sets
himself, in the light of this fuller knowledge, to obtain a deeper insight into the life and teaching of Jesus himself.

16. *Controversial Interests*

There is one respect in which the Gospel cannot be rightly
appreciated unless we view it in its relation to its own time.
Its chief aim is undoubtedly a religious one, as the evangelist
himself declares in his emphatic closing words, "These things
are written that ye may believe that Jesus is the Christ, the
Son of God, and that believing ye may have life in his name"
(20:31). Yet it cannot be doubted that this Gospel, moving
though it does in a timeless spiritual atmosphere, is in some
of its aspects a controversial work. At least three motives of
a polemical nature can be distinguished. (1) The enemies with
whom Jesus came into conflict are described in general terms
as "the Jews," and from the historical point of view this account of them is meaningless. Jesus was himself a Jew, and
all the people with whom he held intercourse were Jews. It
was not the Jews as a nation, but certain groups of them, par-

ticularly the Pharisees and Sadducees, who were antagonistic
to Jesus. But when the Fourth Gospel was written, the Jewish
people as a whole had become hostile to the church, and their
enmity was especially dangerous, since they were furnished
with weapons taken directly from Scripture. In every city the
church and the synagogue were in bitter opposition, and it is
this Jewish controversy of his own day which the evangelist
reads back into the lifetime of Jesus. He puts in the mouth of
Jesus' opponents the criticisms which were constantly urged,
at the beginning of the second century, by the Jewish enemies
of the church — that it was blasphemous to make a man equal
with God, that the facts of Jesus' life were in conflict with
Messianic prophecy, that the Eucharistic beliefs were absurd
and childish. Objections of this kind, so different from those
which Jesus himself had to answer, have plainly grown out
of the later controversy. (2) Again, the evangelist shows a
peculiar interest in John the Baptist, and is at pains to show
that while he was a noble figure, he was subordinate to Jesus,
and came only to bear witness to him. This attitude toward John
the Baptist becomes intelligible when it is remembered that he
founded a sect which continued long after his death and had
established itself, as we can infer from the book of Acts (19:-
3, 4) in Ephesus. These followers of John apparently sought
to exalt their own master to the rank of Messiah, and one of
the evangelist's aims is to answer them, and to win them over,
if possible, to the Christian side. (3) Underlying the whole
Gospel, there is an opposition to Gnostic teaching. The Gnostics had emptied the earthly life of Jesus of all value. They
had distinguished between the man Jesus and a heavenly being
who for a time was united with him. They had denied the
reality of Jesus' death. The First Epistle of John is written
for the direct purpose of counteracting these errors, and there
can be little doubt that a similar motive runs through the Gospel. This is clearly announced in the great opening statement,
"The Word was made Flesh," that is, the eternal divine principle became truly man. But while opposing Gnosticism, the

writer shows a curious sympathy with some of its positions —
so much so that his work was early accepted in Gnostic circles
and has sometimes been ascribed, both in ancient and modern
times, to Gnostic authorship. It aims at overcoming Gnosticism by meeting it in a broadminded and sympathetic spirit.
The evangelist perceives that in this heresy there are elements
of truth which largely explain its success, and for which he
would like to make room in the orthodox Christian faith.

17. *The Church*

Apart from these controversial interests, there is a practical one which plays a great part in the Gospel. It never mentions the church by name, but in some respects it is the most
ecclesiastical book in the New Testament. Writing at a time
when the idea of a Catholic church was taking shape in men's
minds, the evangelist is anxious to help it forward. His Gospel
culminates in the seventeenth chapter, the prayer which Jesus
utters just before his death, on behalf of the future church.

I pray not for these alone but for those who shall believe on me
through their word; that they all may be one, I in them and thou in me,
that they may be made perfect in one. [17:20 f.]

Those inconsistencies in the thought of the Gospel, which have
been taken as evidence of composite authorship, are more
probably due to this desire for a church that will be truly
united. Christianity is presented in such a manner as to comprehend all the elements which have hitherto been in conflict.
Men of all parties are to recognize in the message of Christ
the very things they have been standing for, so that they may
give up their hostile attitude to one another and all join together in one universal church.

18. *The Logos Doctrine*

All other interests in the Gospel are subsidiary to the religious one. The evangelist writes in order that "you may believe
that Jesus Christ is the Son of God, and that believing you
may have life in his name" (20:31). He sets himself, there-

fore, to tell who Jesus was, what he did and taught while he lived on earth, how he had passed through death into a higher state of being, in which he is still present with his people. Thus far it may be said that John's purpose is the same as that of the other evangelists, but he goes about it in a different way. The others rest their appeal on the assumptions of Jewish apocalyptic. They try to show that Jesus was the promised Messiah, and tell how he proclaimed the Kingdom of God, and the conditions on which men may enter it. John gives up the apocalyptic ideas altogether. He interprets the Christian message in terms of that conception which had grown up in Greek philosophy and had been developed by the famous Jewish thinker, Philo of Alexandria.

In Greek thought, the ultimate principle of the world was Reason (Logos), which in the Stoic teaching took the place of God. Philo, with his strong Jewish convictions, could not accept Reason as ultimate. He made it subordinate to God, who is himself transcendent and unknowable, but projects from his being a second divine principle by which he creates and governs the world. The term "Logos" is used in Greek for both "reason" and "word," and Philo took advantage of this double meaning. To the Logos he attributes all the functions which belong in the Old Testament to the sovereign Word of God. We have seen that already, in writings like Colossians and Hebrews, the idea of the Logos had made its entrance into Christian thought. The evangelist takes hold of it and makes it the basis of his interpretation. Christ was the Logos or divine Word, and in this light the whole significance of his life and of his work for men must be explained.

The Gospel thus opens with a Prologue of eighteen verses, which may be regarded as John's substitute for the account of the miraculous birth in Matthew and Luke. For the Fourth Evangelist, it did not matter how Jesus had entered into the world, for he had been divine from all eternity.

In the beginning was the Word, and the Word was with God, and the Word was of divine nature. All things were made by him, and without him was not anything made that was made. In him was life, and the life was the light of men.

In the body of the Gospel Jesus is never called Logos or described in the metaphysical language of the Prologue; but the reason doubtless is that when he became flesh, the name Logos ceased to be applicable to him. The ideas of the Prologue are those which pervade the Gospel. They are stated explicitly at the very outset, that we may carry them with us and so understand the life that follows. The Prologue might be compared to the opening of an old fairy tale, in which the true origin of the hero is recounted. He is to wander into sordid surroundings and endure contumely and hardship; but we follow his history, knowing that all the time he is born a king.

19. *Christ as Life-Giver*

As the Logos, Christ came forth from God and shared in his nature, and it is from this point of view that John explains his work. Men are creatures of flesh and are thereby debarred from that true life which exists only in God. But Christ, who is himself divine, possessed that life of God and imparted it to his people. The great word of the Gospel is Life; the Synoptic idea of the Kingdom of God disappears, and in place of it we have the message of "eternal life." It is everywhere assumed that through Christ we obtain a higher kind of life, compared with which our natural state is more truly one of death. "I came that they might have life, and have it more abundantly" (10:10).

John has much to say as to how this divine life is imparted. It exists in Christ, and men obtain it by believing in him, by knowing him, by doing his commandments. But all this is not enough. The life was inherent in Christ's personality, and it cannot pass from Christ to men unless they in some way become one with him. In the last resort John's thought is mystical. He conceives of the believer as entering into a relation to Christ like that of the branches to the vine (15:1-7). In that union with Christ, men draw into themselves like an actual substance the life which resides in him.

20. *The Return of Christ*

Here we come on one of the characteristic ideas of John, and one which determines all his presentation of the Gospel history. Since in his own Person Christ is the life-giver and can impart the life only through immediate union with himself, it might appear as if his work could be valid merely for the brief time when he sojourned with men. John himself insists on the primary value of those days when the Word was manifested in the flesh. Yet he holds that this revelation was only the prelude to another, in which Christ communicates himself no less directly. It had always been the Christian belief that the Lord had departed in order to return, not in weakness as he had come at first, but in his Messianic glory. More than two generations had now gone by and there was still no sign of that glorious advent, and many had begun to fear that the hope was vain. In several of the later New Testament books there is an effort to convince the doubters that, in spite of the long delay, the Lord's promise will presently be fulfilled. The Fourth Evangelist adopts a different method. He declares that Christ has already returned, not in visible form on the clouds of heaven, but as an inward presence in the hearts of his people.

I will not leave you desolate; I will come unto you. Yet a little while and the world beholdeth me no more, but ye behold me. If a man love me he will keep my word, and my Father will love him, and we will come unto him and make our abode with him. [14:18 f.]

This is the significance which John assigns to the death of Christ. He thinks of it as the act in which Christ threw off the limitations of space and time and entered on a larger spiritual existence, in which he would continue always and be present everywhere and dwell with men inwardly like part of their own being. In a real sense, he would be closer to his people after his death than in his lifetime. Under conditions of ordinary human intercourse they had been separated from him; they could apprehend his mind only imperfectly. In the future, when they knew him as a spiritual presence, there would be no barriers. Their communion with him would be complete and unbroken. Sometimes John speaks of Christ himself as returning; sometimes he declares that after Christ's departure the Spirit will be sent as a "Comforter," or Supporter, to take his place. Between the two ideas of the indwelling Christ and the Spirit, there is no real distinction. The Comforter of whom the believer is conscious in his inward experience is no other than Christ himself in his new and higher manifestation. Throughout the Supper discourses the promise, "I will come to you," keeps interchanging with the other, "The Spirit will come to you."

21. *Christ in History and in Faith*

This conception, that Christ has returned and is now present with his disciples just as really as when he lived on earth, is central to the Gospel, and serves to explain much in it that is perplexing. Its portrait of Jesus, as compared with that in the Synoptic Gospels, seems lacking in reality. We feel at times that what we have before us is not a human figure at all. But the reason is that the evangelist is trying to read back into the earthly life of Jesus his inward experience of the abiding Christ. More than once the thought is expressed that there was much in the life that was hidden at the time, and has only now begun to disclose itself.

I have many things to say unto you, but ye cannot bear them now. When he, the Spirit of truth, is come he will guide you unto all truth. [16:12, 13.]

He shall glorify me, for he will take of mine and will show it unto you. [16:14.]

The aim of the Gospel is to present the life, not merely as it happened, but in that fuller light which has now been thrown on it by the Spirit. Yet to this aim there is another side which is equally prominent. It is impressed on us that while we know the life through the later revelation, yet we are to find the key to all later revelation in the life itself. Paul had declared that, for those to whom the glorified Lord had revealed himself, the knowledge of "Christ after the flesh" had ceased to be necessary. John has realized the value of the actual history. He is aware that the more we ponder it, the more fully we shall apprehend the work of Christ as it is now, in the world's progress and in the experience of faith. All that the Spirit does is to unfold, ever more largely and clearly, the revelation which was given once for all in the actual life of Christ.

The Fourth Gospel is thus at once a historical narrative and a record of spiritual facts. It describes how Jesus was known in his lifetime to his immediate disciples, and how he is known as an inward presence to those in every generation who believe on him. John is convinced that the invisible Christ whom we apprehend by faith is the same with Jesus, who appeared at a given time in Palestine, and his aim is to blend together the two phases of the manifestation, so that through the one we may better understand the other. It is owing to this double purpose that the Gospel has so often been misjudged. Sometimes it has been taken as literal history, and the author has been condemned for misrepresenting the facts. Sometimes it has been set down as nothing but an allegory or spiritual romance, of no value whatever for our knowledge of the real Jesus. Both these estimates are wrong, for the Gospel is at once a work of history and a book of Christian devotion. The writer has kept far more closely to the facts than is often supposed, and appears to have had sources of information which were historically of great value. But the history is everywhere interpreted in the light of Christian reflection and mystical experience. The evangelist has himself tried to realize the promise which he ascribes to Jesus: "The Spirit will take of the things which are mine, and will show them unto you."

22. *Theology and Religion*

There can be no question that he has succeeded marvelously in his purpose. In all ages, men have turned to his Gospel as the profoundest and most satisfying of all interpretations of

the life of Christ. His spiritual insight is never at fault; and
yet we feel, as we examine his work carefully, that he was
hampered by his theological assumptions. He accepts the belief, current in the Christian thought of his time, that the
Logos manifested itself in Christ, and he tries to reconcile the
facts of the history with this conception. But the task was
an impossible one. The Logos doctrine was metaphysical,
taken over from Greek philosophy, and the many-sided personality of Jesus could not be rightly defined in terms of this
abstract idea. In the attempt to bring the historical life into
harmony with all the requirements of Logos speculation, there
is something forced and unnatural. Too often as he passes
before us in the Fourth Gospel Jesus becomes little more than
a theological principle or a symbol of the divine nature. Those
profitless controversies on the Person of Christ which occupied the church from the third to the sixth century and at last
emptied Christianity of much of its meaning, had their roots
in the metaphysic of the Fourth Gospel. It was in those centuries that the evangelist was given the proud title of John
the Divine, that is, the master theologian. Yet the religious
value of the Gospel lies quite apart from its theology. Multi-
tudes of readers have treasured it as the most inspiring of all
books, without ever suspecting that behind its simple record
there is a philosophical theory. For this evangelist, like the
others, is concerned in the last resort with the actual history.
In scenes of matchless power and beauty he describes Jesus as
the immortal Friend who gave himself for men and who,
through the vision of his own life, taught them to see God.
John is at his greatest when he forgets his theology and is content to make us feel, as he had felt it himself, this meaning of
the life of Jesus.

23. *Additions to the Gospel*

Although the composite authorship of the Gospel cannot be
admitted, it contains at least two passages which were not in
the original work. One of them is that closing chapter which

was added by the early editors. In itself the chapter is one of the most exquisite in the New Testament, but it is different in character from the rest of the Gospel. That story of the risen Christ appearing to his disciples at the lake of Galilee, may be compared to Luke's account of the journey to Emmaus, and is possibly drawn from the same source. It may be conjectured that the editors, wishing to add a final chapter, availed themselves of one of the traditions which the Synoptic writers had omitted, and which they wished to preserve for its own sake. Into this story they weave their testimony as to the authorship of the Gospel by the Beloved Disciple. The other extraneous passage is that concerning the woman taken in adultery (8 :1-11). In the oldest manuscripts this passage is wanting, and in others it is marked as doubtful, or assigned to a different place or to another Gospel altogether. The best modern editions of the Greek text print it by itself, at the end of the Gospels. In this passage also we are to see a stray fragment of tradition which the church was unwilling to lose. Possibly it had been handed down by word of mouth; more likely it had a place in one of the early documents which had gone to the making of the Synoptic Gospels. Why it had been left out from Matthew and Luke we cannot tell; but though it has no right to stand in the Fourth Gospel, we may be grateful to the early editors who inserted it, and thus preserved for us a priceless addition to our record of the life of Christ.

CHAPTER XXVII

THE FIRST EPISTLE OF JOHN

1. *Epistolary Form*

The longest of the three letters assigned to John is classed in our Bibles among the "general Epistles," but this view of it is almost certainly wrong. Although it bears no address and mentions nobody by name, it seems to have been intended for some definite community. This, indeed, is the chief reason why much in the Epistle is now obscure. The writer is concerned throughout with a given situation. He takes for granted that his readers are acquainted with the persons and events he has in mind, and makes allusions, in almost every paragraph, to which the clue has now been lost.

It has sometimes been held that the so-called "Epistle" ought rather to be regarded as a homily. There are no salutations at the beginning or end; the writer has nothing to say about himself, and touches on no matters of everyday interest. At the same time, he explicitly states that he is not speaking but writing (2:1, 7, 12, 13, 14) and, if he does not use the set epistolary forms, it is probably because he addresses the community as a whole. He writes a letter, but a pastoral letter, in which there seems to be no occasion for specific notices and greetings.

2. *Date*

The date of the letter can be roughly determined, both from external and internal evidence. A quotation from it is found in the Epistle of Polycarp, which was written about 117 A.D., and everything in the letter itself points to some year in the beginning of the second century. The distinction of Jews and Gentiles in the church is never mentioned, and has apparently

disappeared; the Christian religion has been so long in existence that its precepts may be spoken of as "old commandments"
(2:7); the Gnostic movement had begun, but had not yet
grown to its developed form. In its teaching, too, the Epistle
reflects the period about the beginning of the second century.
It is tinged with the philosophic ideas which had come in after
the Apostolic Age, but still retains the freshness of outlook
and the religious glow which marked the earlier days. On
every ground, the Epistle may be assigned to much the same
time as the Fourth Gospel.

3. *Authorship*

That it was by the same author there is no good reason for
doubting, though in some respects it shows points of difference. For instance, the return of Christ, to which a spiritual
meaning is given in the Gospel, seems to be understood literally (2:28 f.); the name "Paraclete" is applied, not to the
Spirit, but to Christ himself (2:1); much more emphasis is
laid than in the Gospel on the fact of sin and on the death of
Christ as the propitiation for sin. It must be remembered,
however, that the Epistle is written for a special purpose, in
view of which the Christian teaching has to be presented from
a new point of view. The differences, indeed, are themselves
a proof that the evangelist himself wrote the letter. An imitator would have been careful to copy his model exactly, while
the original teacher could feel himself free to deal as he
pleased with his own ideas.

The differences need to be searched for, but the agreements
lie on the surface. For almost every verse in the Epistle some
analogy can be found in the Gospel. We meet everywhere with
the same style and vocabulary, the same type of thought. Not
only so, but the writer handles all the great Johannine ideas
with complete mastery, and in some respects they are more
finely expressed in the Epistle than in the Gospel. Two works
so like one another and both so excellent, cannot reasonably
be assigned to any but the same author.

4. *Relation to the Fourth Gospel*

It has often been debated whether the Epistle was written before the Gospel, or after it. On the one side, it is argued that the simpler work must have preceded the more elaborate one. On the other hand, the Epistle appears to presuppose the teaching of the Gospel — so much so that sometimes it is not fully intelligible unless we take the Gospel as our guide. This argument for the priority of the Gospel is strong, but not decisive; for the man who wrote such a work as the Fourth Gospel must have been living for years with the great conceptions on which it is based. They would become part of his very nature and find utterance, without his knowing it, in everything he thought and said.

If the Epistle was written before the Gospel, it may have been intended to prepare the way for the greater work, much as Bacon and Darwin drew up preliminary sketches of their new theories before presenting them in elaborate form. If the Epistle was written later, it may have aimed at removing difficulties which the Gospel was likely to create. According to this view, the evangelist was conscious that the church would look doubtfully on his account of Jesus' teaching and might even suspect him of heresy. He took pains in the Epistle to express his ideas more simply, and to show that they were not merely speculative, but had a direct bearing on Christian practice. He condemned in plain terms those heretical positions which the Gospel might wrongly be supposed to favor. But against all such conjectures, it must be noted that the Epistle has a well-defined purpose of its own, and there is no need to read into it the further purpose of anticipating or defending the Gospel. The two works are closely related, in so far as they both bear the impress of the same mind and set forth the Christian message from the same point of view. Otherwise, they do not appear to have any connection with each other. The Epistle, for that part, becomes far more interesting and significant when we assume that, while similar to the Gospel, it is quite independent. It shows us this profound religious thinker applying his conceptions to matters of common life and to the practical issues of his own day.

5. Contents

Before examining the purpose of the Epistle, it is necessary to have before us some general idea of its contents. There have been many attempts to reduce it to an ordered plan, but they all break down. The writer seems to be anxious to avoid any suggestion of formal discourse. He does not lecture his readers, but talks to them, and to its artless, spontaneous character the charm of his letter is largely due. We feel as if he is engaged in meditation and allows us to overhear his thoughts as they arise in his mind. Yet there are two or three ideas around which the meditation revolves, and which give it coherence. They connect themselves with a phrase which keeps constantly recurring: "hereby we know" (2:2; 3:16, 19, 24; 4:2, 13; 5:2). The writer is trying to discover tests or criteria for the Christian life. Men believe that through Christ they have fellowship with God, but how are they to know that they have truly attained to this fellowship? The doubts of Christians have usually centered on some question of fact: is the Bible trustworthy? Was Christ the Son of God? Is it certain that I am saved? For John everything depends on an inward condition of soul. He would say "I know that I am saved because I am sensible of communion with God." But the question arises, "How can I tell that this sense of communion is not delusive?" His object, therefore, is to prove the validity of his inward experience, and this he does by offering three main tests. (1) There is the test of ethical conduct.

Hereby we know that we know him if we keep his commandments. He that saith, I know him, and keepeth not his commandments is a liar and the truth is not in him. [2:3 f.]

The Christian life is bound up with a rule of right action, and if we live instinctively by that rule we may be sure of our inward condition. (2) There is the test of belief.

Hereby know ye the Spirit of God; every spirit that confesseth that Jesus Christ is come in the flesh is of God, and every spirit that confesseth not Jesus is not of God. [4:2 f.]

Right belief, as John sees it, is more than a formal confession. It signifies that the Spirit of God is working in a man's heart, leading him to all truth. (3) There is finally the test of brotherly love, and to this the thought of the Epistle continually returns.

Beloved let us love one another for love is of God; and every one that loveth is begotten of God and knoweth God. He that loveth not knoweth not God, for God is love. [4:7 f.]

Here the reason is given us why love is the supreme test. Since love is the very nature of God, those who possess love are sharing in the life of God. We are human beings and our love can manifest itself only in the daily intercourse with our fellow men; but in its essence it is divine. "He that loveth not his brother whom he has seen, how can he love God whom he hath not seen?" (4:20.)

So the Epistle rings the changes on these three tests, with the main emphasis on that of love. The writer shows us in a variety of aspects what the tests mean, and how they act, and how they work in with one another. Ever and again he breaks off into digressions, suggested by one point or another of his main theme. Mystical and practical religion are everywhere exquisitely blended. The mood of thought is that of the Fourth Gospel and, at the same time, we are reminded continually of the matter-of-fact Epistle of James.

6. *Purpose*

The broad purpose of the writer is to confirm his readers in their Christian faith and life. Several times he disclaims the intention of telling them anything they do not know already (2:7; 2:20; 4:16). What he wishes to give them is not new knowledge, but a firmer assurance that the knowledge which they have is sufficient.

These things I have written unto you that ye may know that ye have eternal life, — even unto you who believe in the name of the Son of God. [5:13.]

But this broad religious purpose is combined with a more special one. We can gather that a division had lately taken place in the church to which John writes. Some of its members had been attracted to heretical teachings, which seemed to offer them a deeper truth and a larger liberty than the traditional Gospel. They had formed a group by themselves, and the remaining members were much troubled by this cleavage in the church, especially since those who had broken off were more intellectual than themselves, and professed a higher religious experience. John writes to reassure them. He lays down the tests whereby they may judge for themselves whether they truly know God. If they feel sure that they satisfy those tests, they need have no doubts as to the validity of their faith.

The Epistle is written, therefore, with constant reference to a heresy which we can pretty confidently identify with a form of Gnosticism. It denied that Christ came in the flesh (2:22; 5:5), in other words, that the man Jesus was one with the heavenly Christ. It minimized the significance of the death of Christ (1:7; 5:6, 8) and made the Gospel depend on the Baptism by which the divine Christ united himself with the man Jesus. It allowed no place to the idea of sin, holding that the higher, spiritual natures were exempt from sin, in virtue of their inborn affinity with God. It rejected the moral law as belonging to an inferior stage of religion, and fostered a spirit of pride and exclusiveness. On this lack of brotherly love to which the Gnostic beliefs had inevitably led, John places the chief emphasis. He finds in this attitude the very negation of all that Christianity stands for. The essential test of our love for God is love of our brethren, and those self-centered intellectuals, despite their claim to be the only "spiritual men," have no fellowship with God.

The Epistle has to be interpreted at almost every point in

relation to the heresy and the misgivings which it had caused
in the minds of ordinary Christians. All the tests have a direct
bearing on Gnostic error. By his application of them, John
seeks to show that the new teachers, so far from carrying
Christianity to a higher plane, are the clearest examples of
what it is not and cannot be. Possibly he is unjust in some of
his judgments, but undoubtedly he lays bare the fatal weak-
nesses of the Gnostic teaching, and his criticism of it ensured
its final rejection by the church. The principles on which it was
based were seen, in the light of John's exposure, to be directly
contrary to those of the Christian message.

7. *Ethical Teaching*

The ideas of the Fourth Gospel almost all reappear in the
Epistle, but in much briefer and more general form. Some of
them are not definitely stated, but are present only by implica-
tion. At the same time, the Epistle supplements the Gospel
by bringing clearly to light its practical demands. It has been
said, not altogether unjustly, that the Fourth Gospel has nothing to say about the real message of Jesus. It tells us, no doubt,
of the new commandment to love one another, and illustrates
the duty of service by the beautiful example of Jesus washing
his disciples' feet. But apart from these incidental touches, the
ethical side of the message is kept in the shadow. It might
almost seem as if the evangelist had forgotten the Parables
and the Sermon on the Mount, and had made Christianity consist wholly in a mystical devotion. In the Epistle, however, the
chief stress is laid on Christian action. We are shown how the
principles set forth in the Gospel have their inevitable outcome in obedience to the moral law, and above all in brotherly
love. The new life is an inward condition, but this condition
cannot be separated from the practical activities laid on us
by Christ. By our willingness to perform them, we know that
the new life has been born in our hearts. Here, as in other
respects, the Epistle affords the key to the purpose of the Gospel, and needs to be read along with it. Taken by itself, the

Gospel might seem to displace the earlier Christian teaching but, when we study it in the light of the Epistle, we can see that it preserves it. From the empty speculations which were gaining favor in his time, the evangelist goes back to Jesus' own message and shows how the larger knowledge has made it more real and practical than ever.

> Brethren, I write no new commandment unto you but the old commandment which you had from the beginning. [2:7.]

This is the watchword of the Epistle, and also, when we look beneath the surface, of the Fourth Gospel.

8. *The Witness to Christianity*

In this connection, we require to note that one of the characteristic ideas of the Epistle is that of "witness." Since the validity of the "old commandment" had been questioned by the false teachers, the writer sets himself to prove that it has been fully attested. Witness has been borne to it, not only by Christian experience, but by sanctions ordained by God.

> For there are three that bear witness, the Spirit and the water and the blood, and these three agree in one. [5:8.]

This is one of the most difficult verses in the Epistle, and it has been explained in many different ways; but the reference is most probably to the two sacraments of Baptism and the Lord's Supper, and to the spiritual manifestations in Christian worship. These all testify to Christ, who had lived and died for men, and is still present among his people. The verse is preceded in our authorized translation of the Bible by another, which was once a storm center in controversy:

> For there are three that bear witness in heaven, the Father, the Word and the Holy Spirit, and these three are one.

This verse is found in no ancient manuscript, and can be proved to have been inserted, perhaps in the fifth century, to support the doctrine of the Trinity. It is the one verse in the New Testament which is entirely spurious, and has now been struck out from every good text. But while he appeals to various witnesses, the writer insists most of all on the inward witness of the Spirit.

If we receive the witness of men the witness of God is greater; for the witness of God is this, — that he hath borne witness concerning his Son. He that believeth on the Son of God hath the witness in him, and the witness is this, that God gave unto us eternal life, and this life is in his Son. [5:9 f.]

This is the thought which underlies the whole Epistle, that the message is vouched for by that which is truest and deepest in our own nature. The divine element in man responds to the voice of God, as it speaks to us through Christ. It is the pervasive sense of this inward witness which gives enduring value to the Epistle. The writer has little to say about mere dogmas and speculations. He takes his stand on the eternal facts of love, goodness, fellowship with God. These are the things which all men know in their hearts to be greatest, and the Christian message is bound up with them. It requires no proof from theological argument, for the truth of it is vouched for by an inward witness, by the instincts that lie deepest in the nature of every man. The aim of the Epistle is to bring into clear relief the ultimate and unchanging elements in the Christian message. No book has ever been written which takes us nearer to the very heart of our religion.

CHAPTER XXVIII

THE SECOND AND THIRD EPISTLES OF JOHN

1. *Genuineness*

Along with the First Epistle, we possess two others which are likewise ascribed to John. Both of them are personal notes, of almost exactly the same length, and containing just the number of words which could conveniently be written on a single sheet of papyrus. Neither of them is of any theological value, and for this reason they were slow in obtaining a place in the New Testament; but the very slightness of their contents is the best proof that they are genuine early writings. No motive for inventing them can be conceived, and they must have been preserved for no other reason than that they were the work of a highly revered teacher.

2. *Historical Value*

Brief and casual as they are, they have a very great historical interest, and it is only in recent years that their importance has been fully recognized. It consists chiefly in this, that they afford us a vivid glimpse into the momentous change from the primitive apostolic ministry to the episcopal system. Hitherto the church had been controlled by itinerant missionaries, whose authority depended on the "spiritual gifts" with which they were endowed. In place of this original form of government, there gradually arose a local, official ministry, and the two Epistles come to us from the very time when this transition was in process. They indicate how it came about, and reveal to us something of the friction and misgiving with which it was accompanied.

3. *The Elder*

Both of the Epistles state in their opening verses that they were written by the "elder," but he does not name himself.

Apparently he was so well known to those whom he addressed that he did not require to give his name. We know of one man in that age who was afterwards remembered as "the elder," but this, as we have seen, provides no ground for assuming that the author of these letters was the elder John. The title seems to have been borne by all the older teachers who could link themselves, in some direct manner, with the Apostles.

The two letters are evidently by the same author, and were probably written at the same time, for II John 12, 13 is almost word for word the same as III John 13, 14. It is equally evident that the man who wrote the two short Epistles also wrote the First Epistle. Second John, more particularly, is full of phrases and sentences that are found in the longer letter, and the author cannot be seeking in this way to disguise himself, for he is writing to those who knew him well. If I John is by the author of the Fourth Gospel (as there is every reason to believe), a peculiar interest attaches to these brief letters. They bring us face to face in his ordinary life with the sublime teacher to whom we owe the Gospel. Unfortunately, they throw no light on the mystery of who he was. If that "elder" had only written one word more and given us his name, how much baffling investigation would have been spared us!

4. The Second Epistle

The Second Epistle is addressed "to the elect lady and her children," and these words have sometimes been construed literally and have given rise to fantastic theories. Romances have been woven around this imaginary "lady" and her relation to the great evangelist. But there can be little question that the reference is to a church, and similar language is used, obviously in this symbolic sense, in I Peter 5:13. It is evident, too, that the writer is thinking of some definite church, and not of the church at large. The purpose of his letter is to warn this church against certain missionaries who plan to visit it, teaching what he considers to be a false doctrine. They seem to have called themselves by a name which has a curiously modern sound, "the Progressives." (This is doubtless the true explanation of the phrase in verse 9: "He who progresses, and abides not in the teaching of Christ, has not God.") In the first half of his note, the elder utters his warning against these men who claimed to be advanced thinkers. He insists that the simple truths of faith in Christ and love to one's fellow men are also the everlasting ones, beyond which the Christian message can never advance. He then declares in emphatic terms that the "progressive" teachers are not to be received by the church. Although they come ostensibly in the name of Christ, they are not true missionaries.

5. The Third Epistle

The Third Epistle is also concerned with itinerant teachers, but the Elder's grievance is now of a different kind. He writes to his friend Gaius, of whom we know nothing except what may be gathered from the letter itself. Apparently he was a man of some means and position, who took on himself the duty of entertaining the missionaries who visited the church. Some teachers closely associated with the Elder had been on the point of coming, and he had written to the church on their behalf; but his request had been met ungraciously. A man called Diotrephes was aspiring to be the sole leader of the church, and was jealous of any rivalry. He had spread malicious rumours about the Elder and his friends, and had used his influence to have them excluded (9, 10). The elder therefore writes privately to Gaius, asking him to show due respect to the visitors, and promises that he himself will appear before long and deal fittingly with Diotrephes.

Thus in the Third Epistle the curtain is lifted for a moment on church conditions in the beginning of the second century. Up to this time, traveling missionaries had been treated with honor, and whenever they entered a community had taken rank, as a matter of course, over the local officers. The Elder himself had been accustomed to this deference, and writes in a tone of authority. But a new state of affairs had arisen. The communities had grown in strength and self-reliance, and each of them had now its local officers who were impatient of outside interference. Instead of taking precedence, as in former days, the traveling missionaries had difficulty in being received at all. Not only so, but a new type of church government was coming into existence. In each church there had previously been a number of leaders, all of the same standing; but now we learn of one man who had taken on himself the chief authority. Diotrephes, in fact, is the first Bishop whom we know by name. He has assumed the direction of this particular church, and has even gone the length of expelling fellow members who do not obey him (verse 10). The Elder appears to think that this action of Diotrephes is due simply to personal ambition, but it is fairly certain, in the light of the later history, that he had not grasped the full significance of the change which was in process. He is the champion of an old order, in face of a new one which has become inevitable. In earlier days, the system of itinerant missionaries had been the only possible one, but it had outlived its usefulness. The churches had grown capable of standing by themselves, and what they now needed was strong local government.

6. *True and False Missionaries*

In the Second Epistle, the Elder himself throws light on one reason why the itinerant system had ceased to be desirable. Gnosticism in its various forms was making dangerous progress, and the old arrangement had offered a tempting opportunity to the false teachers. Men whose antecedents were unknown, and who were sometimes impostors and adventurers, could find easy entrance as traveling evangelists, and so implant their errors. With resident teachers, the church was on safe ground. Their character and record were known, and there was no danger of their carrying on a pagan propaganda under a Christian mask.

Taken together, therefore, the two Epistles illustrate the

anomalous situation in that time of transition. In the Second
Epistle, the Elder calls on a church to exclude certain wandering teachers; in the Third Epistle, he protests against such
exclusion, since it is being applied to some of his own colleagues. We can plainly see, as we thus compare the two
Epistles, that the old system had become unworkable. It was
necessary for the church to organize itself afresh, on the basis
of a local and official ministry.

There is a passage in the Fourth Gospel, where the evangelist seems to be dealing with the general question which
faces him in concrete form as he writes the two short Epistles.
It is the discourse which accompanies the parable of the Good
Shepherd (John 10:1 ff.) :

He that entereth not by the door into the sheep-fold but climbeth up
some other way is a thief and a robber. The thief cometh not but to
steal and kill and destroy. — The hireling fleeth because he is an hireling and careth not for the sheep.

Here, in figurative language, the contrast is drawn between
true and false missionaries. There was no longer an assurance,
as in Apostolic days, that all who came in the name of Christ
were doing his work, and the church was often confronted by
a very serious problem. John proposes to solve it, alike in the
Gospel and the Epistles, by a more careful scrutiny of the credentials of traveling teachers. He does not realize that
the whole primitive system is in need of changing, and that the
Christian ministry will henceforth be organized on new lines.

CHAPTER XXIX

THE BOOK OF REVELATION

1. *Christian Apocalyptic*

Jesus himself had announced his message in terms of Jewish apocalyptic, and the earliest disciples had understood his sayings about the approaching Judgment and the future Kingdom of God in the most literal sense. As the church identified itself more and more with the Gentile world, the primitive ideas fell into the background. The message of Jesus was now interpreted in the light of conceptions taken over from the Greek philosophical thinkers. Yet the apocalyptic beliefs, with which the church had set out, were never entirely laid aside. Paul and the other great teachers allowed room for them; and in the more popular Christianity they maintained a central place and have continued to do so to this day.

Not only did the church avail itself of the Jewish apocalyptic literature, but from the outset it produced apocalypses of its own. We hear repeatedly in the New Testament of Christian "prophets," whose chief function was to make apocalyptic forecasts. Paul himself, among his other gifts, had that of prophecy, and several times in his Epistles (most notably in I Cor. 15 and II Thess. 2) he gives us examples of his visions of the future. One early apocalypse is embodied in the thirteenth chapter of Mark, and another, of much later date, forms the basis of Jude and Second Peter. Most of the Christian apocalypses were probably never committed to writing. By their nature they were ecstatic utterances, thrown out by "prophets" when suddenly possessed by the Spirit. They would hardly be intelligible to those who spoke and heard them, and would be forgotten as soon as the momentary excitement was past. But there was one Christian apocalypse which was written down and preserved. Historically it is of the highest value, as illustrating the mode of thought which was more characteristic than any other of primitive Christianity. It must never be forgotten that the New Testament is mainly the work of thinkers, who stood on a different level from the church at large. A book written today by one of our advanced theologians would carry little meaning to the ordinary church member; and it may be surmised that Paul's Epistles to the Romans and Ephesians were quite over the heads of most of his audience. From the book of Revelation, we learn something of what the mass of Christians in that age were thinking. It was written for the people, and reflects the beliefs and emotions of the plain men and women who must always make up the great majority of the Christian church.

2. *Wrong Interpretations*

Revelation used to be considered a book so mysterious that all effort to understand it must necessarily be futile. "This is a book," says an old commentator, "which either finds a man mad or leaves him so"; and it is still regarded by many people as a secret writing which is better not to be meddled with, and which has more to do with occult science than with religion. This idea of the book arose out of two misapprehensions, both of which have been dispelled by critical inquiry. We have grown aware, for one thing, that it by no means stands alone, as was formerly assumed. It belongs to a class of literature which was widely cultivated in later Judaism, and of which many examples have been recovered within the last century. These Jewish apocalyptic writings have obviously served as models for the Christian book, and throw a flood of light on the nature of its symbolism. Even more important has been the recognition, on the part of almost all scholars, that it was meant for its own time. The old assumption was that it had reference to a distant future, and endless attempts were made to apply its prophecies to the events and personages of later history, and to the coming destinies of the world. This was a strange error, since the writer himself declares more than once that he is dealing with his own age. Even in his opening verse, he says plainly: "The revelation of Jesus Christ concerning the things which must shortly come to pass"; while at the close, a warning is given: "Seal not the words of the prophecy of this book for the time is at hand" (22:10). It is implied here that this apocalypse is not like the ancient ones which had to be sealed and laid aside until the days should come when their fulfillment was near. This book was to be left open, since all that was predicted in it would take place almost immediately.

As soon as we accept the writer's own account of his work, most of its difficulties disappear. It is composed in the regular apocalyptic manner, and its forecasts are found to agree with things that were happening in the church, or in the Roman Empire, towards the end of the first century. Instead of being the most mysterious of New Testament books, it is, in fact, the simplest; for it does not move, like the Gospels and Epistles, in regions of profound religious thought, and any secrets it contains are mainly of the nature of historical puzzles. Perhaps the chief problem of the book is now the purely literary one. In its present form, it bears all the marks of unity. Its various parts all fit together, and it advances towards a great climax with real dramatic power. But there are many indications that this unity has been imposed on a number of documents which were originally separate, and which were drawn up at different times and in different circumstances. The sifting of these diverse sources of the book has given rise to critical questions of much complexity, which have not yet by any means been answered.

3. *Authorship*

The book, then, out of whatever materials it was composed, now bears the stamp of a single author. He calls himself John, and some have maintained that he merely adopts the usual apocalyptic convention, by which prophecies were given out under the names of revered figures of the past. But this cannot be, since he wrote to churches which were well acquainted with him, and which he addressed with a personal authority. There can be no doubt that his name was John, and it is more than likely that he was John the Elder, to whom reference has been made already in our survey of the Johannine problem. The time and place of the book are in keeping with this conjecture; and one of the few facts recorded of John the Elder is that he was deeply interested in apocalyptic speculation. If it was he to whom we owe the book, he must have been a man of remarkable genius. Revelation, on its own merits, is incomparably finer than anything else in apocalyptic literature. One has only to think of the splendor of some of the descriptions — the worship in heaven (4), the fall of Rome (18), the general resurrection (20:11-15), the New Jerusalem (21). Christian art and poetry in all ages have been profoundly influenced by the book. Apart from all other claims, it may fairly rank as one of the loftiest works of imagination that the world can show.

4. *Occasion and Purpose*

Whoever wrote it, the book was evoked by the terrible crisis which had burst on the church in Asia Minor owing to the enforcement of Cæsar-worship in the reign of the Emperor Domitian, about the year 95 A.D. By their refusal to observe this official cult, the Christians had exposed themselves to persecution, and John, who himself had been exiled to the island of Patmos, writes to seven churches in the region most gravely affected. His immediate purpose is to encourage them to faith and fortitude; but after he has done this in a series of messages, thrown into the form of letters (2, 3) he proceeds to tell them why they can afford to bear up patiently. Their suffering will soon be over, for they are living in the last days, and the triumph of Christ and his cause is just at hand. This is the theme of the book, which is not a book of doom, as is generally supposed, but a summons to faith and courage.

According to apocalyptic teaching, the world's evil must come to a head before God can interpose and bring in the great deliverance. With this in his mind, John sets himself to paint the wickedness and calamity of his time in the darkest colors. Most of all, he dwells on the crowning iniquity whereby an earthly king demanded the worship which was due to God alone. Evil has now reached its height. The last days have come, and the dawn of the new age may be looked for at any moment. So the real note of the book is one of exultation. The writer seeks to impress on the church that, in the very extremity of its present suffering, it is to find the assurance of its approaching victory.

5. Contents

Apart from the preliminary letters to the churches, the book is built around three conceptions, all of them taken over from Jewish apocalyptic. (1) It was believed that the coming of the Messiah, to judge the world and bring in the new order, would be heralded by a series of disasters, known as "the Messianic woes." (2) Before the Messiah himself appeared, there would arise an "Antichrist," — a mysterious figure, half man and half demon, in whom the forces of evil would be incarnated and who would represent Satan himself in the final struggle. (3) The earthly Jerusalem is the counterpart of a Jerusalem in heaven and, in the new age, this heavenly city will take the place of the present earthly one, and will be the abode of God's redeemed people.

With these conceptions before him, John describes how in a vision he saw the throne of God, surrounded by the hosts of angels. In the hand of God was a sealed book, containing the final woes, and it was given to Christ, who began to break the seals, one by one (4 and 5). As each seal is broken a calamity falls on the earth (6 and 7), and, after the seventh seal, there appear seven angels with trumpets. The blowing of each trumpet is the signal for a new woe (8-10). There follow three chapters, which are plainly meant to be the most significant in

the book and which tell in cryptic language of the appearance
of Antichrist (12-14). Another series of woes is now introduced, parallel to the previous ones, and this time typified by
the pouring out on earth of seven bowls of wrath (15-18).
When these last calamities have taken effect, the end is come.
Antichrist and Satan himself are made captive, and all men
are brought up for judgment before God (19, 20). The last
two chapters (21, 22) describe the glorious opening of the
new age, when the heavenly Jerusalem will descend to earth
and the people of God will be gathered into it.

6. The Antichrist

The larger part of the book is thus occupied with the triple
series of woes, culminating in the appearance of Antichrist,
who is conceived as Nero, the great persecutor, come to life
again. The writer here avails himself of a popular belief
which long persisted, that Nero had not slain himself after
the victory of his rival, but had escaped to Parthia and was
one day to return with an avenging army. Revelation, in its
final form, was written thirty years after Nero's downfall,
and no one could now reasonably doubt that he was dead.
John therefore conceives of him as coming back, not from
some place of exile, but from the "abyss" into which he had
descended, and making war in the power of Satan on God's
people. He is not named, but is indicated by a number, 666,
which represents the numerical value of the letters in "Nero
Cæsar" when added together (13:18). The wicked emperor
is portrayed as a kind of Satanic caricature of Christ. He
claimed to be divine, not through spiritual power, but through
brute force. He suffered a violent death, and passed through
death to the abyss. He is to have a resurrection and a second
coming, but will come again from beneath and accompanied
by the hosts of darkness. The end will come when the Christ
of God will encounter this devil's Messiah and will destroy
him.

7. *Value of the Prophecy*

The book of Revelation is thus a forecast, in the apocalyptic manner, of events which are to happen in the immediate future. John believed himself to be living in the last days, and in calamities taking place around him — wars, famines, pestilences — he saw the final woes already begun. Everything had come about thus far as the old prophets had foretold, and John makes it his task to look a little further forward and trace the world's drama to its close. Rome, the impious power through which Satan had ruled over mankind, is presently to go down in fire and blood; and its fall will mean the end of this age and the coming of God's Kingdom. It is always dangerous to forecast the future, and John's prediction was to prove utterly at fault. The wicked Domitian was succeeded, not by Antichrist, but by the five good emperors. Rome did not fall, but continued to rule for centuries and at last became the citadel of that church in whose name John had condemned it to perdition. It was this failure of the book, as a literal prophecy, which led to the later misconceptions. The church could not bring itself to acknowledge that the seer who had so confidently proclaimed "the things that must shortly come to pass" had been mistaken. His predictions were now interpreted in a symbolical sense, and their fulfillment was thrown forward into a distant future.

As a prophecy in the literal sense, the book of Revelation has no value, or serves only to illustrate the outlook of the church in the closing years of the first century. Its real significance is to be found in the splendid faith, by which it judges present events in the light of religion. The writer lived in the darkest days that have ever fallen on the church, when the all-powerful empire had put forth its might to destroy the cause of Christ. To all human appearance, the church was pitifully weak and could never stand up before the forces which were bent on crushing it. Yet John does not doubt for a moment that it will prove victorious. He sees God enthroned above the world's tumult and protecting his own people. He

believes that the church, in its hour of calamity, is stronger
than the great empire, and is destined to endure when it has
fallen. The book is, throughout, a magnificent expression of
faith — faith in God, in the truth of Christ's message, in the
supremacy of spiritual over material power. It is this which
gives it a permanent value, in spite of the fantastic imagery
and old-world beliefs whereby its meaning is conveyed. In
every age, the contest seems a hopeless one between the visible
forces of this world and the struggling cause of God, and the
book of Revelation will always be, what it was to its first
readers, a trumpet call to courage and endurance.

8. *Religious Teaching*

When we turn from its great underlying idea to its specific
teaching, the book is somewhat disappointing. The real elements of Jesus' message might seem to fall away altogether.
God is conceived as an absolute King, of the Oriental type,
who is surrounded by a retinue of angels doing him homage.
The heavenly world is a place glittering with gold and jewels,
where the saints dwell in endless delight. Over against it, there
is a dungeon where sinners are tormented. The promised salvation is understood in a crudely literal, not to say a vindic-
tive, sense. Christians are now at the mercy of their enemies,
but their turn is coming. They have only to bear up for a
little while longer, and Christ will appear as conqueror and
will reign in the midst of his people. The Roman Empire will
give place to a divine kingdom and the Christians will inherit
the earth. In the ethical teaching of the book, very little is
made of the distinctively Christian virtues. Nothing is said of
humility, forgiveness, love for one's enemies; there is hardly
an echo anywhere in the book of the Sermon on the Mount.
Christianity consists for this writer in unwavering confession
of Jesus, loyalty to his church, patience until the day of his
coming. No doubt a great deal in the book must be explained
from the special circumstances in which it was written. It was
not meant to commend the normal Christian virtues, but to

nerve men to heroic effort in a time of crisis, when the one thing needful was fidelity to the Christian confession. But when all this is granted, the book cannot be placed on the same religious level as the other New Testament writings. It represents a type of piety which appealed in that age to the popular mind, and which has never really been displaced. The mass of men, it has to be admitted, are not reflective, or mystical, or sensitive to the finer moral values. They apprehend ideas most easily in a pictorial form and are apt to mistake the picture for the inward reality. For such a public the book was written and will always have a special attraction.

9. Christian Character

It has often been remarked that much in John's thought is more Jewish than Christian, and the theory has been advanced that his book was originally a Jewish apocalypse, which was revised in a Christian sense and adapted to the use of the church. This theory breaks down on closer examination, for in its own way the book is Christian through and through. It is indeed modeled on the Jewish apocalypses and borrows many of their images and ideas; but these are all transformed by the central place which is everywhere assigned to Christ. In Jewish apocalyptic, the Messiah was never more than a subordinate figure; in Revelation, Christ is seated on the right hand of God, and all that happens in heaven or on earth is in some manner related to him.

Not only is Christ made central, but his preëminent act is his death. In Jewish apocalypses, the Messiah is never conceived as suffering, while, in Revelation, Christ is exalted to the highest place because he died.

They sung a new song saying. Thou art worthy to take the book and open the seals thereof; for thou wast slain and hast redeemed us to God by thy blood. [5:9.]

The name which is most commonly assigned to him is "the Lamb," a name which has often caused difficulty, since it does not seem to be associated with any ideas of gentleness. It alternates with the name of "the Lion of Judah," and we hear of the "wrath of the Lamb" (6:16), and of the Lamb over-coming his enemies in war (17:14). All that the name signifies is the fact of sacrifice. Christ has redeemed the world and won for himself an eternal kingdom through his death.

The supreme function attributed to Christ is that of Lord and champion of the church. By his death, he called the church into being. From his place in heaven, he watches over it. A day is coming when he will appear again to lead it to victory. The consummation of all things will be when the perfected church will come forth as the Bride of Christ (21:9). If the book is regarded as a kind of sacred drama, the two characters around which it revolves are Christ and the Church. As John thinks of the church, it is in the first instance the visible community on earth, the elect people of God who have been drawn together by the magnetic power of the Cross (5:9, 10; 7:9 f.). This idea of the visible church is conjoined, however, with that of a heavenly community. The church on earth is only an outpost of the true church, which has its place in heaven and is already victorious. In the last days, the earthly and heavenly companies of God's people will be united in the New Jerusalem.

It is noticeable that the book shows practically no trace of Pauline influence. This is most strikingly evident in its teach-ing on salvation, which is never associated with faith. The writer appears to think of a certain number of men whom God has chosen, and who are inevitably drawn into the church by the power of the Cross. So far as they have themselves part in their salvation, the whole emphasis is thrown on good works. They appear clothed in "white garments," in "robes of fine linen which are the righteous deeds of the saints" (19:8). A conspicuous place is given to martyrdom, the highest deed of merit which a Christian can render. Salvation, obtained as it is by works, is described as a reward, bestowed on "him that overcometh." This reduction of Christianity to a higher mo-rality is characteristic of the church after Paul, and perhaps belonged to the more popular type of religion from the first. In the great heathen cities, the most obvious mark of the Christian was that he kept aloof from the prevailing vices, and this purer mode of living was accepted by the ordinary mind as the saving factor in the new faith.

10. *Permanent Significance*

The religious value of the book of Revelation is not to be sought in its theology, but in the great convictions which lie behind it. The writer believes with his whole heart that God is ruling the world, that material power, however strongly intrenched, is only for a time, that the service of Christ leads to eternal life. These were the beliefs that sustained the early church, and though they were commonly held in a crude, unreasoned fashion, as they have been in most times since, they were intensely realized. The religion which finds expression in the book may not have been profound and spiritual, but it was a living one, and drew its vitality from truths that were central in the message of Christ. There was ground for John's confidence that the church which held to it would, in the end, "overcome the world."

CHAPTER XXX

The Formation of the New Testament

1. *Primitive Christian Literature*

The New Testament may be described in general terms as the literature of the first Christian age; but this definition must be largely qualified. Although the primitive church had little concern with the making of books, it produced many more than the twenty-seven which are now included in the New Testament. As we have already seen, there were records of the life and teaching of Jesus which preceded our present Gospels and supplied the basis for them. There were early documents of which Luke availed himself in composing the book of Acts. Paul wrote a number of letters which have now disappeared, or survive only in fragments embedded in the present Epistles. We have traces of other lost literature, of which the precise nature and extent cannot now be determined. In the existing books, for example, we meet again and again with lyrical outbursts which have all the appearance of early Christian hymns. Sometimes they are definitely marked as quotations.

Wherefore he saith: Awake thou that sleepest and arise from the dead, and Christ shall shine upon thee. [Eph. 5:14.]

And without controversy great is the mystery of godliness: He who was manifested in the flesh, justified in the Spirit, seen of angels, preached among the nations, believed on in the world, received up in glory. [I Tim. 3:16.]

The opening chapters of Luke contain the songs of Mary, Zacharias, Simeon (the Magnificat, Benedictus and Nunc Dimittis), and the book of Revelation is interspersed with lyrics, sometimes of great beauty. They rarely fit with any exactness into their context, and were taken, most probably, from some collection of hymns, employed in Christian worship. It may be gathered, too, that a number of Apocalypses were current in the church. One of them is preserved in the thirteenth chapter of Mark, others are built into his larger work by the author of Revelation, and can still be distinguished as separate pieces.

Besides this lost literature, of which the remnants are incorporated in our New Testament, there were writings which were just as early in date as some of the present books. A few of them are still extant, in whole or in part. The Epistle of Clement was written before the end of the first century, and the Epistles of Ignatius, Polycarp, Barnabas, the Shepherd of Hermas, the Teaching of the Twelve Apostles, not long afterwards. The Gospel of the Hebrews and the Gospel of Peter — to name only two works of this class — cannot have been much later than the Gospel of John. Before the last writings of the New Testament came into existence, the church had a fairly extensive literature, and all of it, on the mere ground of date, had a right to be included in the sacred book. For a long time, indeed, there was a feeling that those other early writings must not be rejected, and several of them find a place in the most ancient manuscripts of the New Testament. On the other hand, the church was by no means unanimous as to some of the books which were ultimately accepted. Hebrews, Revelation, James, the two short Epistles of John, were long in dispute. The three Pastoral Epistles and Second Peter were always considered doubtful, and have never to this day been fully recognized.

The New Testament, therefore, is not so much the literature of the early church, as a selection from that literature. What was the process by which the selection was made? This is a question very difficult to answer, and belongs rather to general church history than to the study of the New Testament itself. Yet there are several points with regard to the formation of the Canon of which notice must be taken, however briefly. Before we can rightly appreciate the New Testament, we need to have some assurance that it is no mere fortuitous collection, but does indeed contain the primary books of Christianity.

2. *Beginnings of a New Testament*

For more than a hundred years, the only Bible of the church was the Old Testament. This was the book which Jesus himself, and the Apostles after him, had accepted as the Word of God, and it continued to be sacred for the church. All Christian teaching was based on the Old Testament, though it was now interpreted in the light of the belief that Prophets and Psalmists had consciously looked forward to the appearance of Christ. From the outset, however, a peculiar reverence was attached to Jesus' own sayings. He had been God's messenger, in an even higher sense than the Prophets, and the message he had brought was placed on the same level as the inspired scriptures.

In order to understand how writings by the Apostles came gradually to be regarded as sacred, we must bear in mind the nature of early Christian worship. It was modeled on the worship of the synagogue, and consisted of prayer, singing of a psalm or hymn, reading of Scripture, and finally an address. When a letter arrived from Paul or some other honored Apostle, it would be read out at the public meeting in place of the address. The letters of Paul, as even his enemies acknowledged, were "weighty and powerful" (II Cor. 10:10), and would require to be read several times before their full meaning could be taken in. A custom would begin of repeating them at intervals, so that their ideas and language became familiar. As yet they were regarded only as the utterances of a highly gifted teacher, but in course of time, and more than ever when Paul had been martyred and was a consecrated figure, his words would be listened to with reverence. Instead of serving as the address, they would tend to take the place of Scripture, and would themselves afford texts for exposition.

A change had meanwhile come over the method whereby

the teaching of Jesus himself was imparted. At first the word "Gospel" was not associated with a written book. The message of Jesus was proclaimed by word of mouth, each instructor reporting it in his own fashion; and all these accounts of it were known as "the Gospel." But a time came when this oral Gospel was put into writing. Records like those of Matthew and Mark were accepted everywhere as authoritative, and began to rank as sacred books. Shortly after the beginning of the second century, Ignatius spoke of the "Gospel and the Apostle" as the two indisputable sources of Christian knowledge. The church was feeling its way towards a Scripture of its own, supplementary to the Old Testament.

3. Idea of a Christian Bible

The decisive step was taken in the middle of the second century, and it was due, strangely enough, to Marcion the great heretic. Christianity for Marcion was an entirely new revelation, having nothing in common with that which had formerly been offered to the Jews. He held, indeed, that the God of the Jews was an inferior God, who had tyrannized over men through a law of strict justice, instead of drawing them to himself by love. The work of Christ, according to Marcion, had been to reveal the true God and so deliver men from their taskmaster, and from this he inferred that the Old Testament must be abandoned altogether and replaced by a Christian Bible. For the use of his own sect, he drew up the first New Testament. Believing, as he did, that Paul had been the one teacher who had truly understood the message of Christ, he included only Pauline writings. The book consisted of ten Epistles of Paul (the Pastorals being omitted), and the Gospel of Luke, which was written by Paul's companion and might be assumed to be indirectly the work of Paul. This Bible of Marcion was rejected by the church, but his conception of a Christian Scripture at once took root. It commended itself all the more, because of the alarming progress of those heresies which had found one of their champions in Marcion himself. In view of the prevalence of false doctrine, it had become imperative to have some standard by which the teaching of the church could be regulated. Not only so, but the heretics had adopted the practice of issuing their propaganda under the names of venerated Apostles, and of composing fantastic Gospels which professed to convey the true account of Jesus' life and message. It was evident that, unless the new religion was to fall into utter chaos, the church must single out the genuine writings and make them authoritative. The idea of a Christian Bible was now established, and it was necessary to decide on the writings which it should contain.

4. *Principles of Selection*

There was never any question as to some of the writings, and these the most important. The Four Gospels, the Epistles of Paul, the book of Acts, the First Epistle of Peter, the First Epistle of John, had secured a firm hold on the Christian mind, and passed of their own accord into the new Bible. But there were many other writings which were by no means so certain, and various criteria were suggested by which they might be valued. The three main tests are indicated by Irenæus (180 A.D.). (1) A writing could not be scriptural unless it had an Apostle as its author. This test of apostolicity was the decisive one, but it could not be strictly applied, since it would have excluded two of the Gospels. It was therefore modified to allow room for books written by men so closely associated with Apostles that their teaching might be considered Apostolic. (2) No book could be admitted which taught anything contrary to the "rule of faith," the type of doctrine which was generally held by the church. (3) In order to be fully accepted, a book must be vouched for by one or more of the leading churches. There was fair ground for assuming that these churches, founded in the early years by actual Apostles, had preserved the genuine Christian tradition.

The tests were well devised but, in their practical application, they furnished little real guidance. In some respects, they were positively misleading. There were books, for instance, which were obviously of inferior worth, and yet professed to have come from the hands of Apostles; and it was impossible by the critical methods of those days to disprove their claim. On the strength of a mere title, were they to be received as Scripture? There were other books of the highest excellence, which lacked the stamp of Apostolic authorship; were they on that account to be discarded? A conspicuous example was the Epistle to the Hebrews. It was undoubtedly one of the finest of Christian books, and had come down from the early times. The eastern churches were anxious to have it included, but in the west, where it was known to be non-Apostolic in origin, its right was long disputed. An agreement was finally arrived at, by a sort of pious fiction, that, whoever was its real author, it should be classed among the Epistles of Paul. The test of sound doctrine likewise proved embarrassing. About the middle of the second century, arose the wild millennarian movement known as Montanism. In view of the dangerous excitement to which it gave rise, all apocalyptic teaching was condemned as heretical, and doubts were thus thrown on the book of Revelation. The church had hitherto treasured it, but for some time it shared the fate of other Apocalypses which had now been deservedly thrown aside.

5. Disputed Books

Hebrews and Revelation eventually won their place, in spite of their failure to meet the required tests; but there were five writings which were long kept outside of the New Testament, or remained only on the outer fringe of it — Second Peter, Jude, James, Second and Third John. The Epistle of James was highly esteemed, but its authorship by a great Apostle was acknowledged to be uncertain. Still more dubious was the origin of Jude and Second Peter. Against the two Epistles of John, there seems to have been no objection except that they were so short and theologically so unimportant. If books that taught unsound doctrine were to be excluded, must not the rule be also enforced against writings which apparently taught no doctrine at all?

The chief trouble was with books which have now disappeared from our New Testament. Some of them, like the Epistle of Barnabas, were generally attributed to Apostles. All of them were written in an edifying strain and contained nothing to which exception might be taken. In several instances, too, they were closely connected with a church of high standing, which was unwilling to part with them. This was particularly true of the First Epistle of Clement and the Shepherd of Hermas, which had originated in the great church of Rome.

Throughout the third century, the New Testament was a term to which no precise meaning could be attached. It was fully recognized that Christianity had its sacred book, worthy to be ranked with the Jewish Scriptures or even above them. But the limits of this Christian Bible were not defined, and as yet there was no central authority which could speak for the whole church and impose its judgment. The question as to which books should be included was left open, and different lists were drawn up by different outstanding teachers. On the principal books, all were agreed; but others were placed on a secondary list of "disputed books." The use of these was permitted for purposes of edification, but they were not to be regarded as in the full sense inspired. In course of time, this class of "disputed books" resolved itself into two — books which were not altogether certain, and books which might pretty confidently be rejected. Those in the former division tended more and more to be frankly accepted, while the others fell out altogether. It was not till after the middle of the fourth century that the New Testament took its definite form. In the year 367 A.D., Athanasius, who had come to be acknowledged as the foremost man in the whole church, issued his famous Easter letter, in which he enumerated the books as we now have them, and declared that these henceforth were to form the Christian Scriptures.

6. *The Final New Testament*

As we look back on this process by which the New Testament took shape, our first impression is one of misgiving. We have been accustomed to think of this book as apart from all others, but it seems to have grown up quite fortuitously. For several centuries, there was no agreement as to its contents. Writings which once were part of it have dropped out; others, which are now Holy Scripture, were long considered doubtful. Have we any guarantee that the final choice was the right one, or that a book which was put together in that accidental manner has any peculiar claim?

The answer to these questions is to be found in the very fact that the selection was made by a gradual, tentative process. There is nothing more difficult than to appraise the true quality of a work of literature. Until at least a hundred years have gone by, the best judges are at fault, and even then the position of the book is not secure. There have been countless books which, in their own day, were acclaimed as masterpieces, and are now utterly forgotten; there have been others which, at first, were hardly noticed, and have finally taken their place among the world's great possessions. The only judgment which can be relied on is that of time. When a book has survived all changes of fashion, when it has appealed to all kinds of readers and they have responded, only then can we be sure that it is a living book. It was by this test of time that the New Testament books were selected. We can never be sufficiently thankful that in the early days there was no ecclesiastical council, no committee of trained critics, which could impose its decisions on the church. However well qualified it might have been, it would have failed in its task. It would have judged the writings by some temporary and artificial standard, and have given us a New Testament which would long ago have become antiquated, like most of the sacred books of other religions. The selection was made unconsciously by the mind of the church at large. All the writings were at first accepted without much discrimination but, as time went on, some of them grew arid and meaningless and ceased to be read; others retained their freshness, and seemed to become always richer and deeper. The church, in the end, selected those writings which had already selected themselves.

The judgment of the early church has been more than confirmed by that of the centuries since. When we compare the books which now stand in the New Testament with those which were excluded, we feel at once that they stand on a different plane. Not only do they express, with unerring instinct, those things which are vital and permanent in the Christian message, but they bear on them everywhere the stamp of great literature. It was by their intrinsic worth that the writings won their place, and by the same right they have maintained it to this day. Some of the beliefs which once threw a halo around the New Testament may have been dispelled in the light of criticism; but it will always stand out by its own excellence as the supreme religious book.

BIBLIOGRAPHY

BIBLIOGRAPHY

Books on the New Testament are innumerable, and nothing has been attempted here but to name two or three in each of the main departments of study, and to append a list of commentaries on the particular writings. The books selected are not necessarily the best, but those which seem to be most useful and accessible. The list is confined to English books or books translated into English, except in a few instances where the most adequate treatment is to be found in a French or German work.

GENERAL HISTORY

ANGUS, S. The Environment of Early Christianity, 1915.
DEISSMANN, A. Light from the Ancient East, 1911.
DILL, SAMUEL. Roman Society from Nero to Marcus Aurelius, 1904.
JONES, H. STUART. The Roman Empire, "Story of the Nations," 1910.

JEWISH HISTORY

FAIRWEATHER, W. The Background of the Gospels, 1908.
JACKSON, F J. F. Josephus and the Jews, 1931.
SCHÜRER, E. The Jewish People in the time of Christ, 1891.

JEWISH RELIGION

BRANSCOMB, B. H. Jesus and the Law of Moses, 1930.
HERFORD, R. T. Pharisaism, its Aim and its Method, 1912.
MOORE, G. F. Judaism in the first Centuries of the Christian Era, 3 vols., 1927-1930.
STRACK, H. L., AND P. BILLERBECK. Kommentar zum Neuen Testament, 1922-1928.

APOCALYPTIC

CHARLES, R. H. The Apocrypha and Pseudepigrapha of the Old Testament, 1913.
LECKIE, J. H. The World to Come and Final Destiny, 1918.
OESTERLEY, W. O. E., AND G. H. BOX. Translations of Early Documents, 1917 ff. The chief apocalyptic books in separate small volumes.
PORTER, F. C. Messages of the Apocalyptical Writers, 1905.

HELLENISTIC RELIGION

ANGUS, S. The Mystery-Religions and Christianity, 1925.

BEVAN, E. R. Stoics and Sceptics, 1913.
CUMONT, F. The Oriental Religions in Roman Paganism, 1911.
―――― Astrology and Religion among the Greeks and Romans, 1912.
―――― The Mysteries of Mithra, 1903.
KENNEDY, H. A. A. Philo's Contribution to Religion, 1919.
WILLOUGHBY, H. R. Pagan Regeneration, 1929.

CANON AND TEXT

GOODSPEED, E. J. The Formation of the New Testament, 1926.
GREGORY, C. R. Canon and Text of the New Testament, 1907.
KENYON, F. G. Handbook to the Textual Criticism of the New Testament, 1912.
LAKE, K. Text of the New Testament, revised edition, 1928.

LEXICONS

ABBOTT-SMITH, G. A Manual Greek Lexicon of the New Testament, 1922.
SOUTER, A. A Pocket Lexicon to the Greek New Testament, 1917.
THAYER, J. H. A Greek English Lexicon of the New Testament, 1889.

GRAMMARS

MOULTON, J. H., AND W. F. HOWARD. A Grammar of New Testament Greek, 1906-1929.
NUNN, H. P. V. A Short Syntax of New Testament Greek, 1912.
ROBERTSON, A. T. A Grammar of the Greek New Testament, 1914.

EDITIONS OF THE GREEK TEXT

NESTLE, E. Novum Testamentum Graece, revised edition, 1927.
SODEN, H. VON. Griechisches Neues Testament, 1913.
SOUTER, A. Novum Testamentum Graece, 1910.
WESTCOTT, B. F., AND F. J. A. HORT. The New Testament in the Original Greek, first issued, 1882.

MODERN TRANSLATIONS

GOODSPEED, E. J. The New Testament; an American Translation, 1923.
MOFFATT, J. The New Testament; A New Translation, first issued, 1913.
WEYMOUTH, R. F. The Modern Speech New Testament, 1904.

INTRODUCTION

BACON, B. W. The Making of the New Testament, 1912.
MOFFATT, J. An Introduction to the Literature of the New Testament, 1911.

PEAKE, A. S. A critical Introduction to the New Testament, 1910.

SYNOPSES

BURTON, E. D., AND E. J. GOODSPEED. Harmony of the Synoptic Gospels, 1917.
HUCK, A. Synopse der drei ersten Evangelien (in Greek), revised edition, 1931. In English, edited by R. L. Finney, 1907.

LIFE OF JESUS

BOUSSET, W. Jesus, 1906.
CASE, S. J. Jesus; A New Biography, 1927.
GOGUEL, M. Vie de Jésus, 1932.
KLAUSNER, J. Jesus of Nazareth, 1925. Written from the Jewish point of view, but instructive and fair-minded.
MACKINNON, J. The Historic Jesus, 1931.
RENAN, E. Vie de Jésus. Written in 1873 and critically out of date, but still from a literary point of view the most beautiful of all the modern Lives.
SANDAY, W. Outlines of the Life of Christ, 1905.
SCHWEITZER, A. Quest of the Historical Jesus, 1910.
WARSCHAUER, J. The Historical Life of Christ, 1926.

PRIMITIVE CHRISTIAN HISTORY

HARNACK, A. Mission and Expansion of Christianity in the First Three Centuries, 1908.
JACKSON, F. J. F. The Life of St. Paul, 1926.
McGIFFERT, A. C. A History of Christianity in the Apostolic Age, 1898.
RAMSAY, W. St. Paul the Traveller and Roman Citizen, 1896.
ROBINSON, B. W. Life of Paul, 1918.
ROPES, J. H. The Apostolic Age, 1906.
WERNLE, P. Beginnings of Christianity, 1903-1904.

NEW TESTAMENT THEOLOGY

No satisfactory treatment of the whole subject has yet appeared in English, but excellent outlines will be found in the books on the Apostolic Age by McGiffert and Wernle. In German there are three standard works on New Testament Theology by H. J. Holtzmann (1911), P. Feine (1919), and H. Weinel (1921). The English books mentioned below deal with the separate divisions of the subject.

PAULINE THEOLOGY

MORGAN, W. Religion and Theology of Paul, 1917.

PORTER, F. C. The Mind of Christ in Paul, 1930.
SCHWEITZER, A. Paul and his Interpreters, 1912.
—— The Mysticism of Paul, 1931.
WREDE, W. Paul, 1907.

JOHANNINE THEOLOGY

CARPENTER, J. R. Phases of Early Christianity, 1916.
LYMAN, MARY E. The Fourth Gospel and the Life of To-day, 1931.
SCOTT, E. F. The Fourth Gospel; Its Purpose and Theology, 1926.

THEOLOGY OF HEBREWS

NAIRNE, A. The Epistle of Priesthood, 1913.
SCOTT, E. F. The Epistle to the Hebrews, 1922.

THE SYNOPTIC PROBLEM

BACON, B. W. Studies in Matthew, 1930.
BUCKLEY, E. R. An Introduction to the Synoptic Problem, 1912.
BURKITT, F. C. Gospel History and its Transmission, 1907.
EASTON, B. S. The Gospel before the Gospels, 1928.
—— Christ in the Gospels, 1930.
HAWKINS, J. C. Horae Synopticae, 1909.
STREETER, B. H. The Four Gospels, 1924.
TAYLOR, V. The Gospels, 1930.

THE JOHANNINE PROBLEM

HOWARD, W. F. The Fourth Gospel in Recent Criticism and Interpretation, 1931.
JACKSON, H. L. The Problem of the Fourth Gospel, 1918.

PAULINE CRITICISM

LAKE, K. The Earlier Epistles of St. Paul, 1911.
MACNEILE, A. H. St. Paul, his Life, Letters and Christian Doctrine, 1920.

CRITICISM OF ACTS

CADBURY, H. J. The Making of Luke-Acts, 1927.
JACKSON, F. J. F., AND K. LAKE. Beginnings of Christianity. Publication begun in 1920 and still in process.
HARNACK, A. The Acts of the Apostles, 1909.

BOOK OF REVELATION

CASE, S. J. The Revelation of John, 1919.

APOCRYPHAL WRITINGS

JAMES, M. R. The Apocryphal New Testament, 1924.

APOSTOLIC FATHERS

LIGHTFOOT, J. B. Apostolic Fathers (text and commentary) 5 vols., 1890.
——— Apostolic Fathers (text and translation), 1898.

COMMENTARIES

The fullest English commentary on the whole New Testament is the *International Critical Commentary*, now almost completed. The volumes are of unequal value, and the best of them are selected in the following list (marked with the letters ICC). Another full commentary is the *Expositor's Greek Testament*. Some of the sections retain their value, although the work as a whole, and especially in the earlier volumes, is passing out of date. The new *Commentary* under the general editorship of Moffatt (based on the English text in his translation) may be highly recommended. Other commentaries which cover the whole New Testament and employ the English text as their basis are the *New Century*, the *Clarendon* and the *Westminster*. Two *Commentaries* have been published in recent years which include the whole Bible in one volume. The task is an impossible one, but these works, under the editorship of A. S. Peake and C. Gore, are useful for the purpose of rapid review. Besides commentary proper they contain a number of excellent special articles on matters of Biblical interest.

Several comprehensive commentaries deal with the Synoptic Gospels, which cannot be rightly interpreted unless they are taken together. The most interesting and judicious work of this kind in English is that by C. G. Montefiore (new edition, 1927). The author is a Jew, of liberal and deeply religious temper, and gives an exposition of Jesus' teaching which no Christian scholar can afford to neglect. The outstanding Synoptic commentary is that by A. Loisy (*Les Évangiles synoptiques*, 1907-1908). A commentary of more popular character but of first-rate value is that of J. Weiss in *Die Schriften des Neuen Testaments*, 1907-1908. This German work, of moderate compass and price, is excellent throughout, and all who can use the language will do well to possess it.

MATTHEW

McNEILE, A. H. The Gospel according to St. Matthew, 1915.
ROBINSON, T. H. The Gospel of Matthew, 1928.

Mark

MENZIES, A. The Earliest Gospel, 1901.
RAWLINSON, A. E. J. Gospel of Mark, 1929.

Luke

EASTON, B. S. The Gospel according to St. Luke, 1926.
RAGG, L. The Gospel of Luke, 1926.

John

BERNARD, J. H. The Gospel of John (ICC), 2 vols., 1929.
MACGREGOR, G. H. C. The Gospel of John, 1929.

Acts

JACKSON, F. J. F. The Book of Acts, 1932.
LAKE, K., AND H. J. CADBURY. Commentary on Acts. This, which
will be the standard English commentary, is now in the press.

Romans

BOSWORTH, E. I. Commentary on the Epistle of Paul to the Romans,
1919.
SANDAY, W., AND A. C. HEADLAM. A Critical and Exegetical Commentary on the Epistle of Paul to the Romans (ICC), 1896.

I Corinthians

ROBERTSON, A., AND A. PLUMMER. A Critical and Exegetical Commentary on the First Epistle of Paul to the Corinthians (ICC), 1911.
This is the only full commentary in English, but is by no means
satisfactory. By far the best commentary is that of J. WEISS, in
German.

II Corinthians

MENZIES, A. The Second Epistle of Paul to the Corinthians, 1912.
PLUMMER, A. A Critical and Exegetical Commentary on the Second
Epistle of Paul to the Corinthians (ICC), 1915.

Galatians

BURTON, E. D. A Critical and Exegetical Commentary on the Epistle
of Paul to the Galatians (ICC), 1920.
LIGHTFOOT, J. B. St. Paul's Epistle to the Galatians, 1870.

Ephesians, Colossians, Philemon

ABBOTT, T. K. A Critical and Exegetical Commentary on the Epistle
of Paul to the Ephesians, etc. (ICC), 1897.

Scott, E. F. A Critical and Exegetical Commentary on the Epistle of Paul to the Ephesians, etc., 1930.

Ephesians

Robinson, J. A. St. Paul's Epistle to the Ephesians, 1904.

Colossians (with Philemon)

Lightfoot, J. B. Commentary on Colossians. Published in 1876, but not yet superseded.

Philippians

Lightfoot, J. B. St. Paul's Epistle to the Philippians, 1894.
Michael, J. H. The Epistle of Paul to the Philippians, 1929.

I and II Thessalonians

Frame, J. E. The Thessalonian Epistles (ICC), 1912.

I and II Timothy and Titus

Lock, W. A Critical and Exegetical Commentary on the Pastoral Epistles (ICC), 1924.

Hebrews

Davidson, A. B. The Epistle to the Hebrews, 1882. Still valuable.
Moffatt, J. The Epistle to the Hebrews (ICC), 1924.

James

Mayor, J. B. The Epistle of St. James, 1907.
Ropes, J. H. A Critical and Exegetical Commentary on the Epistle of James (ICC), 1916.

I and II Peter and Jude

Bigg, C. A Critical and Exegetical Commentary on the Epistles of St. Peter and St. Jude (ICC), 1901.

The Johannine Epistles

Brooks, A. E. The Epistles of John (ICC), 1912.
Frame, J. E. The Epistles of John. In preparation.

Revelation

Beckwith, J. T. The Apocalypse of St. John, 1919.
Charles, R. H. A Critical and Exegetical Commentary on the Revelation of St. John (ICC), 2 vols., 1920.

INDEX

INDEX

RECORDS OF CIVILIZATION

SOURCES AND STUDIES

Edited under the auspices of the

DEPARTMENT OF HISTORY, COLUMBIA UNIVERSITY

XVIII. TRACTS ON LIBERTY IN THE PURITAN REVOLUTION, 1638-1647. Edited, with a commentary, by William Haller. In three volumes. Vol. I, xiv + 197 pages; Vol. II, 339 pages; Vol. III, 405 pages. $12.50.

XIX. PAPAL REVENUES IN THE MIDDLE AGES. By W. E. Lunt. In two volumes. Vol. I, x + 341 pages; Vol. II, v + 665 pages. $12.50.

XX. THE EARLIEST NORWEGIAN LAWS. Translated, with introduction, annotations, and glossary, by Lawrence M. Larson. xi + 451 pages, maps. $5.00.

XXI. THE CHRONICLE OF THE SLAVS, by Helmold. Translated, with introductions and notes by Francis Joseph Tschan. vii + 321 pages, map. $4.00.

XXII. CONCERNING HERETICS; AN ANONYMOUS WORK ATTRIBUTED TO SEBASTIAN CASTELLIO. Now first done into English by Roland H. Bainton. xiv + 342 pages. $4.00.

XXIII. THE CONQUEST OF CONSTANTINOPLE, FROM THE OLD FRENCH OF ROBERT OF CLARI. Translated by Edgar H. McNeal. vii + 150 pages, map. $2.75.

XXIV. DE EXPUGNATIONE LYXBONENSI (THE CONQUEST OF LISBON). Edited from the unique manuscript in Corpus Christi College, Cambridge, with introduction, notes, and an English translation, by Charles Wendell David. xii + 201 pages, maps, illustrations. $3.75.

XXV. THE WARS OF FREDERICK II AGAINST THE IBELINS IN SYRIA AND CYPRUS, BY PHILIP DE NOVARE. Translated, with introduction and notes, by John L. La Monte, and with verse translation of the poems by Merton Jerome Hubert. xi + 230 pages, illustrations, maps, and table. $3.75.

XXVI. SEVEN BOOKS OF HISTORY AGAINST THE PAGANS; THE APOLOGY OF PAULUS OROSIUS. Translated, with introduction and notes, by Irving Woodworth Raymond. xi + 436 pages, map. $4.50.

XXVII. THE EDUCATION OF A CHRISTIAN PRINCE, BY DESIDERIUS ERASMUS. Translated, with an introduction on Erasmus and on ancient and medieval political thought, by Lester K. Born. xiii + 275 pages. $3.75.

FORTHCOMING VOLUMES

ABELARD: SIC ET NON. By Richard McKeon, Dean of the Division of the Humanities, University of Chicago, and Mary Sweet Bell.

CORRESPONDENCE OF BISHOP BONIFACE. By Ephraim Emerton, Late Professor Emeritus, Harvard University.

ENGLISH TRANSLATIONS FROM MEDIEVAL SOURCES; A BIBLIOGRAPHY. By Austin P. Evans, Professor of History, Judith Bernstein, and Clarissa P. Farrar, Columbia University.

EUDES OF ROUEN; THE DIARY OF A BISHOP. By Sidney M. Brown, Professor of History, Lehigh University.

MEDIEVAL HANDBOOKS OF PENANCE. By John T. McNeill, Professor of the History of European Christianity. University of Chicago, and Helena M. Gamer, Instructor in Latin, Mt. Holyoke College.

MEDIEVAL UNIVERSITIES AND INTELLECTUAL LIFE. By Lynn Thorndike, Professor of History, Columbia University.

PASCAL: ON THE EQUILIBRIUM OF FLUIDS. By A. G. H. Spiers, Professor of French, and Frederick Barry, Associate Professor of the History of Science, Columbia University.

SOURCES FOR THE EARLY HISTORY OF IRELAND, THE. Volume Two: Secular. By Dr. James F. Kenney.

WILLIAM OF TYRE: HISTORY OF THINGS DONE IN THE LANDS BEYOND THE SEA. By Mrs. Emily Atwater Babcock, Instructor in Latin, and A. C. Krey, Professor of History, University of Minnesota.